# The Remaking of the Chinese Character and Identity in the 21st Century

**Recent Titles in**
**Civic Discourse for the Third Millennium**
*Michael H. Prosser, Series Editor*

Civic Discourse: Intercultural, International, and Global Media, Volume 2
*Michael H. Prosser and K. S. Sitaram, editors*

The Double Helix: Technology and Democracy in the American Future
*Edward Wenk, Jr.*

Civic Discourse, Civil Society, and Chinese Communities
*Randy Kluver and John H. Powers, editors*

Human Rights in the International Public Sphere: Civic Discourse for the 21st
Century
*William Over*

Civic Discourse and Digital Age Communications in the Middle East
*Leo A. Gehr and Hussein Y. Amin, editors*

Culture and Technology in the New Europe: Civic Discourse in Transformation
in Post-Communist Nations
*Laura Lengel, editor*

Civic Discourse: Communication, Technology, and Cultural Values, Volume 3
*K. S. Sitaram and Michael H. Prosser, editors*

In Search of Greatness: Russia's Communications with Africa and the World
*Festus Eribo*

Social Justice in World Cinema and Theatre
*William Over*

Exploring Japaneseness: On Japanese Enactments of Culture and Consciousness
*Ray T. Donahue, editor*

Working at the Bar: Sex Work and Health Communication in Thailand
*Thomas M. Steinfatt*

# The Remaking of the Chinese Character and Identity in the 21st Century

## The Chinese Face Practices

Wenshan Jia

Foreword by Vernon E. Cronen

Civic Discourse for the Third Millennium
Michael H. Prosser, Series Editor

**Ablex Publishing**
**Westport, Connecticut • London**

**Library of Congress Cataloging-in-Publication Data**

Jia, Wenshan, 1961–
    The remaking of the Chinese character and identity in the 21st century : the
    Chinese face practices / Wenshan Jia; foreword by Vernon E. Cronen.
        p. cm.—(Civic discourse for the third millennium)
    Includes bibliographical references.
    ISBN 1-56750-554-6 (alk. paper)—ISBN 1-56750-555-4 (pbk. : alk. paper)
        1. National characteristics, Chinese. 2. Dignity. 3. Self-respect. I. Title.
    II. Series.

DS727.J53 2001
306′.0951—dc21        00-052552

British Library Cataloguing in Publication Data is available.

Library of Congress Catalog Card Number: 00-052552
ISBN:  1-56750-554-6
        1-56750-555-4 (pbk.)

First published in 2001

Ablex Publishing, 88 Post Road West, Westport, CT 06881
An imprint of Greenwood Publishing Group, Inc.
www.ablexbooks.com

Printed in the United States of America

The paper used in this book complies with the
Permanent Paper Standard issued by the National
Information Standards Organization (Z39.48-1984).

10  9  8  7  6  5  4  3  2  1

This book is dedicated to those—be they Chinese
or other—who are committed to transforming Chinese
culture by starting to transform
the Chinese face practices.

# Contents

viii Contents

# Foreword

There is little reason to doubt that our sense of who we are is related to culture. The phrase "cultural identity" has become common coin. We have come a long way from the time when identity was thought to be an internal possession and culture an external matter that could be rejected without impairing the worth of the individual. However, the recognition that individuality is a cultural and sometimes a multicultural achievement has not been accompanied by an equivalent understanding of what is meant by preserving culture. Some years ago, Israeli author and peace activist Amos Oz offered two views of culture. One view treats culture on the museum model, in which each feature is placed in a case to be preserved and protected from the defamation of change. The other model is that of a varied, complex living tradition in which evolution, change, and contact with other traditions are intrinsic to culture.

If we adopt the latter view, can we not simply appropriate whatever another culture offers that we find useful? The answer is complex. We can import Chinese acupuncture and use it along with Western medicine in relieving pain, and China can adopt particular Western economic practices, but what will be the long-term consequences? There are cases in which the importation of foreign practices and materials has been highly destructive to the recipient, other cases in which features of a foreign culture have been tried and rejected, and still others in which foreign features have been uniquely woven into a host's cultural patterns to create something new and useful.

Since I knew him, Wenshan Jia has been concerned with the relationship between Chinese culture and modern Western culture. He rejects the idea that China should be "Westernized" in the sense of just adopting Western practices; he does believe that China can develop useful new practices in contact with the West. In this book, Wenshan Jia discusses change in China and the relationship of change to the Chinese understanding of selfhood. His route into the subject is examining the Chinese conception of "face." He challenges Western appropriations of the term "face" and their use in the social science literature. His historical examination of how the term has evolved shows its profound connection to the Chinese understanding of what it means to be a human being. The understanding of "face" that he presents is highly useful for improving communication between China and the West. He rejects the idea that face is an unchanging feature of reified Chinese identity.

In this important book, Professor Jia also introduces the beginning of a methodology for encouraging the further evolution of the Chinese conception of face. His method is to encourage reflection on actual episodes of Chinese life by the use of a modified form of Circular Questioning, a method of interviewing originally developed for systemic therapy and consultation. It does not presume a "correct" solution to social or personal problems. The approach is highly innovative and consistent with Jia's historical constructionist view and culture as a living tradition. It has promise for opening new possibilities for communication.

Vernon E. Cronen

# Preface

This book is written when contemporary Chinese society is characterized by the deepening macroeconomic reform and social change and by irreversible and increasing contact with the rest of the world. It is based on the assumption that behind every human face lurks a distinct but rarely self-evident cultural grammar for feeling, acting, and speaking. It is my goal here to describe the unique cultural grammar behind the Chinese face, to account for its functions and social consequences in contemporary Chinese society, and to explore the possibility of transforming this grammar for feeling, acting, and speaking in light of a unique communication perspective—social constructionism.

I attempt to answer the following questions in this book: What is the status of Chinese culture from the perspective of communication as transformation or reconstruction? What might be the most significant of the dynamics that enspirit Chinese culture, character, and identity? Why should the transformation of the Chinese character be facilitated? How could this transformation be an enhancement instead of a mere addition, deduction, or even division? What might be the most useful method? This effort critiques the philosophies and strategies for change of various modern Chinese intellectuals. It offers both an alternative view of change and an alternative means of change.

Chinese face practices lie at the heart of Chinese culture. These practices constitute a systematic grammar of action and a unique way of life, both of which are proving unequal to the challenges of modern instrumental rationality. They must be transformed. Transformation of such a system of cultural practices entails an appropriate perspective and method. The living Chinese tradition and modern Western culture must be creatively and selectively merged, allowing Chinese culture to emerge as a rejuvenated, open, and flexible culture that is both sustainable and adaptable.

This book presents a social constructionist account of Chinese face practices, covering their historical, emotional, and consequential dimensions. It also offers a social constructionist critique of generalist theories of face and ethnocultural studies of Chinese face practices. Using a social constructionist tool called circular questioning (CQ) together with the case-study method, the book presents a tentative model of creative engagement with and grounded transformation of Chinese face-centered social practices. The model is based on the social constructionist critique of revolutionary and individualistic models of transformation of Chinese face practices.

The book concludes that in order to reshape Chinese character and identity in the twenty-first century, social constructionists in the Chinese context have a dual research agenda. On one hand, they have to curtail the excess of communalism due to face practices that undermines individual agency; on the other, they must prevent the complete triumph of unrestrained individual agency over community that would result from the abandonment of face practices in a rush for individual interests.

I also examine CQ in the Chinese context and identify major similarities and differences between the Chinese version of social constructionism and its Western communication version. Western social constructionism, a constructive modification of modern Western culture, is one big step closer to Chinese culture than modern Western culture. The modified Western culture and Chinese culture have a lot to learn from each other. My study implies a promising future for intercultural relations between the East and the West, one that social constructionists with a research agenda in the East can jointly construct with those in the West.

I hope that this social constructionist study of Chinese face practices will help renew the New Culture Movement of 1919 in China by means of a civic discourse, a discourse of transformation that is free, dialogic, participatory, responsible, exploratory, pluralistic, integrative, and cumulative, instead of monologic, iconoclastic, radical, hegemonic, and absolute. Such a new communication process could make Chinese character and identity more expansive, pluralistic, and resilient.

This book is one volume in the series entitled "Civic Discourse for the Third Millennium." Embedded in my book are three major assumptions about civic discourse: Social science can be a new type of civic discourse; communication can be a powerful force of social transformation; and the key to the transformation of Chinese culture and Chinese national character and identity is to transform Chinese face practices as a system of traditional Chinese cultural practices and to facilitate the growth of a new system of communication.

I view the social science research presented here as a kind of civic discourse, rather than a journey of discovery about Truth or External Reality. This view is consistent with Richard Harvey Brown's argument that social science should be transformed as a truly democratic civic discourse (1989) that functions as a tool of self-reflection on citizens' own cultural practices, a tool of self-emancipation from their cultural helplessness, and a tool of empowerment of their own agency in reshaping who they will be.

Informed by the social constructionist view, I define communication as a group, interpersonal, or individual effort to transform and reconstruct an individual member's emotions, social behavior, view of self, and cultural character and identity, eventually transforming the society. I illustrate with case studies that a systemic consultation by means of CQ in a group or interpersonal context could help generate a new type of civic discourse that would enter and alter the fabric of the routine lives of common folk, a non-elitist discourse of the people, by the people, and for the people. This social constructionist discourse on Chinese face practices belongs to the common Chinese folk because they will recognize that the culture the discourse tries to transform is their culture; the new culture and new character and identity emerging out of the discourse will ultimately be theirs, too. In other words, they own the discourse. Furthermore, this discourse is chiefly created by the common folk, among whom everyone is a co-architect of the new culture and the new character and identity. It is the common folk who address each other's concerns and build their future in the form of an artful dialogue. In the process, they help to change themselves by changing each other for the good of all.

Finally, the ways that common Chinese folk speak, act, and emote are governed by their system of face practices. However, this interpersonal system—the traditional triad of face, favor, and fate—is increasingly inadequate to deal with the new social issues brought about by the growth of the market, law, and technology in China in the manner demanded by the instrumental rationality underlying this emergent triad. Is there an alternative, lying between the traditional triad and the emergent triad, that will favor neither and reject neither completely but selectively and creatively draw upon both? What new Chinese national character and identity can be shaped out of the contradictory interplay of these factors? To answer these questions cannot and should not be the job of China-related social scientists only. It should be a conjoint project involving as many Chinese common folk as possible, because it concerns what kind of persons they will become and would like to become. It is with the hope of rebuilding Chinese character and identity that this study makes its contribution to the Chinese civic discourse.

This book articulates a new and systematic view of Chinese face practices and their relationship to Chinese character and Chinese culture. It is of value to scholars, students, professionals, and practitioners with a strong interest in China, Chinese people, and Chinese culture. Its unique communication perspective and its theoretical and methodological import make it especially valuable to scholars and students of intercultural and international communication and of discourse and change, to social theorists, and to social science philosophers.

# Acknowledgments

Throughout this book project, many people and institutions have been of help. My deep gratitude first goes to Professors Vernon E. Cronen, James Averill, and Leda Cooks, who have provided valuable theoretical stimulation and critical reviews of the dissertation out of which this book comes. I especially thank Michael Prosser, Series Editor, whose unique intellectual judgment and insight made the publication of this book possible. I also thank Professors Lucian Pye, Chung-Ying Cheng, and Tu Weiming for their intellectual support at different stages of the project. I thank the Department of Communication and the Graduate School of the University of Massachusetts at Amherst for offering me the graduate fellowship that gave me time and financial resources for my research. My thanks also go to Harvard's Yenching Library and Fairbank Center Library, which provided free access to their resources on China and Chinese culture during my research stay in Boston. I also thank William Cody, former Acquisitions Editor of Ablex, Pamela St. Clair, Acquisitions Editor for Culture and Media Studies at Greenwood Publishing Group, and Linda Robinson, copyeditor for Publishing Synthesis, Ltd. Last but not least, I am thankful for my anonymous consultants, my family and parents, for their strong support.

The views presented here are my own, not necessarily shared by the parties and institutions I have named here. I bear full responsibility for any errors found in the book.

# Introduction

In *The World Daily* of November 29, 1997, Xinhua News Agency reported the following piece of news, entitled "Beijing University plans to renovate its *menmian* (gate-face) to celebrate its centennial anniversary," from Beijing:

> The most distinguished university in China, Peking University, has invested 50,000 Chinese dollars for a renovation of its symbol, the Western Gate, formerly named the Alumni Gate, in order to celebrate its upcoming Centennial Anniversary next year. Today, the project has been accomplished with the last finish. Its scarlet gate, golden lintel and stone lions display the glory of its past.

> The Western Gate was named the Alumni Gate. It is also the University's Main Gate. It was built with the gifts of the alumni of Peking University in 1926. This is one of the few university gates in classical style of traditional Chinese architecture. The Western Gate had been renovated twice in the past—once during the Cultural Revolution and once at the end of the 1970s. With the tear and wear of more than 20 years in the past, the Gate has been worn down in coloring and glamour. A Beijing University official says, the principle of this renovation is to make the Gate take on the same look as its original in design, style, coloring and oil (Xinhua, 1997, p. A9).

This news would elicit a host of divergent responses. Most readers would find the news commonplace. Reflective readers would raise questions such as: Why was news about a university gate reported in order to attract its alumni? Why was such an investment made on the renovation of a gate, instead of on educational and research projects in the University? Will university alumni be willing to donate more when their alma mater has spent so much on such a project?

The present study is neither a scholarly project on traditional Chinese architecture nor a piece about a Chinese institution of higher learning. This study merely aims to sensitize readers to a presently latent but profound issue lurking behind the behavior of renovating a university gate—the Chinese face practices or *lian/mian* behaviors. *Lian/mian* may define the true nature of Chinese communication, Chinese culture, and the Chinese character and may indicate the route to social and cultural change in China.

The gate-face renovation story carries significant information about the status of tradition and cultural change in China. It is the received view that Peking University has been the most significant university introducing and disseminating ideas for social change and campaigning for social transformation in China during the past century. However, this news tells a different story about Peking University—the story of the University's maintenance and glorification of its gate (*menmian* literally meaning gate-face) in extension of its face (*mianzi*). In revealing the University's traditional Chinese cultural persona, it raises a profound question about what social and cultural changes Peking University has helped produce in China with its incessant production of modern Chinese discourse and its critique of traditional China culture over the past 100 years. It raises intellectual doubts about the validity and reliability of theoretical perspectives taken and the consequences of strategies used for social change in China in the modern period. Indeed, the story points to the possibility of reconceptualizing and strategizing social change in China from the vantage point of face (*lian/mian*) transformation.

The study of the Chinese concept of face (*lian/mian*) has become urgent. In Zai Xuewei's words, "Whether *lian/mian* should be studied, whether it can be studied or not; if so, how it should be studied and what results such studies would yield, all relate to the issues of to what extent Chinese will be able to understand their own society-culture-psychology and where the Chinese destiny lies" (1995, p. 387).

Study of the Chinese *lian/mian* is also practical. Chen Zhizhao makes the best argument on the practicality of face research. Chen argues:

> The systematic studies of "*mianzi*" are not only very important, but also practical. Through such studies, we can see where the values of the society and the values of social groups lie and what the aspirations of social actors are. They are helpful in our assessment and evaluation of *mianzi*'s negative and positive social functions in the society. They will be also effective in promoting the Chinese psychological building, in nurturing mature and effective means to save face, in getting rid of unnecessary face concerns.

They would also be helpful in developing individual potential and in realization of self values. (1988, p. 156)

The beginning of *lian/mian* research may portend a fundamental social transformation of the Chinese persona, the awakening of self-reflexivity in the Chinese national consciousness and culture.[1] The era of Lu Xun and Lin Yutang (1920s–1930s) represents the modern critical approach to *lian/mian* practices. The present era, at the beginning of the third millennium, could usher in an alternative approach to Chinese *lian/mian* practices—a microsocial transformation. The *lian/mian* research in Taiwan and Hong Kong in the 1970s and 1980s signaled the social and cultural transformation underway in those regions. When social/cultural transformation reaches a point where people are capable of reflecting upon their own most commonsensical social and cultural practices, it may signal that this culture is undergoing or could undergo a fundamental transformation. Study of *lian/mian* as a central part of the fundamental dynamics of Chinese social/cultural practices in Mainland China and throughout Cultural China may help reshape the Chinese character in the twenty-first century.

Unfortunately, the Chinese concept of face has rarely become a serious research topic for Sinologists, China specialists, and the Chinese *guoxue* (Chinese classical canon) scholars, perhaps because of the limitations of these disciplines. Sinology, which is purely humanistic and classics-centered, is primarily concerned with literary, historical, philosophical, and religious writings from Ancient China. It is an extension of the *guoxue* studies in the modern West. Characterized by a dash of elitism, the Chinese classical canon would view research into *lian/mian* practices as unscholarly. China studies, primarily concerned with modern China, is an extension of the area studies approach developed in the United States when the Cold War began. Preoccupied with political prediction about and control of the region called China, China studies is primarily concerned with geopolitical visions and strategies, marginalizing systematic inquiries into commonsensical cultural practices.

Study of Chinese face practices began when an American missionary named Arthur Smith wrote a book entitled *Chinese Characteristics* (1894), based on his 24 years of participant observation of the everyday practices of Chinese from all walks of life. Smith's study triggered social/cultural criticisms of the Chinese *lian/mian* practices by some well-known modern Chinese intellectuals such as Lu Xun (1934/1960) and Lin Yutang (1935). It was later picked up by social scientists, first in the United States (Hu, 1944; Stover, 1962), then in Hong Kong (Ho, 1976; Bond and Lee, 1981; Redding and Ng, 1982), Taiwan (Hwang, 1987; King, 1988), Mainland China (Zai, 1995; Zuo, 1997), Japan (Doi, 1971;

Matsumoto, 1988), and Korea (Choi and Choi, 1996). Both quantitative (Bond and Lee, 1981; Redding and Ng, 1982) and qualitative methods have been applied, with the qualitative approach predominanant.

While there is some diversity in the studies of Chinese concepts of face, the research literature largely concentrates on the description and interpretation of the concept of *lian/mian* situated in the here and now. Research literature is scarce on *lian/mian* as an evolving system of cultural practices, to understand its dynamic primacy over its structure or as a concept of emotion, to understand its social primacy—which I term "soft rationality"—over its biological and psychological nature—which I term "hard rationality." Research is also lacking on the concept of *lian/mian* as a benchmark for gauging social and cultural change and as a social/cultural practice to be assessed, evaluated, and critiqued. Such research might help activate social and cultural change, given multiple case studies of interactive episodes of face enactment within Chinese communities, viewed from both a macrohistorical and a microsocial constructionist point of view. Some practical and activist efforts have been made to transform Chinese *lian/mian* practices (Lin, 1935; Lu, 1934/1960), but well-defined and well-refined models for change centering on *lian/mian* practices are lacking. The state of the art of *lian/mian* research can be best described as diverse but chaotic, prolific but uncreative.

The present book attempts to address these needs. From a social constructionist perspective, it attempts to create a conceptual and practical alternative to the ways of life now confronting Chinese peoples—the traditional Chinese way of life embodied by face and the modern Western way of life embodied by self—without abandoning either. It hopes to demonstrate how an alternative way of life is possible for Chinese who seem caught between Chinese tradition and Western modernity.

First, this book offers a particular social constructionist perspective, which embraces Vernon E. Cronen's practical theory (1994, 1995a; 1995b; 1996; Cronen and Lang 1994) and the social constructionist theory of emotions of scholars such as James Averill (1990, 1992). From this perspective, Chapter 2 offers a social constructionist conceptualization and definition of *lian/mian*. Chapter 3 presents a social reconstruction of *lian/mian* in its various dimensions. Chapter 4 is a comprehensive review and a social constructionist critique of the literature, which demonstrates the promise and uniqueness of the social constructionist perspective as used in *lian/mian* research. Chapter 5 is a detailed description of the study's social constructionist methodology. Based on the two case studies presented in Chapter 6 and 7, I generate a new model for *lian/mian* transformation in Mainland China in Chapter 8. Finally, I discuss implications and future directions for studies of *lian/mian* transformation, with theoretical reflection upon and revision of both social constructionism and circular questioning, in light of social constructionist case studies in the Chinese context.

In this book, the Chinese *lian/mian* practices are defined as an evolving system of communication processes, deeply rooted in Chinese culture and history, that constructs and maintains both social harmony and social inequality. "Social constructionist approach" mainly refers to the practical theory developed by Cronen, that treats communication research as both a fundamental instrument and an ethical process of cultural transformation and reconstruction.

The goal of this study is to apply social constructionist theory and the circular questioning method in the Chinese context. The purpose of the study is twofold: to offer a social constructionist account of Chinese face dynamics for English readers and to generate an alternative approach to social and cultural transformation in China.

## NOTE

1. While the present study is grounded in contemporary culture in Mainland China and is of special relevance to the transformation of *lian/mian* practices there, it is also intended to be of general heuristic and practical value to cultural China. I do not equate culture with nation-state or ethnicity because I view culture more as a process than an entity.

# 2

# Social Constructionism and Practical Theory

## A Theoretical Perspective on *Lian/Mian* Research

### SOCIAL CONSTRUCTIONISM

Social constructionism, as used in this book, refers to a realist version of social constructionist writings in communication that consists of the practical theory developed by Vernon Cronen (1994, 1995a, 1995b, 1996; Cronen and Lang, 1994) and social constructionist theories in other social and human science disciplines such as James Averill's social constructionist studies of emotions (1990, 1991, 1992; Morgan and Averill, 1992), social constructionist writings by John Shotter (1984, 1993), Rom Harre' (1983, 1987, 1994), John Stewart (1995), and Kenneth Gergen (1973, 1994), which are either communication centered or communication sensitive. This body of theory is significantly informed by American pragmatism (Dewey, 1934, 1958, 1929/1960, 1916/1966), symbolic interactionism (Mead, 1934), systems theory (Bateson, 1972; Watzlawick, Beavin, and Jackson, 1967; Maturana and Varela, 1987), and Ludwig Wittgenstein's later philosophy of language (1958). It is significantly inspired by Thomas Kuhn's ideas about science and the paradigmatic shift (1962) and Richard Bernstein's critical reflection on modern Western philosophy (1983).

The body of theory I call social constructionism shares the following theoretical strengths, which are of heuristic value for the present inquiry.

1. Social constructionism gives up the nineteenth-century scientific view of human interaction as trans-situational. Instead, it highlights the historicity of human interaction and the way (inter)action points into the future.

2. Instead of treating human interactions as epiphenomena of immutable law-like social structure or products of pregiven individual constructs, social constructionism argues that the essence of the social world is human interaction itself.

3. Instead of treating what communication achieves as consequences that are outside communication, social constructionism views what communication does as consequentiality that "can be observed in ways of thinking, feeling, and so on that arise integral to the process of communication at the moment of action" (Cronen, 1995a, pp. 20-21). In other words, communicative acts that constitute a given type of personhood, a social mechanism, and even a social institution can transform other communicative acts constituted by another type of personhood, social mechanism, or social institution.

4. Instead of treating emotion as innate, irrational, individual, and universal, social constructionism reclaims emotion as an inseparable dimension of human communication that is both socially constructed and socially constructionist. First of all, emotions are cultural constructions. James Averill (1990) argues that emotions are cultural creations, cultural performances, and cultural participation that "are more central to a culture than to an individual" (p. 126); they are "a shared experience that is informed by many of the same conventions that govern the use of language" (p. 116). Emotions are also active in the construction of a given type of personhood and a given type of society. Morgan and Averill, through their study of the American discourse of true feelings (1992), have found that true feelings, as a privileged emotion in middle-class American life, have helped reconstitute, reclaim, and strengthen a typical middle-class person's sense of self.

5. Social constructionism does not believe in either a dichotomous worldview confined by the close-ended vocabulary of modern rationality that stifles human experience by means of polarization, compartmentalization, and isolation or a unitary indivisible world that stifles open-endedness and diversity. Significantly invigorated by American pragmatism, it believes in a world that is a result of social uses of language—a world that is multivariate, unfinished, uncertain, and ongoing in nature. Informed by the dichotomous modern rationalist view of the world, for example, Brown and Levinson posit that face, as the core of politeness in human interaction, consists primarily of the negative face and the positive

face. Informed by social constructionism, which liberates researchers from a dichotomous worldview, researchers can discover many dimensions to the concept of face.

6. Instead of viewing human interaction as a reflection of invisible laws, social constructionism sees that human interaction is the very process by which and the very force with which these so-called invisible laws and structures are made. Therefore, it believes that transforming human interaction is the key to transforming social rules and structures.

7. Instead of treating human communication as a transmission of information, social constructionism holds that communication is conjoint action, "wherein different kinds of connections emerge to be extended, critiqued, changed, or discarded" (Cronen, 1996, p. 44).

## PRACTICAL THEORY

On the basis of the preceding social constructionist assumptions, Vernon Cronen, a leading social constructionist in communication, has been consistently inquiring into the transformative potential of communicative acts or the consequentiality of communication (Cronen 1994, 1995a, 1995b, 1996; Cronen and Lang, 1994). He explicitly states, "I want to encourage the development of theory with this same emphasis: providing a way of intelligently joining into the activity of the world so as to enrich it" (1996, p. 38). He calls this theory "practical theory" (1996).

The *function* of practical theory is to inform "our ability to describe, interpret, critique and influence real communication processes" (p. 61) and "patterns of human communication" (1996, p. 39) and to "facilitate the *engagement* of theorist/practitioner in the process of liberating persons for creative forms of life" (p. 25). This engagement is based on a high-level reflexivity in a fusion of thinking, action, and feeling and should be future oriented.

The theory also stresses stronger agency on the part of researchers/practitioners and social actors/clients who will not succumb to the pressure for social conformity and who will be able proactively to improve means to affirm and rejuvenate humanity. As Cronen argues, "The process of attunement in humans may usefully involve episodes of reflection, analysis, planning, etc. However, the heart of the process remains the same, how to so attune to situations so as to make conditions better. This view of attunement includes, of course, projection into the future. A living organism does not simply correct a deficit. It acts in a way that creates affordances for continuing attunement" (p. 22).

In terms of *methodology*, Cronen argues for a continuum of situated-ness—historicity—culturality. This continuum links three levels of analysis—micro, mezzo, and macro—with situatedness as micro, historicity as mezzo, and culture as macro. He states, "To study communication from the orientation I have suggested is to inquire—in a situated, historical-cultural way—into how we are cocreating who we are and what we are doing, and with a view as to how we might do better" (p. 61).

Consistent with practical theory, several communication models of engagement have been developed. One of them is circular questioning (CQ), and another is appreciative inquiry (AI). These have been used extensively by Kingsington Consultation Center in London to offer training and consultation for professionals and organizations seeking to create new ways to communicate so that life will become more meaningful and business will become more prosperous. I discuss CQ and AI in detail in Chapter 6.

## A SOCIAL CONSTRUCTIONIST CONCEPTUALIZATION OF *LIAN/MIAN*

Modern social science approaches and modern macro-critical approaches to the study of the concept of face tend to view face as an immutable entity, to objectify it and analyze it as an independent variable, and to generalize about it regardless of cultural context. These approaches fail in the following aspects: First, they fail to address the issue of face from a historical/cultural perspective. Furthermore, they fail to look at the concept of face in relationship to its family resemblances. Finally, they fail to address undesirable social consequences of face from a consultative or interventionist approach. A systematic critique of these approaches is offered in Chapter 4.

Social constructionism-cum-practical theory, as outlined, constitutes a heuristic for the study of face. It is potentially capable of addressing issues of face not addressed by traditional approaches. From the social constructionist perspective, the following aspects of face can be addressed. Face can be regarded (1) as a conceptual product of interaction; (2) as an object of conceptual transformation within a given system of cultural and historical practices at various levels; (3) as a complex cultural grammar of action within a family of practical concepts which are interrelated to one another; (4) as a starting point for cultural reflexivity and social change; and (5) as a cultural grammar of social interaction.

What aspects of *lian/mian* hidden within traditional approaches are highlighted in the social constructionist approach? With social constructionism as a heuristic, the following points are highlighted:

1. Interpretation of *lian/mian* from the social constructionist perspective is unlike the conventional interpretation in the ethnographic sense. It is better termed "interactional engagement" with or "communicative intervention in *lian/mian* practices." The goal is not to describe and inform, but to enlighten and help actors of *lian/mian* practices reflect on them and (inter)act in a way conducive to the healthy growth of a more open-ended and more inclusive personhood, community, and culture capable of drawing upon all the cultural resources—tradition, modernity, and postmodernity.

2. From the microsocial/cultural/historical perspective on the Chinese concept of *lian/mian*, the history of face as a history of social practices consists of several time-bound periods of *lian/mian* concepts/practices, as described in the early part of Chapter 3.

3. Conceptual transformation is possible through different practices: The *lian/mian* concepts are holistic and undifferentiated and even hardly differentiable. Once the Chinese are able to understand the various dimensions of face and their interrelationships, able to reflect on the social implications and social consequences of *lian/mian* practices in contemporary China, and able to differentiate them, the way of life embodied by the concepts could become open-ended and cultural change could become possible.

4. Emphasis is placed on uncovering the consequentiality and functions of *lian/mian* practices in Chinese life. *Lian/mian* practices in China can function as a form of government, a substitute for law, social control/sanction, and a mechanism for distributing political, relational, and material resources. They can be harmony building, conflict preventive and conflict minimizing, pregnant with social crisis and social chaos, conflict igniting and conflict escalating, conflict resolving and conflict mediating, depending on the context. They can also maintain social hierarchy, the status quo, and social injustice.

5. The focus is on light intervention or consultation as a method (1) to enhance self-reflexivity on *lian/mian* practices; (2) to solve the practical issues of *lian/mian*; (3) to enable people to cope with emotional distress such as the five *lian/mian* anxieties—anxiety over expressions of love, anxiety over talk about sex, anxiety over one's social status, anxiety over admitting one's weaknesses, and anxiety over social performances—elaborated in *Teacher Zhang Monthly*'s book *Chinese renqing and mianzi* (Editorial Board 1990); and (4) to better manage confusions arising out of the process of Chinese identity transformation at the individual and interpersonal levels coupled with ongoing societal change in contemporary China.

## A SOCIAL CONSTRUCTIONIST DEFINITION OF *LIAN/MIAN*

According to the preceding social constructionist propositions, I define *lian/mian* as a unique interactive dynamism and mechanism that members of Chinese communities continually co-construct in order to maintain the harmony of coexistence and social hierarchy. This definition implicates an evolving grammar of morality, an evolving cultural syntax of emotions, given patterns of communication, and a given hierarchy of personhoods characterized by situatedness, continuity, and open-endedness. Together, these factors constitute the actual workings of *lian/mian* and bring unexpected and undesirable political, social, interpersonal, and individual consequences. Such consequences call for the development of an alternative to modern social-scientific, ethnocultural, and critical approaches to help people intellectually and pragmatically prepare to deal with and live with such undesirable consequences and change the *lian/mian* practices.

This definition embraces and emphasizes change, unlike the generalist and ethnocultural definitions that are interested only in description and interpretation.

My rationale for social transformation of *lian/mian* practices can be described briefly as follows.

1. Due to *lian/mian* concerns, Chinese personhood is too culturalized, ethicalized, moralized, and communalized/nationalized to be ready to integrate other cultural values into its everyday living. For example, John Fitzgerald, talking about Liang Qi Chao's thought, writes, "Individual physical existence was transitory and that continuity was to be found only in nations. Variation in space was then matched by difference over time, and both helped to establish the preeminence of the national self over the individual one. The individual self derived its value from membership of the Chinese nation" (1993, p. 31). Fitzgerald also said of Chinese self, "What mattered was that, over the first half of this century, the Chinese self was neither national nor class conscious, it was 'asleep'" (1993, p. 40).

   Indeed, even Liang Chi Chao's attempt to modernize the Chinese self hardly respects the Western concept of self within an individual as something prior to, more sacred than, and constitutive of the so-called national self. The Chinese self is suppressed and is vulnerable to the communal gaze. Liang is a typical Chinese example of devaluing and negating the modern Western type of self within a Chinese individual. Although Liang was regarded as a social and cultural reformer, he remained largely Confucian.

2. *Lian/mian* and the harmony associated with it in Chinese society minimizes the individual agency of the society's members. Many individual members lack even a minimal level of independence in thinking, action, and emotions. In reconstructing Chinese person-hood, *lian/mian* and harmony should be treated as tools to maxi-mize individual happiness while respecting the right of others to it, not as ends in themselves. Because people develop their indi-viduality out of interaction with the community, the community needs to respect individuality. The very goal of harmony is to maximize the happiness of every individual. If the goal of har-mony brings unhappiness to most members of the community, pressures people to slavishly follow the rules and norms of the society, suppresses their basic individual needs, and even drives them to madness and suicide, the mechanism needs to be adjusted.

3. *Lian/mian* discourse and ritual, while intended to be conflict pre-ventive and harmony building, are inherently pregnant with crisis or disorder in modern Chinese society. The excessive emphasis on harmony originates from Confucianism, which regards differ-ences, uncertainty, and change as sources of disorder and hence to be avoided at all costs. This "harmony" is actually a euphemism for homogeneity and conformity. As Hall and Ames point out, "Just as the conductor addressing his orchestra is not concerned to elaborate upon the innumerable possibilities for discord, so Confucius too has little interest in the topic of variations in social disorder" (1998, p. 275).

*Lian/mian* invokes cultural continuity, perpetuates the traditional sys-tem of living, and tends to reinforce the close-ended Chinese identity in the contemporary era of global diversification and multiple inven-tions. Through a social constructionist conceptualization and construc-tion of and intervention into the *lian/mian* practices, I attempt to show how to liberate the Chinese from overemphasis on *renqing, guanxi*, and *lian/mian*. With the Chinese *lian/mian* discourse and ritual transformed to be more open, dynamic, and pluralistic, Chinese personhood and society will be able to preserve the necessary *renqing, guanxi*, and *lian/mian* practices and to be receptive to individuality, equality, free-dom, and diversity.

# 3

# A Social Reconstruction
# of *Lian/Mian*

This chapter maps out the developmental history of *lian/mian* concepts with the historical method of Collingwood, as delineated in the first part of Chapter 4. From historical materials about Chinese etymology, folk songs in early history, biographies, and the like, *lian/mian* history is seen to consist of four stages: the formative phase; the mature phase; the phase of discovery, criticism, revolution, analysis, reflection, and transformation; and the phase of social construction.

## A HISTORICAL DEVELOPMENT OF *LIAN/MIAN* CONCEPTS

The evolution of the Chinese concept of *mian* seems to have been consistent with the evolution of the Chinese character *mian*. Found on a tortoise shell from the Shang Dynasty (1000 B.C.), the original character resembles the current Chinese character for "eye" (Xu, 1988, p. 993). I call it *Mian* 1 (目). An overview of studies of primitive religions in Chinese society before the Shang Dynasty identifies the frequent involvement of the Chinese in creating all kinds of totems and gods and maintaining an intense interaction with them. *Mian* 1 may have symbolized the formation of a society chiefly defined by man-god interactions and the possible emergence of one chiefly defined by man-man face-to-face interactions. The character *Mian* 1 takes the shape of the human eye in a vertical relationship. The shape does not include the two cheeks. Such eyes are primarily used for looking at gods, not at fellow humans. I would characterize the society this character stands for as predominantly defined by the mythical. Scrutiny of the character

"日" seems to suggest that in this phase, the two cheeks do not count as part of the face because a human being is largely defined by his/her eyes not in combination with his/her cheeks.

The transformation of *Mian* 1 into *Mian* 2 (面) marks the emergence of the human-centric Chinese society, whose view of a human being includes more than just eyes. *Mian* 2 incorporates the two cheeks, the forehead, and the chin, encasing the two eyes. It signals the emergence of the social nature of face through human group life and humanity's awareness of its own existence through the sensitivity of the two cheeks. It shows the thinning of the mythical view of human beings and the growth of this-worldly human activity. The human face is found to be able to maintain communal order. The meaning of *Mian* 2 may have been an early source of early Confucianism. *Mian* 2 became a character in classic Chinese.

In the early twentieth century, classic Chinese was simplified, and *Mian* 2 lost the eye. The resulting *Mian* 3 (面) is written such that the lower part of the character is just a square without the eye. While *Mian* 2 is still used as a character of the official version of the Chinese language in Taiwan and Hong Kong and among overseas Chinese communities, *Mian* 3 is used in Mainland China.

The phases of the evolution of the *lian/mian* character in Chinese history can be characterized by a chain of simplicity-complexity-simplicity. The first two phases can be said to be descriptive of the actual *lian/mian* practices, and the last phase can be said to be partially descriptive and partially prescriptive of the *lian/mian* practices. In other words, *Mian* 3 was reinvented in the early twentieth century in order to deconstruct and reconstruct the *lian/mian* practices embodied by *Mian* 2. At the same time, it can be used to signify that the traditional *lian/mian* practices have been significantly but perhaps inappropriately simplified.

While a more sophisticated history of the development of the Chinese concept of *lian/mian* remains to be written, on the basis of further systematic ethnographic and archaeological research, a historical sketch seems due.

As suggested by the historical evolution of the Chinese character *mian* coupled with the emergence and transformation of Chinese culture, the concept of *lian/mian* seems to have experienced the following developmental phases.

1. The formative phase, which is pre-Confucian (before 551 B.C.) is symbolized by *Mian* 1; *mian* 1 emerged in the formative phase of the Chinese culture.
2. The mature phase, which is symbolized by *Mian* 2 (between 551 B.C. and the late 1800s), accompanies full-blown Chinese culture.

3. The phase of discovery, criticism, revolution, analysis, reflection, and transformation symbolized by *Mian* 3 (1800s–1980s) consists of challenges from modern Western civilizations in general and from both communism and the free-market economy to the concepts of *lian/mian* in particular. Bo Yang's *Ugly Chinaman* and Su Xiao-kang's *He shang* mark the end of this phase. This phase originated with the beginning of the modernization movement of Chinese culture and has lasted till today.

4. The fourth phase can be called the phase of social construction. It is imagined as a creative reconstruction of Chinese personhood by way of synthesizing Chinese *lian/mian* culture and the modern and postmodern cultural resources of the West. This reconstruction will be based on a critique of *Mian* 2 and *Mian* 3, which represent a close-ended and homogeneous Chinese cultural personality split between the East and the West, tradition and revolution. The initiation of the phase of social construction is attempted in this present inquiry.

## The Formative Phase

The history of the development of *lian/mian* dates back to the Shang Dynasty. According to Meiling Zhou and David Ho (1992, p. 207), the Chinese character *mian* first appeared in inscriptions on bones or tortoise shells in the Shang Dynasty (the 16th to the 11th century B.C.). According to Chen (1988, p. 157), the concept of *mian*, which fully meant status and fame, originated around the 14th century B.C.; the character *lian* originated in the Yuan Dynasty (1206–1368) and became popular in North China, as *The Kangxi Dictionary* records.

Zhongtian Yi (1996, p. 127) speculates that *mianzi* , as a virtual homonym of *mianju*, meaning "face tool" or mask, may have derived from *mianju*, which was used by the tribal chiefs and masters of funeral ceremony as a medium to communicate with and invite the presence of spirits and deities in the primitive period of Chinese history. By implication, *mianju* became a symbol of status and power in the tribes, as did *mianzi* in later societies. Even today, people with *mianzi* are usually described as "*shen tong guang da*," meaning "to be able to have broad access to spirits and deities." Yu further argues that *mianju* also functioned as an identity card for tribal members in primitive society. The *mianju* for each tribe would carry a different totem. Each person could be identified as a tribal member only by the *mianju* he or she was wearing. A person who lost the *mianju* would be suspected of being a spy from another tribe and would be killed. Losing *mianju*, the mask, equalled losing *mianzi*, the face, which further meant to lose one's life. Therefore, the loss of *mianju/mianzi* originally brought with it a feeling of fear and terror. It was much later that the loss of *mianzi* meant a feeling of shame.

According to Zhou and Ho (1992, p. 207), terms equivalent to *mianzi*, such as *mianmu* (face and eyes), were used to describe the appropriateness of people's social and moral behavior and emotional response to the face threat for the first time in *The Book of Songs*. Wenshan Jia (1996, p. 8) also finds the use of an equivalent of *mianzi*, *ho yen* (thick-faced) in "Wise Words, *Xiaoya*" from *The Book of Songs* (Education Bureau of Changzhou City, 1981, p. 310), as in "The silver-tongued people are thick-faced," meaning that fast talkers do not feel a sense of shame. It suggests that people should cultivate themselves morally through learning to be humble and to talk less and do more. *The Book of Songs* came into being before Confucius, or before 551 B.C.

Confucianism obviously played a very important function in the early development of the concept of *lian/mian*. There may have been a Confucianization of the concepts of *lian/mian*. Chung-ying Cheng, a well-known contemporary Chinese-American philosopher of Chinese philosophy, has equated the roots of the concept of *lian/mian* with Confucianism (1986). However, he seems to have changed his idea recently. He broadened the roots of *lian/mian* by tracing a significant part of the roots of Confucianism to *Zhou yi*, a classic before Confucius that philosophizes *wei*, meaning "positioning" or "positions" (Cheng, 1996). Cheng argues that "*wei* can be said to define the worth and raison d'etre of anything, particularly those of the human person" (1996, p. 149). He further argues that Confucius affirmed the idea of *wei* in *Zhou yi* in his ideal constructions of government, society, family and morality, and human relations in general, which later became the source of *li*, the rites (p. 170).

Confucianism cannot be regarded as the ultimate and only source of the concept of *lian/mian*. The birth of Confucianism and its subsequent dominance in government, education, social, and family life in China affirmed, rationalized, ideologized, and reified the practices to such an extent that most Chinese do not like them and yet cannot do without them. Rather, *wei* may have been a major conceptual source of *lian/mian*. I would argue that the concepts of *lian/mian* may constitute the very foundation and rationale on which Confucius established Confucianism. That process in turn Confucianized the concepts of *lian/mian*, for as documented earlier, the *lian/mian* concepts first came into being more than a thousand years before Confucius.

### The Mature Phase

In the mature phase, *lian/mian* seems to have been concerned about basic human feelings such as shame and fear due to social blunders and was first developed and refined through social interaction in a tightly knit community. As Zito suggests, "But even more important is the fundamental process made possible by the connection of inner and outer: in the gaze of the community, the mediating 'layer' called *mianzi* that is positioned between the inner *lian* and the outer world is the site of the social construction of the self, simultaneously articulated with interior and exterior" (1994, p. 120). With Confucius' recognition of the centrality of cultivating and maintaining *lian/mian* to full humanity, a set of ethical rules and rituals developed around *lian/mian* to regulate social interaction. When the concepts of *lian/mian* were ethicalized and ritualized, they became stable and institutionalized (Zai, 1995, p. 299).

The mature stage began with the emergence of Confucianism around 551 B.C. and ended around the 1800s. Confucianism may have come into being on the basis of Confucius' discovery and creative development of the value of *lian/mian*. Lu Zheng suggests this when he states:

> The most important of our ancestors' scholarships is *renqing* and *mianzi* in the social life. As a result, the less attention given to scholarship other than that of *renqing* and *mianzi*, the more concentration we have on the scholarship of *renqing* and *mianzi*. In other words, the more concentration we have on the scholarship of *renqing* and *mianzi*, the less attention we pay to other types of scholarship. Hence, the most advanced (not necessarily correct) scholarship is the scholarship of *renqing* and *mianzi*. Confucianism is the representative and embodiment of such a scholarship. In this sense, *Confucianism is a study of* renqing *and* mianzi. (1996, p. 150)

The last sentence suggests that *renqing* and *mianzi* are not just social consequences of Confucianism, but fields of inquiry for Confucianism. In other words, Confucianism is but one interpretation of *lian/mian*. While it has imprinted its strong accent on the concepts of *lian/mian*, Confucianism alone is not able to fully account for Chinese *lian/mian* practices. Since the source of *lian/mian* practices is not classical texts of a given abstract ideology or philosophy but social interaction or communication itself, one needs to inquire into the process of communication beyond Confucius to identify their conceptual formation, pragmatic functions, and transformation. More specific than Lu Zheng's argument is that of Hu Wenzhong and C. L. Grove. They argue that Confucianism *affirms* each person's need to maintain face, which constitutes the very order of the society. For example, instead of equating Confucius' concept of *li* with the concept of face, they understand *li* as a Confucian means to "accept and respect each person's need to preserve face" (1991, p. 117). They suggest that Confucius made Chinese more acutely conscious of face needs.

While the *lian/mian* practices constitute the cultural roots of Confucianism, it was Confucianism that brought *lian/mian* to a higher level of sophistication. It is perhaps largely due to Confucianism that *lian/mian* became a sacred object that can be lost, saved, given, sold and bought, and so on. It is perhaps also due to Confucianism that *lian/mian* became a central mechanism or a diffuse social institution that governs and regulates, constrains, and affords Chinese political, economic, military, diplomatic, and social lives and a defining dimension of Chinese personhood. Specifically, Confucianism played a crucial role in making the Chinese concept of *lian/mian* a more pervasive, more deeply rooted, and more dominant form of life and government in Chinese society.

In this stage, *lian/mian* would be a cultural practice of common sense and it would be taken for granted. No Chinese scholar-official ever explicitly made a systematic observation or a study of it before Smith (1894), though folk sayings on face were in circulation, such as those recorded and analyzed for the first time by Hu (1944). Although *lian/mian* was most systematically practiced, the concept was not found to be of academic interest or value during this stage, let alone recognized as central in Chinese society. However, Confucius' discovery, creative expansion, and systematic institutionalization of the *lian/mian* practices before him changed Chinese culture and significantly determined the formation of Chinese personhood for almost 2,000 years.

### The Phase of Discovery, Criticism, Revolution, Analysis, Reflection, and Transformation

The third phase consists of many small steps. Those steps include Arthur Smith's rediscovery of *lian/mian*, which took him more than 20 years' travel and study in all corners of Chinese society in the late nineteenth century (1894); the criticism of *lian/mian* practices by Lin Yu-tang (1935) and Lu Xun (1934/1960); the revolutionary method represented by Mao Tse-Tung, who urged Chinese people to be iron-faced and get rid of human feelings in order to achieve his communist victory; and the scientific analysis started by H. C. Hu (1944) and continued till today by the generalist school represented by Goffman, by Brown and Levinson and their followers, and by the ethnocultural school represented by Chung-Ying Cheng (1986, King 1988). This phase is represented by *Mian* 3.

While Confucius can be said to be the first discoverer of *lian/mian* and the first major reinforcer of *lian/mian* values, Arthur Smith can be said to be the second discoverer of *lian/mian* and the first critic of *lian/mian* from a modern Western perspective, almost 2,000 years after Confucius. Of course, the *lian/mian* he discovered was a Confucianized version. His rediscovery ushered in the formation of *Mian* 3. Like Confucius',

Smith's rediscovery also changed the fate of Chinese culture, making it possible to transform *lian/mian*-centered Chinese personhood. He inspired many well-known modern Chinese intellectuals such as Lin Yu-tang and Lu Xun, who were both influential critics of traditional Chinese culture and who both made their own critiques of the Chinese *lian/mian* practices as institutionalized cultural practices (Lin, 1935; Lu, 1934/1960). The problem with this phase is that the methods used to understand *lian/mian* tend to be biased and the methods used to change *lian/mian* practices are too radical to achieve practical results, as I will elaborate in Chapter 4.

### The Phase of Social Construction

The phase of social construction is a proactive and pragmatic reintegration of all available cultural resources, including the *lian/mian* values, in reconstituting a more expansive, richer, pluralistic, flexible, and open-ended Chinese character with *lian/mian* values as one of its important constituents. It differs from the mature phase, in which *Mian* 2 dominates the Chinese character, and the third phase, of *Mian* 3, which radically negates/marginalizes the values of *lian/mian*. This reintegration is primarily achieved not through sweeping social criticism as represented by Lu Xun and Lin Yu-tang, nor by a revolution like that of Mao Tse-Tung, nor by mere scientific research, but by actual engagement or consultation with groups of Chinese such as families, social groups, or organizations. This consultation is operationalized as Circular Questioning (CQ), which aims at enhancing the self-reflexivity of the Chinese groups or families being consulted.

### Summary of the Historical Development of *Lian/Mian* Concepts

Historically, the concept of face is like a rolling snowball. It gets bigger and more complex through human action and interaction over the course of several thousand years. Originally a physiological concept, it first became a concept of emotion and a set of tacit rules for interaction on the basis of *mianju*, "face tool" or "face piece." It then became a quasi-ethical concept, as is reflected in the adage in *The Book of Songs* that says that "Fast talkers have thick face," which suggests that they sound boastful and lack credibility. These developments constitute the formative stage of the *lian/mian* concept.

In the time of Confucius, the concept of *lian/mian* and the values associated with it were discovered by Confucius, who fully ethicalized and ritualized, or Confucianized them in order to maintain social order and create social harmony. It was further institutionalized by Confucius to maintain social order and harmony. It naturally became the sacred object of central value for every member of society after institutionalization, when it could be lost, earned, exchanged, shattered, torn, or got rid of (*po chu*). These developments constitute the mature phase.

Between the 1880s and the 1970s, the concept became an ossified ideal of personhood, one that was hardly achievable but was still used as a system of social constraints and oppression that maintained the status quo of social hierarchy. Recently it has been used primarily as symbolic capital or social resources by which to gain more power, prestige, and material benefits (Luo, 1997; Yang, 1994). This has triggered a series of efforts along a continuum consisting of social/cultural criticism, revolution, and scientific control. These developments constitute the third phase.

All these historically formed dimensions of *lian/mian* intertwine one another synchronically and dichronically, so much so that they function as a complex whole, nullifying all other modern Western forces such as law, democracy, freedom, and rights, while maintaining social order and harmony.

From the previous inquiry and speculation, I tentatively formulate a theory of face I will call Face Discourse Genres. There are generally four genres of face discourse: (1) Face-Explicit Discourse. The discourse of traditional Chinese culture represented by the mature phase and symbolized by *Mian* 2 can be described as face-ful discourse, or self-less discourse. (2) Face-Muted Discourse: The discourse of modern and contemporary Chinese culture can be described as phase-it-out (face-out) discourse, which aims to get rid of face, and face-it discourse, which means to embrace self. (3) Face-Free Discourse: Face-less discourse is law-ful and self-ful in the modern West. (4) Face-lift Discourse. This refers to the social constructionist discourse of face that I am attempting to generate. Face-lift here not only refers to bringing the face discourse to a more explicit level, out of the Face-Muted Discourse that has negated and marginalized the face discourse, but also refers to an effort to remake *lian/mian* values to incorporate other alien but useful cultural substances.

### The Social Constructionist Perspective: The Conceptual and Practical Centrality of *Lian/Mian* in Chinese Culture

*Lian/mian* practices not only have a long history but also play a central role in Chinese culture. The past studies on face and facework in the West have failed to systematically recognize the practical centrality of face as a concept of cultural communication and personhood in Chinese culture. Drawing upon a divergent body of literature in both Chinese and English, which has been ignored by communication scholars and other social scientists in the West, I argue that the conceptual centrality of *lian/mian* in understanding Chinese character and society has been recognized for the past 100 years, though not as part of facework scholars' own awareness. This recognition has been constantly affirmed and expanded in more academic disciplines both at home and abroad. It is high time the centrality of *lian/mian* in Chinese culture was recognized in mainstream facework research.

In 1894, Arthur Smith found the Chinese cultural concept of *lian/mian* to be central to understanding Chinese personhood, after 24 years of investigations in China. The very first chapter of his book *Chinese Characteristics* is on the Chinese concept of face. He argues, "Once rightly apprehended, 'face' will be found to be in itself a key to the combination lock of many of the most important characteristics of the Chinese" (1894, p. 17). Lu Xun's words seem to be more emphatic about the centrality of *lian/mian* in the Chinese society. He wrote in 1934 that "face is the key to the Chinese spirit and that grasping it will be like grabbing a queue twenty-four years ago—everything will follow" (1934/1960, p. 129). Lin Yu-tang (1935), in his well-known book *My Country and My People*, argues that face, fate, and favor are the three "immutable laws of the Chinese universe," which "have always ruled China, and are ruling China still" (p. 195). Among the three, face occupies the most central position.

Talking about face, Lin states that he does not refer to it in the physiological sense; he refers to something elusive yet substantial by which Chinese social interaction is enspirited. He further argues that face is the most fundamental attribute of the Chinese psychology, which outweighs any kind of legal code; it is the sacred symbolic code Chinese live by. Richard Wilson, through an intensive study of the political socialization process in Taiwan, finds that shaming and face-related techniques have been very formative of one's becoming a Chinese person (1970). Chung-Ying Cheng, a distinguished scholar of Chinese philosophy and comparative cultural studies, argues that *lian/mian* is as central to the functioning of Chinese society as the modern Western concept of law is to the functioning of Western society (1986, p. 340). Hwang Kwang-Kuo, a Chinese social psychologist, argues that *lian/mian* is one of the two core concepts necessary for understanding Chinese social behaviors (1987).

Ambrose King, a sociologist, extends Reischauer's argument for the significance of saving *mian-tzu* in Japanese culture (1962, p. 145) to *lian/mian* in Chinese culture and holds that *lian/mian* is so fundamental to Chinese culture that without it the whole ethical/moral system would collapse (1988, p. 332). Kiyoko Sueda, a Japanese scholar of communication, argues, "Chinese people value *mian-tzu* no matter how rich or poor or high or low in status one is" (1994, p. 24). Hu Wen-Zhong and C. L. Grove argue for the centrality of face in Chinese society from a cross-cultural studies perspective. They state, "The difference in the idea of face between the Chinese and Americans is that face simply has greater social significance for the Chinese. In the United States, concern for face exists but remains largely out of most people's awareness. In the People's Republic, everyone is conscious of face all the time" (1991, p. 115). Ge Gao, Stella Ting-Toomey, and William B. Gudykunst, scholars of Chinese communication and/or intercultural communication, state, "The notion of face permeates every aspect of interpersonal relationships in Chinese culture because of the culture's overarching relational orientation," and "Face concern not only explains but also influences the appropriate use of various communication strategies in Chinese culture" (1996, p. 289). Ringo Ma, a scholar of Chinese communication studies, finds that face maintenance through unofficial intermediaries has been perceived as one of the two crucial factors (the other one being impartiality) in successful mediation of interpersonal conflicts among Chinese (1992). Victoria Chen, also a communication scholar, argues that "the term *mien tze* is a crucial cultural concept that provides a basis for social actors' meaning and action in Chinese society" (1990/1991, p. 130). Jia finds through discourse analysis that facework is a major conflict-preventive and harmony-building mechanism in Chinese everyday life (1997/1998).

It is no exaggeration when David Ho, a sociologist, argues that "face is a concept of central importance because of the pervasiveness with which it asserts its influence in social intercourse" (1976, p. 883). He claims that face can be more important than life itself, for committing suicide is often used as a last attempt to avoid the complete loss of face. Yi Zhong-Tian, a Chinese aesthetician, makes a similar argument that people often die or let die for *lian/mian* or fight for post-death *mianzi*; "*mianzi* is of such significance that relationships among Chinese are dealt with in terms of *mianzi* and are maintained by *mianzi*; the social life of Chinese is often determined and managed in light of *mianzi*" (1996, p. 101). Hairong Yan, a folklorist, in her study of the widely used proverbs of *mianzi* and *lian*, finds that in Chinese society, "'*lian*' is the most essential thing for an individual, without which the individual can have neither trust nor respect from the society. The worst thing that one can do to the other is to make the other lose '*lian*'" (1995, p. 363). She concludes, "The concepts of '*lian*' and '*mianzi*' have great significance in Chinese culture and both of them help maintain the social order and hierarchy" (p. 372). Lu Zheng thinks that *lian/mian* has been the most significant and most effective mechanism through which Chinese distribute and gain access to resources necessary for social survival (1996, p. 149); it has created and sustained rule by men instead of rule by law (p. 152). Zai seems to have most comprehensively summarized the ideas on the centrality of *lian/mian* in Chinese society. He concludes, after a systematic study of *lian/mian*, "it [face] has been always exercising a tremendous influence on and even playing a decisive role in the politics, economy, education, physical training, military arts and all aspects of Chinese everyday life" (1995, p. 367). Many other *lian/mian* scholars share a similar view (Hsu, 1996; Zuo, 1997).

While several studies on face and facework do not specifically ground themselves in Chinese culture or any other culture, all acknowledge that face and facework are central to communication in general. To William R. Cupach and Sandra Metts, "the management of face is particularly relevant to the formation and erosion of interpersonal relationships" (1994, p. 15). Sarah Tracy and Karen Tracy argue, after a nuanced analysis of a rude call to 911, "Facework is an embedded activity; any feature of communication that varies is potentially doing facework" (1997, p. 23).

There are several practical advantages to using *lian/mian* as a central analytical framework in interpreting Chinese social interaction and inducing social and cultural change. First, *lian/mian* as an all-pervasive indigenous interpersonal concept is the organizational center of the grammar of Chinese life. Other indigenous Chinese interpersonal concepts such as *guanxi* and *renqing* are less so. Besides, many indigenous Chinese interpersonal concepts, such as *guanxi* and *renqing* and *bao*, are already either explicitly or implicitly embraced in the concepts of *lian/mian*. Furthermore, the *lian/mian* concept emerges out of and functions and survives in Chinese interpersonal life. The *lian/mian* practices may be better said to be an active and constant constitution of, participation in, and affirmation of Chinese culture. Many other concepts— ethical concepts like *li* (ritual) and *zhun* (respect) and philosophical concepts—are invented by scholar-officials and imposed on Chinese in their everyday life; they are far from central and thus much less revealing about Chinese life than the concepts of *lian/mian*. If those concepts invented by scholars were as central to or as influential on Chinese life, so many *lian/mian* idioms and so many uses of such idioms and related concepts in Chinese life would not have emerged. The failure of the concepts invented by scholars to enter into the central dynamics of Chinese life shows how irrelevant these concepts are to the lives of average Chinese. Finally, the *lian/mian* concepts and practices are not pure inventions. They are the result of the creative integration and transformation of all kinds of native cultural resources available in Chinese everyday living. The concepts of *lian/mian* are the products of interaction between the transformativeness of everyday life and the cultural resources produced by the elitists. One can not say that the roots of *lian/mian* lie in Confucianism; rather, its roots lie in the interactive process of integrating cultural resources with living or vice versa.

*Lian/mian* is much more expansive than Confucianism and goes far beyond it, epitomizing the history of Chinese interaction in Chinese societies. As different cultural resources are integrated, the grammar of the Chinese *lian/mian* practices is evolving, too. However, such a process of evolution is often implicit. One certainly needs to decipher such a gradual evolution, for it takes a complex form and moves in multiple directions.

Until now, however, such an evolution has not challenged the central position, nature, and character of *lian/mian* concepts and practices in Chinese culture, as Kipnis's study suggests (1995). It is still legitimate to treat the *lian/mian* concepts as the central concepts of Chinese life. Therefore, the concepts are still most useful as the central interpretive lens for Chinese interaction. Social and cultural transformation of Chinese personhood, society, and culture can be most effectively induced by transforming the Chinese concepts and practices of *lian/mian*.

## The Social Constructionist Perspective: The Emotional Dimension of *Lian/Mian*

It is no exaggeration to say that emotions are central to understanding *lian/mian*. The subject has rarely been treated from a social constructionist perspective on emotions. From this perspective, I argue here that emotions permeate communication. "Discourse which focuses entirely on communication, on the exchange of thoughts, which ignores deference and emotion, is apt to damage the bond" (Scheff, 1990, p. 8). The *lian/mian* practices as the core of Chinese communication can be said to be significantly shaped by given types of Confucianistically humanized emotions. Here, I first discuss the unique and inherent Chinese social constructionist theory of emotions. Then I explore the emotional dimension of *lian/mian* and discuss the major emotions related to *lian/mian*. Further, I compare the Chinese social constructionist theory of emotions, modern Western theories of emotions, and social constructionist theories of emotion in the contemporary West. On this basis, I argue that *lian/mian* can be regarded as a practical concept consisting of both emotions and social actions, which can be called emotive actions or active emotions.

### The Indigenous Chinese Social Constructionist Theory of Emotions

The Chinese concept of *renqing*, often mistakenly translated as the equivalent of the modern biological, psychodynamic, and cognitive conceptions of feelings and emotions in English, can be most fruitfully translated as "proper human feelings" or "humanized emotions," suggesting a unique social constructionist orientation. *Renqing* suggests a conscious process of discrimination, selection, and ethical legislation, ritualistic regulation (Chen, 1996), and socialization of proper emotions and proper ways to display them that cultivate a brute into a human being (*ren*). The proper emotions and the proper ways to display them to proper people in proper contexts are believed to best cultivate and maintain interpersonal and communal harmony and the hierarchical social order. The improper emotions and improper ways to display them are regarded as forces threatening social harmony and challenging social order. As constituents of inhumanity and sources of disharmony and chaos, they are to be kept away, suppressed, and overcome. To Chinese, *qing* (not *renqing* or *qingli*, meaning proper feelings and reasonableness), in a natural form, can run wild and rampant like an uncultivated field (Chen, 1996). As a natural reservoir or a wild field, it can be made to serve for the construction of a harmonious society or it can degenerate society into a brutal world. Such a *renqing* project was initiated by the less-known Chinese cultural heroes before Confucius and Laozi and has been carried on by their descendants ever since. This is partially described by Vera Schwarcz, who, in studying Chinese social suffering, concludes that China has a cultural tradition of seeking to silence or at least to soften public expression of disturbing emotions (1997, p. 122).

Many sayings in circulation in China illustrate the Chinese idea that proper human emotions should be displayed in proper forms in proper places. Consistent with this idea, Fan Zhong-yan, a well-known scholar-official during the Northern Song Dynasty (1046 A.D.) warned himself and urged other scholar-officials and officials, "To grieve long before the world grieves; to rejoice only after the world rejoices" (*xian tian xia zhi you er you; ho tian xia zhi le er le*) (Liu, 1957, p. 111). This suggests a morally proper and superior attitude of a social elite toward the world, based on proper timing of the display of proper emotions such as happiness and sadness.

Another well-circulated saying of a similar nature, attributed to the same person, goes: Neither be happy when successful nor be sad when unsuccessful. This seems to contradict the previous saying, but it is more reflective of the negative consequences of displaying improper emotions. The idea is that one can be both successful and unsuccessful at different times. When one is successful, one one should not be too happy to remember how to avoid possible future failures. When one is unsuccessful, one should not be too sad to remember that one may be successful by making more effort or by using different strategies in the future.

Although Mao Tse-Tung was best known for revolutionizing traditional Chinese culture, he knew the importance of proper emotions in cultivating his version of modern Chinese and modern Chinese society. One of his most popular sayings goes somewhat like this: Modesty (*xu xin*, which literally means to weaken or soften your heart-mind) leads to improvements, whereas aggressiveness or a feeling of self-importance makes one fall behind (*Xu xin shi ren jing bu; jiao ao shi ren lou hou*). This suggests Mao's clear thinking that certain emotions such as *xu xin* have desirable social consequences while other emotions such as *jiao ao* have undesirable social consequences.

In social interactions in Mainland China, one often hears things like "Don't be happy too early" (*Bie gao xin de tai zao le*) or "Don't feel sad. It is not good for your health" as customary sayings to comfort people controlled by a given type of emotion. Again, they illustrate the Chinese idea that proper emotions should be displayed to proper degrees in proper times in proper places.

All this suggests that the Chinese grammar of *renqing* is a result of a series of conscious human endeavors such as discrimination, selection, legislation, regulation by the cultural elites, socialization and observation of the rules by ordinary Chinese, and the moral cultivation and internalization of the rules by each individual member of Chinese communities. In extension, *renqing* or the proper human feelings are ethicalized and materialized resources and power for social exchange and for the establishment of mutual identification and bonding. Thus, proper human emotions are integrated into the social interaction built into the social hierarchy. Together with social action and etiquette, the proper human emotions to be displayed to varying proper degrees to varying proper persons in the proper time and contexts constitute major pillars of the ideal Chinese social harmony and order.

Proper emotions and feelings seem to be of central value while rationality seems to be of secondary value in Chinese culture, as is reflected in popular Chinese sayings such as "Propriety is bigger than law" (*Li da yu fa*) and "Things should fit in feelings and then rationality" (*Shi wu yen he qing you he li*; or, *he qing he li*). In Chinese culture, the head is used to display face and face-related emotions and ethics (*qing* or feelings). Physically, face holds the uppermost and frontal part of the body; the thinking self, to Chinese, resides in the chest below the face, on a lower level than face; hips are viewed as so insignificant that they are treated as if they were not part of the body. A story goes that during the military coup called the Xi'an Incident (1936), the president of the Chinese Nationalist government, Chiang Kai-shek, hid himself in a shallow cave in the Li Hill near the City of Xi'an with his head in the cave and his hips protruding outside the cave. If you patted a Chinese on the hips, he or she would feel that you were being playful. However, if you slapped or patted him or her on the face, he or she would feel violated and become outraged, even if you intended to be friendly. The feet occupy the lowest part of the body. To demand that one walk on one's hands with the feet up or to demand that a person cross between someone else's legs are traditional Chinese strategies to humiliate the performer and make him or her lose face. In such postures, the performer's face and body are physically below the demander's legs, thus spatially metaphorizing that the performer is socially inferior. This embodies the Chinese notion of social hierarchy which is inspired by and emulated according to the natural and physical hierarchy of the human body.

This is in sharp contrast to the modern Western ranking of rationality as central and emotions and feelings as inferior or secondary. Averill testifies to this Western view:

> Historically, Plato (427–347 B.C.) provides the best introduction to this myth. Plato divided the soul (*psyche*) into two major parts. He localized the rational/immortal part in the head and the irrational/mortal part in the body below the neck. The rationale behind this localization was explicitly metaphorical. Rational thought was the highest kind of thought; hence its localization in the body should also be "highest" (i.e., nearest the heavens). . . .

> Since the emotions interfere with deliberate, rational behavior, they should be located away from the head, where they can do as little harm as possible. Plato therefore located anger and related "spirited" emotions in the chest, separated from the head by an isthmus (the neck) but close enough to be called upon by reason when needed for the defense of the individual. The baser emotions were situated still farther away, below the midriff. (1990, pp. 108–109)

*Qing gan, renqing, qing feng,* and *qing mian,* while sharing some semantic overlap with "emotions," "affections," "feelings," and "passions" in English, are also quite different. The Chinese concepts have a strong contextual emphasis, whereas English concepts such as "love," "like," "preference," and "attachment" have a strongly abstract, subjective, and individualistic bent. The word *qing* is also used in other Chinese terms such as *qing xing, qing shi,* and *qing jing* to mean "context," "situation," and/or "scene," whereas the English terms have no such connotations. "The range of *qing*," therefore, "is broader than emotive states, and includes all reality inputs" (Hansen, 1995, p. 202). The literal translation of *qing* into the English equivalent and its synonyms is thus culturally biased and misleading.

There seems to exist a Chinese hierarchy of *qing* words, with *qing* as the natural form; *renqing* as the humanized form, creatively transformed out of *qing*; and *ganqing* (*gan* means "sense") or *shengqing* (equivalent of deep love toward significant others; *sheng* means "deep") as a highly specialized form based on *renqing.* If we arrange these three kinds of Chinese emotions hierarchically, they form an Egyptian pyramid with *qing* as its foundation, *renqing* as its body, and *ganqing* or *shengqing* as its top. The higher it goes, the narrower, loftier, and more civilized and special it becomes. This hierarchy can be best understood as an accumulative process of transformation.

Several tentative generalizations can be drawn about the Chinese social constructionist view of emotions. First, emotions are context bound. Second, originally wild emotions can be cultivated into proper emotions or *renqing* and *ganqing* with given cultural resources. Third, emotions are socially consequential in that they can be helpful in creating social order and social harmony after cultural transformation and could bring about social chaos without it. Finally, emotions are originally inborn in brute form, but they remain to be cultivated and managed in a civilized manner to serve human interests.

### The Emotional Dimension of *Lian/Mian*

When I use the term "emotional dimension" of *lian/mian*, I run the danger of implying that emotions within *lian/mian* are somehow practically separable. I am using this as an analytical convenience. In practice, emotions, embodied actions, and etiquettes form a dynamic whole. However, past literature on facework in general (Goffman, 1967; Brown and Levinson, 1987; Scollon and Scollon, 1981; Fraser, 1990; O'Driscoll, 1996) and on the Chinese concepts of face in particular (Hu, 1944; Ho, 1976; Cheng, 1986; Hwang, 1987; Mao, 1994; Huang, 1996; Hwang, 1997-1998; Jia, 1997-1998) has been limited by the rationalist biases of modern Western social theories. Scholars analyze face and facework as if they were emotion-free, or the literature treats emotion implicitly rather than explicitly. In the following, I highlight the emotional grammar of face to counteract such biases.

Because of the central position that Chinese culture attributes to the human face, the Chinese face can be said to have been socialized into a major sensor/feeler, exhibitor, and performer of the cultivated emotions. The face can be said to display the emotional grammar. First of all, a forceful torrent of human feelings flows in this "reservoir" of the Chinese face. The Chinese term *"lianmian"* often merges with *"renqing,"* meaning "human feelings" in English, as *"qing mian,"* meaning "feelings-face." According to Richard Wilson, face and emotions are intimately related because of the childhood socialization process in Taiwan, which is heavily dependent on shaming techniques (1970). According to *Zhong guo ren de renqing he mianzi* (Chinese feelings and face), a book originally published in Chinese in Taiwan (Editorial Board of *Teacher Zhang Monthly*, 1990), in daily conversations among Chinese one hears the frequent use of *"qing mian,"* an idiomatic phrase meaning "feelings-face" or "affective face." During the Chinese Communist Revolution, people were urged to be "*tie mian wu qing,*" meaning "to be iron-faced and rid of feelings" toward anyone, including their loved ones, who had made mistakes according to the ideology of the Chinese Communist Party. These examples show that in Chinese culture, affect or feelings/emotions are a fundamental part of "face."

A primary way to judge if and how much of "*lian*" or "*mianzi*" is given (*ge mianzi*), added (*zen mianzi*), earned (*zeng mianzi*), rewarded (*shang lian/mianzi*), saved (*liu mianzi*) and so on is through subjective feelings. A primary way to measure how large "*mianzi*" is is also through feelings. One has to cultivate a culturally meaningful way to feel to find out what has happened to "face" in order for "face" to be able to function in the given culture. Feelings associated with the Chinese *lian* and *mianzi* tend to be shared by culturally competent members of Chinese society. To feel is not only personal but also cultural. According to *Li-Chi* (*The Book of Rites*), an ancient Chinese classic, there are seven human feelings, "enjoyment, anger, sorrowfulness, happiness, love, disgust and desire" (Legge, 1967, p. 50). Several authors have highlighted the significance of "feelings" in the Chinese concept of face. Cheng (1986) argues that the Confucian ideal of society is social and political harmony. Harmonious human relationships can be assured through appeal to human feelings. Human feelings are a primary motive for the management of "face." Hui-ching Chang and Richard Holt argue that "the central character of Chinese relationship lies in its emphasis upon human emotion (*ren-qing*), the standard against which the quality of mien-tze is measured" (1994, p. 103) and on which *mien-tze* is built (p. 107). Various feelings are not only deeply felt in the heart but also intensely felt and expressed in the face. The Editorial Board of *Teacher Zhang Monthly* in Taiwan (1990) has done a study on human feelings and *mianzi* in Taiwan and has identified five kinds of apprehension generated out of concern over human feelings and *mianzi*. They are fear of expressing love, fear of talking about sex, fear of talking with authority figures, fear of revealing one's shortcomings, and fear of speaking and performance in general.

To conclude, emotion intertwines and overlaps with *lian/mian*. In fact, they implicate each other. In order to transform *lian/mian* to achieve social change, part of the job is to inquire into how the emotions related to *lian/mian* practices have been constructed and how they can be reconstructed.

### Emotions Associated with *Lian/Mian*

Past literature seems to suggest that only shame is associated with the loss of face (King, 1988). Some even equate shame with the concept of face (Pye, 1968; Wilson, 1970; Benedict, 1946). As the case studies in Chapters 6 and 7 illustrate, many types of emotions are associated with *lian/mian* and their variations, depending on the context and the nature of loss of face. In fact, as Mi Lan's case in Chapter 7 illustrates, different kinds of emotions can be associated with the loss of face relative to the different kinds of relationships the face loser has with different kinds of people. In the following, I discuss a few Chinese concepts of emotions that I find particularly related to *lian/mian*.

*Shame and* Lian. Shame is a popular Chinese concept. According to Zhu Linlou, the concept of shame is an important concept treated by Confucius. For example, shame is discussed by Confucius in 58 chapters out of the 498 chapters in *Lun yu* (1989, p. 106). It is also integrated into interpersonal and family communication and has become a significant part of the Chinese humanistic culture (Zhu, 1989). According to Zuo, shame is more intensely associated with loss of *lian* than loss of *mianzi*, and shame can be said to be the core of *lian* (1997, p. 69).

Shame is socially desirable. It functions at the moral level and works both internally and externally (King, 1988). In Chinese culture, when a person does something face-losing to a typical Chinese and does not feel shameful, he or she would be said not to be conscious of shame (*bi zhi lian chi*), thus having no *lian* and running the danger of losing his or her culturally acceptable mode of humanity or being rejected as an indecent member of the community. In this sense, to feel shameful when losing face virtually equals meeting an individual obligation culturally defined. As Thomas J. Scheff writes, "Shame seems to arise from our need to feel the right degree of *connectedness* with others" (1994, p. 40). A sense of shame and a visible demonstration of shame through blushing, for example, while a response to one's own failure to meet the moral expectations of the community, also constitute a sign of one's willingness and possibility to be good again. Lack of such a sign, then, signals a lack of moral consciousness and thus a lack of hope to be good again.

*Anger/Rage and Loss of* Mianzi. As the case studies in Chapters 6 and 7 illustrate, a Chinese person whose *mianzi* is lost feels denied, rejected, or unaccepted either as a person or as a role player. Anger is an immediate emotional response to such denial or negation.

Coupled with anger/rage is a pain of the flesh deeply felt by the insider. Pain is the effect of denial. Usually, the sense of a culturally normal self is erased when anger is triggered by loss of *mianzi*. What is left is an "electrical shock" of feelings and emotions shooting through the human body in confusion. I would call this anger a seizure of reason. Such is an extreme scenario of loss of *mianzi*. In getting rid of this pain, the person either seeks to destroy others (as in the case of the Director in Chapter 6) or to destroy or harm himself or herself (as in the case of Mi Lan in Chapter 7).

*Individual Suffering for the Sake of Face.* This idea comes from the popular Chinese saying, "Love *mianzi* to death only to privately suffer" (*si yao mianzi he shou zui*). This state can be a result of observing the Confucian and Mencian doctrine of overcoming self in order to restore *li* or the communication ritual (*ke ji fu li*). One endeavors to be morally good and socially acceptable only to find oneself suffering too much personally. Such examples include holding a luxurious wedding at the cost of falling into huge debt after the wedding; persisting in not remarrying to show faithfulness to a dead spouse and true love to one's children in order to have *lian/mian* by living up to traditional Chinese virtue, and so on. A story exchanged among Chinese students studying in the U.S. goes that a newly arrived Chinese student was invited by an American professor to a party. When the professor asked him if he would like to drink or eat something, he declined, saying that he was neither thirsty nor hungry. The professor took his words at their face value and never asked the student again. That evening, he ended up eating and drinking nothing and suffering from both thirst and hunger. He wanted to appear polite and cultured by not accepting the host's offer until the offer was repeated insistently. But this is a Chinese hosting pattern that Americans do not usually practice. Many Chinese students in the U.S. tell each other this story to illustrate that this student loves his *mianzi* to death, only to suffer privately.

*Positive Emotions Associated with* Lian/Mian. There seems to be no idiomatic phrase that expresses one's emotions when one has face in Chinese social interaction. But there are descriptions of one's face when one has face that suggest that the person is happy. This is understandable, given the general Chinese observance of the epigram credited to the ancient Chinese scholar Fan Zhong-yan that goes, "Never be happy when successful nor be unhappy when unsuccessful" (*Bu yi wu xi bu yi wu bei*). "To be with shine or brightness on one's face" (*lian shang you guang*), for example, is described from the onlooker's perspective rather than from the first-person perspective. In addition, happiness on the part of the person who has face is implied by the appearance of his or her face—brightness or shine. If there is a positive emotion in this phrase, it is primarily visual, not sensual; public, not private. The ideal proper form of emotion is the same both for those having face and those who have lost face. This form of emotion can be described as "reserved," or Daoist—effortlessly and naturally neutral, very much like the emotions of the heavens.

## Comparison and Contrast

The Chinese social constructionist theory of emotions tends to be largely sociocentric, top-down, and bifurcated. In contrast, the modern

Western theories of emotion tend to be largely individualistic, based on biology and individual/cognitive psychology; they view emotions as something primarily irrational, to be repressed. The social constructionist theory of emotions in the contemporary West can be characterized as socially individualistic, both bottom-up and top-down, coming closer to the Chinese view of socially anchored and socially shared emotions, without bifurcation.

*Sociocentricity versus Individual-Centeredness.* The Chinese concept of emotions called *renqing* is hardly individualistic/psychological and naturalistic/biological. *Renqing* is what Leung-Kee Sun calls "social feelings," which are radically different from the shades of meaning of the English term "emotions," which include "impulses, instincts, libido, or animosity" and so on (1991, p. 10). When I say that emotions are social, I mean that they are not only felt by the concerned party but also visible to the public eye, unlike the modern Western view of emotions as private and therefore individually bounded. The Chinese view of emotions seems especially social. The idiomatic phrase "*lian shang you guang*" is a good example. A person who has a face full of brightness must be happy because his or her bright face is seen by his or her community and invites more respect and deference toward him or her.

Chinese emotions are ethicalized, interpersonalized, and materialized, performative, action-oriented, or sociocentric (Potter, 1988, p. 186), arising out of interaction and discourse. Chinese emotions are of social utility and aim at maintaining the hierarchical social order and cultivating social harmony. Bad emotions in the individual sense dissipate in the very process of harmonizing social interactions. As an ideal, Chinese are socialized to be both properly emotional and reasonable (*qing li jie he*). Sun says it well when he states, "It seems that Chinese emotionality is subdued, diffused into less intense channels, or otherwise sidetracked from its direct target" (1991, p. 10). However, he fails to realize that the Chinese emotionality he describes is the consequence of a cultural transformation of brutal emotions to maintain the Confucian ideal of social harmony.

The modern Western individual type of emotions and its modes of open and direct expression, as described by Sulamith Heinz Potter (1988), is regarded as a sign of social immaturity and lack of emotional composedness (*bu wen zhong*) and is usually frowned upon in the Chinese cultural context. Chinese culture, heavily shaped by Confucianism and Daoism, aims at the golden mean (*zhong yong*, meaning "a point between two extremes") in dealing with emotions. Just as free expressions of individual emotions are generally endorsed by social and cultural institutions in the West, with the rationale that such free expressions constitute social order, Chinese social and cultural institutions prefer regulated expression of pro-social emotions, with the ratio-nale that such regulated expression best maintains social order. Al-though Potter aims at understanding Chinese emotions without ethnocentrism, ethnocentric ideas abound in her interpretation. The major bias is her Orientalist/essentialist understanding of Chinese culture, although she claims that her study is informed by the fledgling social constructionist theories in the contemporary West. It is not that Chinese think that "the social order exists independently of any emo-tion" (Potter, 1988, p. 186) and that "Chinese do not locate significance in the connection between the emotions, the self, and social order" (Potter, 1988, p. 186), but rather that Chinese think that emotions, self, and social order constitute the very stuff of society and that natural and wild emotions, like a wild field, can be cultivated or, like a tree, can be trimmed to be sociocentric. Thus controlled, they reinforce the ideal Chinese personhood (*ren*) or cohumanity, which maintains the hierar-chical social order and social harmony. It is not that emotions are secondary to Chinese, but rather that the cultivation of good emotions and concentration on good emotional experiences for oneself are in moral disfavor. It remains a high priority for Chinese to make each other more than emotionally satisfied or to give each other face (*xiang hu gei mianzi*) when one does not have one; to enhance or elevate each other's face (*tai gao mianzi*) when one does not have a big face (*mianzi bu da*); and to save each other's face (*xiang hu wuan hui mianzi*) when it is on the verge of loss. Chinese understand that emotions are collectively reshaped and shared. For example, a Chinese popular saying goes something like "when there is joy, let's share joy. When there is suffer-ing, let's divide suffering" (*you le tong xiang, you lan tong dang*).

Although a "face" is not a full conceptual equivalent of "emotions" in English, the Chinese concept of face can be said to be saturated with emotions. In fact, the Chinese dependence upon the collectively created and shared emotions embodied by face has created many undesirable social consequences for Chinese in this world of unprecedented com-petition. It is the goal of the present study to generate a more useful alternative to the *renqing-guanxi*–based *lian/mian* mode of life, an alter-native characterized by a balance of emotion and reason.

*Conceptual Inseparability versus Separability.* Another difference among the three—the modern Western view, the social constructionist view of the contemporary West, and the Chinese social constructionist view—is that the Chinese view of emotions or *renqing* is practically inseparable from social action, rituals, ethics, morality, and even religion and per-sonhood. These concepts implicate one another. It also has a bifurcated view of emotions as *renqing* or cultivated proper human emotions versus the primitive, uncultivated, and thus potentially rampant and wild emotions of brutes.

The dominant view of traditional social science in modern Western culture holds that emotions are the very stuff of irrationality. They are primarily related to biological instincts, neurological activity, or mental traits (Averill, 1992, p. 21). They are felt privately within an individual and are to be rationalized away as destructive of rationality and the social order. Instead of inquiring into emotions, the traditional social science approach hardly goes beyond its rationalist bias. Its myth holds that the world is dichotomous; it is made up of rationality and irrationality, according to the book *Anger's Past: The Social Uses of an Emotion in the Middle Ages* (Rosenwein, 1998). The book reveals the social and religious repression of anger as a preparation for the coming of the Renaissance, which hallowed rationality. According to Scheff, because of the historical denial of emotions in modern Western civilization, the field of emotions still remains "a jungle of unexamined assumptions, observations, and theories" (1994, p. 41); and "Our language is deficient in precise, complex, and subtle words describing emotional and relational states" (p. 3).

*Other Differences.* If one says that the modern Western person views emotions as universal and unchanging (Solomon, 1995), one should also say that emotions in the Chinese social constructionist view and the Western social constructionist view are particularistic and situated. The modern Western view wants to get rid of them, whereas the Chinese view wants to harmonize them and the Western constructionist view wants to reintegrate them as a legitimate part of contemporary Western culture. An analogy can be drawn between the modern West's attitude toward emotions and its attitude toward nature: The modern West tames emotions as hard as it tames nature. Like a postmodern effort to restore nature through environmental protection, another postmodern effort is also needed to restore, cultivate, and nurture emotions through the protection or improvement of the emotional environment. While a social constructionist view in the West humanizes emotions and views them as open processes in a changing social/cultural context, the Chinese view seems to offer a social but normative and humanistically ideal perspective on emotions. This is where a social constructionist view of emotions emergent in the West is trying to redefine emotions, and this is where the Chinese social constructionist view of emotions can be of heuristic value to the social constructionist project on emotions in the West.

On the other hand, the open-ended transformation of emotions facilitated through language and communication in the Western constructionist view, which is lacking in the Chinese constructionist view, is of heuristic value to my exploration of the possibility to facilitate the transformation of the Chinese *lian/mian*-related emotions, which often bring about undesirable personal and social consequences, as the case studies in Chapter 6 and Chapter 7 show. Another difference is that while the Western social constructionist view of emotions is culturally diverse, the Chinese view is ethnocultural or Sinocentric. The former especially suggests that emotional performances are afforded and constrained by culture and different cultures tend to view, regulate, and manage emotional performances differently. Furthermore, the Western social constructionist view, as a critical response to the Western biological, individualistic, and mentalistic view of emotions, argues only for the social nature of emotions, sacrificing the biological dimension of emotions; the Chinese view recognizes both the natural and the social dimensions of emotions, with more emphasis on how to transform emotions culturally to help achieve social harmony and social order. Last but not least, the former seems to view emotions as separate from but coexisting with reason, whereas the Chinese social constructionist theory seems to view emotions and reason as interrelated and balanced as well as conceptually and practically inseparable.

*Shared Foundation.* The Chinese social constructionist theory and the Western social constructionist theory, while having some differences, share the following assumptions: Emotional experiences and emotion statements are culturally shaped. They are culturally meaningful, socially participatory, and personally, morally, and socially consequential and transformative. They are inseparable dimensions of social interaction that permeate rationality. They can join the world as a dynamic dimension of culture and self. Including emotions in the study of communication can only deepen our understanding of culture and self and enrich our grammar of communication, since communication is inherently and necessarily emotional-rational.

### *Lian/Mian*: A Practical Concept of Communication and Emotions

I tentatively conclude from the preceding discussion that the Chinese *lian/mian* practice, as a communicative practice in Chinese culture, is a practice thickly permeated by culturally constructed emotions. Only these active emotions make *lian/mian* identifiable in that they function both as motives for *lian/mian* and as shields from and spears for *lian/mian*. They are motives in that striving for *lian/mian* is to make oneself enjoy or suffer socially desirable feelings. They are shields from *lian/mian* in that the fear that one will suffer from socially undesirable feelings and the prospect that one will enjoy socially desirable feelings constitute the *lian/mian* dynamics and prevent one's *lian/mian* from losing in Chinese social interaction. They act as spears in that they can be used to tear other people's face, to make other people lose face, and to threaten other people's face when necessary. Since emotions are definitive of *lian/mian*, I hypothesize that the different historical phases of *lian/mian* transformation sketched earlier must have been accompanied by different grammars of active emotions.

## THE SOCIAL CONSTRUCTIONIST PERSPECTIVE: *LIAN/MIAN* AS A CLUSTER CONCEPT

Surrounding the concept of *lian/mian* are a host of indigenous Chinese interpersonal concepts both similar to and different from one another. Inspired by the works of constructionist/pragmatist philosophers, such as Wittgenstein's notions of language games, family resemblances, and grammar of action (1958); David L. Hall's "cluster concept" (1994, p. 215); and Derrida's concept of "deferrance" (1978), I identify many different but related forms of *lian/mian* concepts and explore their cultural meanings and uses in relation to each other. I also briefly explain how they constitute one another and configure a coherent cultural grammar for social interaction in the Chinese context.

Among these concepts, Hall's "cluster concept" warrants special attention. Hall defines "cluster concept" as "complex of associations which can neither be reduced to a coherent or internally consistent meaning nor seen individually in their respective context-relative meanings" (1994, p. 215). It is "a permanently ambiguous" and yet inexhaustibly meaningful notion. *Lian/mian* is very much like Hall's "cluster concept," as explained here.

The following major practical concepts significantly constitute the complex associations of *lian/mian*, which further configure a grammar of action—the rules of "language games" in Chinese social interaction. Each differs from the others but also shares many fundamental similarities with them; they mutually define one other. Some of the *lian/mian* concepts I am going to elaborate are *lian mian, qing mian, gan ga* (embarrassment), *dioulian, li, guqi, bai jiazi, diao jia, tseng mianzi, da zhong lian chong pangzi* (beat one's own face to make it swell enough to appear fat enough to show off an air of authority), *men mian, pai chang, du chi*, and *chu qi*. With differences and similarities among these concepts identified, the nuances and uniquenesses of the *lian/mian* concepts can be better appreciated. The centrality and prevalence of *lian/mian* practices in Chinese culture and the centrality and pervasiveness of emotions in *lian/mian* concepts are further evidenced by the pervasive uses of these *lian/mian*-related terms in daily conversations in Chinese contexts.

## Fundamental Concepts in Contrast

*Lian* and *mian*, which have been both translated as "face" by Smith, are two related but different concepts in Chinese culture. In contrast and in relation to them are *jiazi*, which is false *lian* or *mian*; *li*, which is a formalization of *lian* and *mian*; and *guqi*, which is an antithesis of *lian/mian*. By pointing out what is *lian/mian* and what is not, what it looks like and what it does not look like, more of the richness of the meanings of *lian/mian* and its variants is uncovered here than in past studies that either just enlist and classify *lian/mian* terms (Cheng, 1987; Zai, 1995; Zuo, 1997) or explain only the *lian/mian* proverbs (Hu, 1944; Yan, 1995).

*Lian and Mian.* Face as *lian* refers to the minimum moral level that defines a person's membership in Chinese society, whereas *mian* refers to one's social respectability on a much higher level than *lian* (Cheng, 1986, p. 335; King, 1988, p. 325). On this basis, *lian* can be translated as "moral face" whereas *mian* can be translated as "social face." Such a differentiation is not drawn by Western scholars of face research such as Irving Goffman and Brown and Levinson, who are interested in making cross-cultural generalizations. Loss of face (*diou lian*) equals loss of humanity (*diou ren*), which means that the community no longer regards the person as a decent human being and instead regards him or her as a sheer animal of a lower form. In fact, loss of *lian* (moral face) and loss of *ren* (personhood) are interchangeable terms in Chinese social interaction. Loss of *mianzi* (*diou mianzi*) would mean loss of a certain amount of symbolic resources and in extension power and means for living. In reality, people who have *mianzi* may not have real *lian*, although everyone is supposed to have *lian* as the necessary basis for *mianzi*. *Mianzi* is not the basis of *lian*. The divorce of *mian* from *lian* suggests the hierarchical nature of human relationships in Chinese society. However, together, *lian* and *mian* constitute the unique Chinese self, which is "self-conscious, not in the sense of being able to isolate and objectify one's essential self, but in the sense of being aware of oneself as a locus of observation by others. The locus of self-consciousness is not in the 'I' detached from the 'me', but in the consciousness of 'me'" (Hall and Ames, 1998, p. 26).

*Jiazi. Jiazi* literally means a crutch used by someone to sustain himself or herself while walking. According to Zai (1995), the concept of *jiazi* lies between the concept of *lian*, primarily a moral image, and the concept of *mian*, primarily a social image. *Jiazi* has a negative connotation. It is an excessive display of *lian* or *mianzi* that is viewed negatively by the public or community. One would hear an idiomatic phrase "*bai jiazi*," meaning "to display one's image by relying on a crutch." This phrase is usually used to refer to someone who, having some *mianzi*, refrains from having it taken advantage of by someone else too easily. For example, a person *bai jiazi* when he or she ritualistically declines an invitation for a social event with the hope that the invitation will be extended again with a formality in full accord with his or her self-perceived social status. In other words, to *bai jiazi* is to enhance one's *mianzi* unreasonably. The concept of *jiazi* suggests that *mianzi* is not just about formality or externality as it is understood by some Western scholars (Stover, 1974). It is substantial to members of the Chinese community. Perhaps, "to *bai jiazi*" is just the opposite of "*you gu qi*," or "to have the bone spirit" (meaning to be as solid and firm as the human bone structure), unbending and unyielding to corrupt or evil forces. The former attempts to feed into the *mianzi* mechanism, whereas the latter refrains from it and even intends to break it.

*Li*. Some Chinese scholars of *lian/mian* research tend to think of the relationship between *lian/mian* and *li* in two ways: (1) *Li* (in extension, Confucianism) is the source of *mianzi* (Cheng, 1986; Zai, 1995, p. 285). For example, Zai states, "The essence of *lian/mian* is *li*. Therefore, to want to have *lian* is to follow *li*." (2) *Li* is regarded as a virtually fully overlapping synonym of *lian/mian* (King, 1988; Zhu, 1988). These scholars seem to strongly suggest that *li* is *lian/mian* and *lian/mian* is *li*. I argue that *lian/mian* is prior to *li*. As mentioned previously in my historical perspective on *lian/mian* practices, according to Zhong-Shu Xu (1988, p. 993), the earliest character of *mian* is found on a tortoise shell dated back to a thousand years before Confucius, in the Shang Dynasty. The character of *mian* is written in the shape of a human eye. Again, in "Wise Words, Xiaoya" from *Book of Songs* (*Shi jing*) before Confucius or around 551 B.C., the phrase "*houyan*" or "thick face" is used for the first time in the adage I have cited to refer to fast talkers who do not feel ashamed (Education Bureau of Changzhou City, 1981, p. 310). These historical records strongly show that the character *mian* is likely to have appeared long before the character *li*. Therefore, *li* should not be interchangeable with *lian/mian* or *mian*.

*Li* is but a Confucian attempt to codify, affirm, expand, ethicalize, and ideologize *lian/mian*. *Lian/mian* is a grammar of social practices that constitute an emergent system of cultural values in action. *Li* is superficial, whereas *lian/mian* is substantial. *Lian/mian* is relatively stable, whereas *li* is changeable. *Li* refers to specifics of *lian/mian*, whereas *lian/mian* is its spirit. *Li* is a formal and elitist term detached from ongoing reality and imposed upon the society, whereas *lian/mian* is from the deep culture and emerged out of popular culture. In conclusion, *lian/mian* is the source and rationale of *li*.

*Guqi. Gu* means bone. *Qi* means air or spirit, literally the spirit around the bone. *Guqi* is related to *mianzi*, but it is much more than *mianzi* and transcends it. Someone who has *guqi* never bows in front of worldly power and authority just because he or she is afraid of losing *mianzi*. *Guqi* stands for moral and ethical uprightness and the Chinese sense of justice, so much so that one's *guqi* is most likely to challenge the *mianzi* of authority. The classic case of dragging the emperor down off his horse to stop him from doing something wrong illustrates this point. Its goal is to break the harmony that belies chaos and crisis and to transform an unjust social order, as well as to maintain individual integrity. In this sense, *guqi* is from within.

*Gu* is essence, whereas *lian/mian* is form: *gu* is internal, whereas *mian* is external; *gu* is whole, whereas *lian/mian* is part. *Guqi* is ideal and loyal to the ideal, whereas *lian/mian* is worldly. *Guqi* is critical of the social order, whereas *lian/mian* maintains the status quo and the social order. The concept of *guqi* may have been developed out of *lian/mian*; it functions as a rival to *lian/mian*. It symbolizes a critical force, countering the vices of the *lian/mian* mechanism. Historically, *lian/mian* has been dominant in social and political life, whereas *guqi* has been on the margin. *Guqi* is like a waterlily in a dirty pond. The waterlily is most beautiful, pure and unpolluted, but it emerges out of dirty mud and water. Likewise, *guqi*, the purest and most admirable human quality, is born out of a social and political environment dominated by the *lian/mian* mechanism full of vices. Someone with *guqi* usually does not have *mianzi*, whereas someone who wants *mianzi* can not afford to have *guqi*. *Guqi* is independent from and even opposed to the establishment. However, it always has a potential to transform *lian/mian*. Chu Yuan, a well-known figure of the State of Chu during the Warring States Period of Chinese history (475 B.C.–221 B.C.) and the father of ancient Chinese literature, is usually treated as someone of *guqi*. He drowned himself because he was unwilling to serve the king of the Chu State, who was full of vices and would refuse to listen to the objective criticisms of loyal inferiors and would entertain himself with flatteries from his deceptive ministers.

### Lian with Different Adjectives

*Guei Lian (Ghostly Face). Guei lian* describes to someone who is sneaky, reluctant to come face-to-face with people, as if he or she has done something wrong and is afraid of being known by the community. It is usually used together with *guei tou* (the ghostly head), as in *guei tou guei lian*.

*Si Lian (Dead Face). Si lian* is used to describe someone who does not smile at all and does not show any sign of friendliness or liveliness toward people. This person appears as if he or she were dead or as if his or her face were not alive.

*Lian Hou (Thick Face). Lian hou* is used to describe someone who always repeats immoral behaviors without any effort or willingness to stop, repent, or apologize, regardless of warnings from his or her community. A person with thick face does not have the culturally defined minimum level of shame consciousness. Such a person is usually regarded as a mean person to be frowned upon by the community.

*Si Pi Lai Lian (Dead Skin and Coarse Face). Si pi lai lian* is even worse than "thick face." It is used to describe someone who is not only unwilling to correct his or her misbehavior but also entertains himself or herself with breaking and defying mockingly the most basic rules for person-making (*zuo ren*). An example would be a man who, although the woman he has been wooing clearly tells him that she dislikes him, still persists without any sense of shame.

*Lian Pi Bao (Thin Face Skin). Lian pi bao* is opposite to "thick face." It is used to describe someone who feels shy and is easily embarrassed. It is regarded as a virtue in Chinese culture, especially of a lady. Someone with a thin face skin is usually humble and peaceful and prefers to be alone or with a few close friends. For example, a teenage girl who feels too shy to attend a social event open to all people can be said to be *lian pi bao*. The use of this phrase is part of the traditional Chinese construction of the ideal feminity.

*Chou O Zui Lian (Ugly and Evil Mouth and Face). Chou o zui lian* is used to describe someone who appears to be very nice and kind but turns out to be full of vices. One often hears married Chinese women use this to ventilate anger and grievances upon their unfaithful husbands. One also hears Chinese use *"chou o zui lian"* to describe cruel and heartless bosses and government leaders, as in the case of the 1989 Chinese Prodemocracy Movement, during which the Chinese government hardliners showed their "ugly and evil mouths and faces" in using tanks and bullets against peaceful demonstrators.

*Hei Lian (Black Face). Hei Lian* describes someone who plays the role of the tough guy who always appeals to the law and believes in punishment instead of appealing to human feelings and believing in patient persuasion. For example, a Chinese parent who is strict with his or her children can be said to play the role of *hei lian*. "Black" is to evoke storm clouds or darkness rather than any skin color.

*Hong Lian (Pink Face)*. *Hong lian* is just the opposite of *hei lian*. *Hong lian* describes someone who plays the role of a nice guy who appeals to human feelings and believes in peaceful persuasion instead of appealing to the law and believing in punishment. For example, a Chinese parent who practices positive reinforcement with his or her children can be said to be a *hong lian*.

*Bai Lian (Pale Face)*. *Bai lain* is a stereotypical character in the Beijing Opera. Chinese people use the term "the pale face" to refer to someone who is a treacherous villain who betrays even the closest friends and relatives for his or her own good and therefore is not to be trusted. People usually avoid dealing with someone called a little *bai lian* on a daily basis.

*Hua Lian (Colored Face)*. The term *hua lian* also originates in the Beijing Opera. *Hua lian* refers to someone who is a little, mean person, someone who remains an outsider within the circle, trying to make a difference with deeds and words incongruent with the situation but ending up with inconsequential but comic effects.

## What Can be Done with *Lian*

Any action verb can be associated with *lian*, as if it were a highly flexible and easily manipulatable object. The following *lian*-plus-verb or verb-plus-*lian* phrases strongly suggest that the concept of *lian* here, while grounded in the two cheeks, is far more than the two cheeks in the biological sense.

*To Yao Lian and to Bu Yao Lian (To Want to Have Face and Not to Want to Have Face)*. Wanting to have one's face and not wanting to have one's face is equivalent to Hamlet's "to be or not to be." The former phrase means that one wants to retain one's humanity through observing the rules and practicing the rituals, whereas the latter means that one does not want to be human.

*To Ge Lian (To Give Face)*. To *ge lian* means to give someone an opportunity to become human again. *Shang lian* (to reward someone with face) can be a synonym for *ge lian* or *ge mianzi*. For example, if a student fails an exam, his father, instead of scolding him as usual, may remain calm and want to discuss peacefully with his son how he can make it up. If the son breaks into hot temper in response to his father's request, his father can say, "I give you *lian* but you do not want it."

*To Tsui Tai (To Remove One's Stage). Tsui tai* is just the opposite of *ge lian* or *shang lian*. It means to damage one's image and reputation. Another version is to *ge* someone's *lian mo hei* (besmear one's face with black color). One can do this in many ways. Gossip is one way, and entrapment or conspiracy is another.

*To Shang Lian (To Reward Someone with Lian). Shang lian* is used to describe someone in a higher position who goes an extra mile to boost up the image of someone in an inferior position by doing something favorable to the inferior such as showing up at the latter's public relations event. *Shang lian* is synonymous with *shang mianzi*. Other versions of *shang lian* can be *shang guang* (reward someone with one's shine on the face) and *ge* someone's *lian shang tie jing* (to add golden color to one's face).

*To Fan Lian Bu Ren Ren (To Turn One's Face Upside Down to Stop Treating the Other Party as a Human Being). Fan lian bu ren ren* is used to describe someone who not only forgets the privileges and favors the other party has supplied in the past, but also refuses to return the privileges and favors and severs the relationship. An extreme and more aggressive form is *si po lian pi* (to tear one's face skin), meaning to radically destroy the relationship with a significant other.

*To Feel Gan Ga and to Diou Lian. Lian* can be lost, whereas the two cheeks can not. Embarrassment or *gan ga* is not an equivalent of loss of face, and loss of face is not an equivalent of embarrassment. Embarrassment is a fully emotional concept. It is an instant and immediate emotional self-awareness of one's own response to one's own inappropriate behavior or thinking. It is primarily grounded within an individual, although it is a social concept. *Diou lian* or loss of face, however, is most likely to be the social consequence of embarrassment. Loss of face would mean degradation of the person's moral and social status and the loss of resources necessary for a decent living, specifically loss of friendships, love of relatives, and even material support, for one's loss of face means one's own relatives' and friends' loss of such resources at the same time. Therefore, loss of face has various emotional connotations such as embarrassment, frustration, regret, anger, and even pain.

Many English readers may tend to equate embarrassment with loss of face. However, in the Chinese context, such an equation is impossible. Loss of face can be an iceberg, whereas *gan ga* or embarrassment is just the tip of the iceberg. An extreme form of loss of *lian* is *diou lian diou dao jia* (to lose one's face to affect the whole family or clan). A lighter version of loss of face is *lian shang wu guang* (there is no shine on one's face). A more serious one is *bu zhi ba lian wang na guo* (one does not know where to put one's face). *Diou ren* (loss of personhood or humanity) is often used in exchange with *diou lian* in Chinese social interaction. Other terms that can be used exchangeably with *diou lian* are *shi ge* (loss of integrity), *chue de* (no morality), and *diou chou* (exposure of one's ugly side).

*To Da Zhong Lian Chong Pangzi.* To *da zhong lian chong pangzi* means beat one's own face so that the face swells to appear heavy enough to show an air of authority. In traditional Chinese culture, a heavy man is regarded as someone of wealth and high social status who demands special respect. This is opposite to the contemporary American notion of a heavy or stout person, who often experiences discrimination. The results of such doings are unsuccessful in most cases. One pays too big a price or makes an unworthy self-sacrifice just to look good to the public. This idiomatic expression is often used by Chinese to satirize those who are excessively concerned about their *lian/mian*. Here is an example: A person *da zhong lian chong pangzi* when he or she holds a grand wedding only to fall into deep debt and to be sued and jailed because of his or her inability to repay the debt.

### Variations of *Mian*

There are so many variations of *mian* that the word "face" used by Smith, Goffman, Brown and Levinson, and many other Western face scholars cannot cover them all. These variations demonstrate that *mian* is a highly contextual and practical concept with a complex system of meanings.

*Qing Mian (Affective Face).* Qing *mian* is a merger of two concepts, with *qing* meaning "affection" and *mian* meaning "owning a large amount of symbolic resources." Thus, *qing mian* is a combination of affective and symbolic resources. *Jiang qing mian* means to treat someone as if a blood relative or to value a particular tie. *Bu jiang qing mian* means to treat someone including a relative as if a person outside the family, or *wai ren*, or to treat someone cold-bloodedly; in extreme cases, to treat someone as a nonperson, or *bu dang ren*.

*Ti Mian (Body-Face).* The word "*ti mian*" is a unitary adjective of common use that endorses the Chinese configuration of the ideal image in and for the society. This image, as the term literally suggests, is a full-body one that includes both the body and the face. The essence of *ti mian* is the Confucian sense and ritual of harmony, balance, and cultivation of the person. Metaphorically, *ti mian* means appropriateness defined in the Chinese sense. A synonym of *ti mian* is *de ti* (being in control of one's body). Related to these is *ti tong* (body unity), which refers to the body ritual system that helps cultivate one into a Confucianist gentleman or *junzi*. *Ti mian*, *de ti*, and *ti tong* all mean one's embodiment of the Confucian virtues, which constitute gentlemanhood.

Future studies should examine *ti mian* and its related terms in relationship to one another (instead of splitting *ti mian* into *ti* and *mian* and studying *ti* and *mian* separately) from an ethnographic and social constructionist perspective. Such a studies could identify the active patterns of *ti mian* in Chinese culture and the historical and regional variations of this concept.

*Men Mian (Gate-Face).* Since I came to the United States, I have always looked for the main gate or *damen* of every university campus or corporate site I visit. When people pointed out the gates, I would always be disappointed, as there are no unique decorations of these main gates or main entrances. In China, the main gate is always distinguishable from any other entrance to every house or every architectural compound. There are usually grand decorations around the main gate or the main entrance, in sharp contrast to a back door/entrance or side door/entrance, which is usually plain, with little or no decoration, or even worn, shabby, and ugly. This gate with grand decorations is called *men mian*, literally meaning gate-face. This gate is called *men mian* or body-face primarily because it is the embodiment, display, and extension of the face or *mianzi* of the institution owner. One can judge how big someone's *mianzi* is by judging how grand the gate of the person's house or the company building looks. In other words, one can see the *mianzi* of the person by seeing and observing his grand gate (*men mian* or gate-face), without seeing the actual person.

*Chang Mian (Site-Face).* *Chang mian* literally means site-face or context-face. It is more extensive than *men mian* or gate-face. Usually, people use "*chang mian da*" (its site-face is big or extravagant) to describe a very grand event such as a wedding or a celebration of a holiday. One may wonder why Chinese like to add "face" to many impersonal objects. My answer is that because of the Chinese value of face-to-face communication, Chinese tend to put a human face to non-human objects to humanize their living environment.

*Pai Chang or Ostentation. Pai chang*, literally meaning "a patterned site," is an instance of having *mianzi*. It is an extravagant scene for an event that displays one's status or signifies one's possession of rich symbolic and material resources.

## *Mian* with an Adjective

One with a big *mianzi* (*mianzi da*) is of high social status and commands special respect, obedience from people around, and special access to resources, whereas one with a small *mianzi* (*mianzi xiao*) is the opposite. The one with a golden *mianzi* is even more privileged than the one with a big *mianzi*. Such a person is regarded as virtually sacred. The term "golden *mianzi*" may have originated from the golden Buddhas that Chinese Buddhists worship. The one with a *xu mianzi* or shallow *mianzi* is like a paper tiger who has no substance.

## What Can be Done to *Mian*

Almost any action verb can be used with *mian* as if it were a very flexible object, easily manipulatable. In the Chinese context, *mianzi* can be given, lost, fought for, protected, made, and so on.

*To Ge Mianzi.* To give face (*ge mianzi*) means to give a protective mask to prevent fear and insecurity, so that the other person can be easily identified by the community and have a sense of belonging. In this sense, to give face is to give the other person opportunities and confidence to interact with other members of the community or to give the other person power and make him or her feel elevated socially. Not to give face is like depriving the person of such opportunities or, in extension, like depriving the person of the social conditions for survival or the sources of humanity (Hall & Ames, 1998, p. 26). Synonymous with *ge mianzi* is *ge* somebody *tsa zhi mu fen* or to powder someone's face. Although the *mianzi* giver does not tell the recipient to give him or her *mianzi* in return, the unspoken assumption is that the recipient is obligated to give the person *mianzi* back in a different form and within an unspecified time period. Failure to be aware of this principle of reciprocity creates conflict.

Another challenge for someone who is not knowledgeable about this dynamic is to become aware of what can constitute an act of *ge mianzi* and an act of *huan mianzi* (to return *mianzi*) in Chinese culture. Many more social acts can be regarded as gestures of *ge mianzi* or *huan mianzi* than one can think of. The verbal "thank you" does not necessarily constitute an act of *huan mianzi*. However, the recipient's nonverbal gesture of humbleness, obedience, conformity, or compliment may fully constitute an act of *ge mianzi*. *Tseng mianzi* is a kind of *ge mianzi* (face giving) and can be viewed as opposite to *diao jia*. It means to help sustain or raise another's *mianzi*. One would *tseng mianzi* for someone who does not have *mianzi*. It is as if one tried to walk for his or her significant other if his or her significant other did not know how to walk. The father will *tseng mianzi* for his son when the father and/or the father's friends go out of his/their own way to attend the first social event hosted by the son. Synonymous with this is *tai mianzi* (to elevate another's *mianzi*).

*Mianzi* can also be sold, bought, and loaned. When one is trying to sell *mianzi*, one is trying to brag about one's special relations with very powerful people so that listeners will give him/her special treatment. Some people in China pretend to be "princelings" of high-ranking officials to cheat people who believe in them. To say that someone has bought (*mai*) *mianzi* from someone else and succeeded in doing something means that the person has been allowed to do something in another person's name, perhaps aided with a phone call to a third party or a letter of recommendation. To loan (*jie*) one's *mianzi* or "to depend one's *mianzi*" (*kao, chong, tuo,* or *kan* one's *mianzi*) can also be phrased as "to loan one's shine" (*jie* one's *guang*). They are synonymous with the phrase "to buy one's *mianzi*." Although these are economic terms, literal financial transactions do not take place. However, since these social and symbolic exchanges do have affective and instrumental, symbolic, and economic values, they are recorded in the social memory and are to be returned in an undifferentiated form and an unspecified time period when there is a need for help on the part of the party who has lent face.

*To Diou Mianzi (To Lose Mianzi)*. *Diou mianzi* is not as serious as *diou lian* and so is hardly exchangeable with *diou ren* (loss of personhood or humanity). It has social rather than moral consequences. Other versions of loss of *mianzi* are *shang mianzi* (to scar one's *mianzi*), *sun mianzi* (to break one's *mianzi*), *sao mianzi* (to sweep away's one's *mianzi*), and so on.

*To Zeng Mianzi (To Fight for Mianzi)*. *Mianzi* is usually earned, although it is sometimes inherited. One has to fight for it (to *zheng mianzi*) through hard work or beg for it (to *qiou mianzi*).

*To Wuan Hui Mianzi (To Save Mianzi)*. There are many ways to say "save *mianzi*" in Chinese. Some of them are *hu mianzi*, meaning to protect *mianzi*; *baohu mianzi*, meaning to guard *mianzi*; *weihu mianzi* (to maintain *mianzi*); *ai mianzi* (to love and take good care of *mianzi*); and *guji mianzi* (to be concerned about *mianzi*).

*To Zuo Mianzi (To Make Mianzi)*. *Zuo mianzi* suggests that this *mianzi* is not earned but fabricated. It is almost opposite to *zeng mianzi*. There are many idiomatic ways in Chinese to say this: *zhuang mianzi* (to make-believe *mianzi*), *zhuang menmian* (to decorate gate-face), *bai mianzi* (to display *mianzi*), *fuyan mianzi* (to idle over *mianzi*), *hun mianzi* (to fish for *mianzi*), and *shua* or *wuan mianzi* (to play with *mianzi*).

## Other *Lian/Mian*-Related Terms

*Diao Jia*. *Diao jia* means to fall off the crutch or to have done something that has lowered one's own superior position in order to go an extra mile to help someone in an inferior position. For example, if a senior extends a genuine invitation to an inferior and the junior declines it, the senior can be said to have done something *diao jia*, a variation of *diou lian* (loss of face).

*Duqi and Chuqi*. The concepts of *duqi and chuqi* came out of my consultants' remarks during my first consultation session on the case of Ms. Huang's kneeling down (see Chapter 6). *Duqi* means an obstruction of air—an unarticulated self-destructive move to attract attention from the public and win more sympathy when a Chinese perceives himself or herself wronged but no one does justice to it. *Duqi* is just opposite to *chuqi*. *Chuqi* means the release of the excessive air that constitutes the built-in anger—an other-destructive or aggressive move of personal revenge. Realizing that no one will do justice to the wrongs one has been inflicted with, one does justice to the wrongs oneself. Both acts are emotionally charged and tend to be snappy.

*Lian/Mian-Related Proverbs*. Many *lian/mian*-related proverbs are in circulation in Chinese social interaction, as documented and explained by Hu (1944), Yan (1995), and Zuo (1997). I will explain one such proverb, which shows that the *lian/mian* pattern has split the Chinese personality. It goes, *Dang mian shi ren, bei hou shi gui*. It means, when one faces another person, one is obliged to do facework as a person or a civilized human being; when one does not face the other person, one would badmouth and curse that other person like a barbarian or a devil. To act like a civilized human being when facing another person is but mere outward social conformity, which belies a crude and uncivilized private self. Although this proverb does not apply to all Chinese, it has become an observable pattern.

### Significance of the Chinese *Lian/Mian* Terms

The large number of *lian/mian* and *lian/mian*-related concepts and idioms used in Chinese daily conversations points to the special significance and centrality of *lian/mian* practices in Chinese culture. These concepts and terms are different and interconnected at the same time. Together, they constitute the Chinese grammar of the *lian/mian* practices and a major working system of Chinese social interaction. Such an active and complex web of terms and concepts not only constitutes the nature of Chinese social interaction but also functions as a critique of the modern rationalist literature on facework by Goffman, Brown and Levinson, and others. To transform Chinese social interaction and the Chinese character should surely start from an analysis of, engagement with, and constructive transformation of this web of practices.

## CONSEQUENCES OF *LIAN/MIAN* PRACTICES FOR CONTEMPORARY CHINESE LIFE

Because of the centrality of *lian/mian* in Chinese culture and the centrality of emotions in *lian/mian* practices, *lian/mian* practices play a central role in defining the nature of Chinese societies and produce negative as well as positive consequences in Chinese societies. In a separate study (Jia, 1997-1998), I have found, on the basis of the ethnographic data, a limited review of literature, and my personal cultural experience, that the Chinese *lian/mian* functions as a conflict-preventive and harmony-building mechanism in Chinese interpersonal or group communication. Today, from a macro perspective of consequences, the study appears limited in that it fails to realize that this very conflict-preventive and harmony-building mechanism masks and reinforces social hierarchy and in-groupness, which may breed inequality, injustice, and close-mindedness. Therefore, in order to better understand the nature of *lian/main* practices, I look at the political, economic, and social/cultural consequences of *lian/mian* practices rather than their functions here.

According to Cronen (1995), communication is consequential in that it is "the locus of the creation of moral communities, and that moral matters are intrinsic to what it means to be living a human life" ( p. 38); "the locus of action, wherein different kinds of connections emerge to be extended, critiqued, changed, or discarded" (p. 44); "therefore," Cronen further argues: "the consequentiality of communication is a call for reversing the old agenda. The first priority must be to develop useful ways to understand and critique patterns of human communication" (p. 39).

In the following, I first critique the biased definitions of *lian/mian* and then document the undesirable consequences of *lian/mian* practices for Chinese life ignored by past studies of *lian/mian*. On this basis, I call for a social constructionist transformation of *lian/mian* practices to improve contemporary Chinese life.

Past definitions of face (Goffman, 1967; Brown and Levinson, 1987) and *lian/mian* (Hu, 1944; Ho, 1976; Chen, 1988; Zhou and Ho, 1992) treat these concepts as either positive or neutral, without any explicit inclusion of the social consequentiality of such cultural/communication concepts. For example, face is viewed as either "the positive social value" (Goffman, 1967, p. 5) or "public self-image" (Brown and Levinson, 1987, p. 62). *Lian*, according to Hu, "is the respect of the group for a man with a good moral reputation," whereas *mianzi* "is prestige that is accumulated by means of personal effort or clever maneuvering" (1944, p. 45). Taking consequentiality into consideration, I realize that such definitions are biased. Zai (1995, p. 98), in response to such bias, argues that the very communicative processes of *lian/mian* and strategies for face and *lian/mian* can be moral, immoral, or amoral, sincere or hypocritical, decent or indecent. Cheng is acutely aware of both desirable and undesirable consequences of the *lian/mian* practices. He argues:

> *Mien-tzu* is the social grace which smooths out social *conflicts* which preserve human relationships and which will weld a sense of community. But insofar as personal ambition and self-interest become the motive force for applying face, *face* becomes a disguise and cover-up of intrigue, conspiracy, arbitrariness, willfulness, and personal self-assertion at the expense of public good, as well as true *virtue* and law. (1986, p. 341)

While the Chinese concepts of *lian/mian* are widely recognized to be central to understanding Chinese social behavior at the conceptual level, as systematic social practices they are also broadly found to produce significant but undesirable social consequences in various spheres of Chinese life. The goal of highlighting such undesirable outcomes is to develop a better way to understand, critique, and transform the Chinese *lian/mian* communication patterns to modernize Chinese life.

First of all, Chinese *lian/mian* has produced significant political consequences, which can be discussed from a comparative perspective. In Chinese culture, loss of *lian* equals loss of personhood. A person who lacks morality is regarded as less human. That is why people who have lost *lian* are sometimes called "wild beasts" or "nonhumans" in China. The fundamental reason is that in Chinese culture, humanity is almost completely defined by a person's sociality, that is, proper enactments of social roles, morality, and social behavior. This explains why to lose *lian* would force *lian* losers to commit suicide or permanently withdraw themselves from the community. Those who have lost *lian* are not given a second chance. In the West, however, humanity is largely defined theologically. The concept of humanity is largely separable from sociality. Since humanity is endowed by God, loss of *lian* would thus hardly equal loss of personhood or humanity. Human dignity is regarded as profound, whereas loss of face due to inappropriate enactments of social roles barely touches upon the iron-strong and invincible personhood. For a Chinese person, however, there is nothing else to sustain meaningful living except *lian*. In the West, by contrast, an individual still has a stronghold of God-endowed humanity that provides alternatives by which to sustain meaningful living in the culture after the loss of face. This may explain why Western politicians still appear dignified, self-confident, optimistic, and friendly to opponents who have defeated them in political campaigns. It may also explain why Chinese politicians tend to maintain their posts by all means, even on the verge of death.

In the West, loss of face is similar to loss of *mianzi* in China. But the former may produce fewer undesirable consequences than the latter. Loss of *mianzi* threatens one's social basis of power, whereas loss of face in the West only slightly undermines one's individual social worth.

While I have criticized Lin's radical approach to changing the Chinese face practices previously, I find that Lin's argument against them testifies that *lian/mian* practices bring many undesirable consequences to Chinese political and social life. To Lin, face is the first and most important of the "triad" (1935, p. 195)—face, fate, and favor—that render all rules, regulations, and laws ineffective. In other words, in Lin's mind, face is an all-round, daily, and incessant interactive perpetuator of an undemocratic and unjust social and political system. He suggests that democracy is an alternative to the face practices.

Echoing and extending Lin is Lu, who asks, "Why is it that only our country has been trapped into the muddy pond of *renqing* and *mianzi* for the past several thousand years without being able to get out of it?" (1996, p. 142). He answers that the dynamics of *renqing* and *mianzi* as a form of political governance produce the following disadvantages to the rulers: Such governance gives the rulers extreme flexibility to deal with inferiors however they want, regardless of social norms and conventions. Since resources for survival are distributed by means of *renqing/mianzi*, the rulers control such resources and thus control life and death. As the *renqing/mianzi* form of governance gives inferiors a sense of extreme uncertainty, profound secrecy, and insecurity, the subjects always live in fear. Finally, this form of governance is deceptively shrouded by an aura of kindness to the subjects, who are carried away with it while hating it (1996, pp. 144-145).

Consequently, according to Lu, because of the supreme power the *renqing/mianzi* system controls, it has enveloped the Chinese national imagination, creativity, and behavioral choices; it defies law, moral codes, the Truth, and facts; it has made Chinese fragile in personality, excessively suspicious, demanding, prone to fighting, difficult to get along with, and even more difficult to cooperate with; it has fundamentally corrupted the power system (1996, pp. 150-151). This has been "a vicious cycle" (p. 144) spanning several thousand years of Chinese history. To Lu Xun, face seems to be a socioeconomic force that maintains class hierarchy, perpetuates social/economic inequality, and reinforces the relationship between the exploiters and the oppressors and the exploited and the oppressed. He argues, "There seem to be many kinds: each class in society has a different face" (1934/1960, p. 129).

In the economic realm, *lian/mian* acts as a primary mechanism of unjust and unequal distribution of economic resources (Yang, 1994; Luo, 1997) that marginalizes the universal principles of the market economy as constructed in the modern West, in addition to its functions as a primary mechanism for political power distribution and a primary form of social control/sanction. On the other hand, it marginalizes economic laws and overwhelms economic concerns. As a matter of fact, people who are solely committed to economic gains are regarded as less human and therefore are looked down upon by society. They are normally placed as the lowest class in the hierarchy of *shi* (scholar-official), *long* (farmers), *gong* (workers), and *shang* (business people) and do not have a big *mianzi* in traditional Chinese society because they usually seek profits at the sacrifice of Confucian ethics and mores. It also produces economic waste and even economic disasters in the form of *paichang*—an ostentatious display of the Chinese concept of *mianzi* by means of expensive banquets, architecture, and other ceremonious events not possible without falling into huge debt (Wilson, 1970; Zai, 1995; Hsu, 1996), without appropriating public funds, or without hurting public and national interests (Lu, 1996).

A story widely circulated in Asia says that the Japanese emperor in the early 1970s offered to compensate for the human and economic losses brought about by the Japanese invasion of China during World War II. The Chinese Communist government declined the offer in order to display its face of moral superiority over Japan in front of the international community. In recent years, from my observations, some current Chinese Communist leaders, in order to demonstrate a strong national image and a desirable individual image and to further maintain the legitimacy and power of the Chinese Communist Party in front of the international community, have signed large purchase deals on behalf of businesses such as the Chinese aviation industry. As a result, the Chinese aviation industry has suffered a huge economic loss because it has purchased too many planes. As early as 1935, Lin lamented and criticized the Chinese practice of ostentation by stating, "Human, all-too-human, this face of ours. And yet, it is the goad of ambition and can overcome the Chinese love of money" (1935, p. 202). His criticism still applies, after more than six decades.

Face prevents conflicts and builds harmony when there is a "balance of 'face'" (Smith, 1894, p. 17), the Confucianist ideal in Chinese social interactions. Jia demonstrates in his analysis of a naturally occurring interactive episode that when social actors are adept at using and appreciating intricate face skills, such as Other-Directed Face, Self-Trivialization, and Redress of Face Threats (p. 49), the balance of face is created and maintained, conflict is prevented, and the whole interaction overflows with good human feelings, mutual respect, peace of mind, and a soothing atmosphere. However, when face dynamics are not in balance at the social and interpersonal level, it is conflict generative (Hwang, 1997-1998), conflict escalating, and disruptive of social harmony (Stelzer, 1998). According to Hwang Kwang-Kuo, striving for face is often the very source of interpersonal confrontation in both horizontal and vertical relationships and even the very reason for the termination of such relationships (1998). Drawing an analogy with the conflict between Qiu Ju and the Village Chief in the Chinese film *Qiu Ju* and the conflict between the conservative gang of the Chinese Communist Party and the student hunger strikers, Leigh Stelzer concludes that fearing the loss of face if either party backed down helped push the conflicts between the two parties to their limits. In the case of Qiu Ju and the Village Chief, the conflict involved more and more parties. In the case of the 1989 Chinese Prodemocracy Movement, the peaceful hunger strike made the then Chinese leader Deng Xiaoping feel a loss of face. He turned the event into a tragedy. In both the cases, the fear of losing face or loss of face itself disrupted the social order.

At the individual level, *lian/mian* practices have been strongly documented to be negative. When face dynamics lose balance, it triggers violence, including suicides (Li, 1917/1989; Lin, 1935; Lu, 1960). A Chinese national myth goes that before the Han Dynasty a great general (between 209 B.C. and 202 B.C.) was defeated by Liu Bang, his rival for the throne. He fled to the bank of the Wei River in the middle of today's Shaanxi Province. On the other side of the river was his hometown. He saw his hometown and could not imagine going back to live with his countrymen for the rest of his life. Having felt that he had lost his face before his relatives and country fellows, he took out his sword and killed himself. Social/emotional suffering is generated within individuals when they are socially expected to maintain interpersonal harmony while suppressing their own desires (Yu, 1991). Furthermore, as I documented previously, such individuals suffer from a series of anxieties, such as fear to express love/affection openly, fear to talk about sex, anxieties about inappropriately representing social positions, fear to confront one's own weaknesses and shortcomings in case one will be laughed at, and fear to fail in impression management (Editorial Board of *Teacher Zhang Monthly*, 1990). The *mianzi* practices also make Chinese emotionally fragile, suspicious, demanding, and prone to fighting and therefore hard to get along with and to cooperate with. Two major dimensions of the Chinese national character—an inflated sense of vanity and excessive face sensitivity—are based on the collective Chinese unconscious, a strong sense of self-superiority and self-centeredness (Lu, 1996, p. 151), which perhaps resists the excessive pressure for selflessness.

Last but not least, the *lian/mian*-centered mode of life encourages conformity with conventions, respect for authority, fitting in with the social hierarchy, and an orientation towards homogeneity. This is consistent with David Hall and Roger Ames's findings in their comparative study of East-West philosophies (1998). They state, "In the Chinese context it is common for images to be invested with their associations through a distinctly communal process. Images so constructed are ritually protected" ( p. 139). Because of the communal participation in the ritualistic construction and maintenance of the *lian/mian* of a small group of social elites, Chinese individuals' potential for originality and innovation in the social sphere and natural sphere are sapped.

Since loss of face (*diou lian*) equals loss of the qualifications for being a member of the Chinese community, one who has lost face is regarded as a literal brute and thus is "cut off from the community of participation and communication that alone can serve to humanize" (Hall and Ames, 1998, p. 26). There is little likelihood that the face loser will be given a second chance. It is inevitable that a strong sense of shame, embarrassment, and other emotional pains such as hopelessness and despair due to the loss of such life-sustaining resources leads to suicide or other self-destructive deeds.

## CONCLUSION

The social constructionist perspective has allowed me to look at *lian/mian* as a historically shaped and reshaped system of deeply emotionally defined social practices that have produced undesirable macrosocial consequences despite playing positive roles in interpersonal communication because of *lian/mian*'s central role in Chinese life. The implications of these social constructionist insights into *lian/mian* include the following ideas: Such a system of practices can be reshaped to help reshape Chinese society and Chinese culture; reshaping such a system of practices can be a key to a fundamental transformation of Chinese culture and society; to understand and help Chinese reflect upon their own emotional experiences of *lian/mian* practices might be a key to an effective transformation of *lian/mian* practices.

With these insights, let us look at the other non–social constructionist perspectives and how they seem to be much less vigorous in generating such insights.

# 4

# Past Studies of *Lian/Mian*

## A Social Constructionist Critique

This chapter critically reviews two bodies of literature from the social constructionist perspective. The first includes social scientific studies, comprising studies of face or facework from a universalist perspective and ethnocultural studies of *lian/mian* in the Chinese context. The second includes literature targeting at face or *lian/mian* as an entry point of cultural change in China, which includes divergent approaches to face-targeted cultural change such as modern intellectual criticism, radical revolution, and gradual evolution.

## SOCIAL SCIENTIFIC STUDIES OF FACE

More than a hundred years ago, Arthur Smith wrote, "But the word 'face' does not in China signify simply the front part of the head, but is literally a compound of multitude, with more meanings than we shall be able to describe, or perhaps to comprehend" (1894, p. 16). Today, this statement of Smith's sounds too pessimistic. During the twentiethth century, studies of the Chinese concepts of face uncovered many of its meanings. This section of the chapter is an overview of such studies during the period. The first part of this section generates a critical review of the allegedly universal theories of face (work) that are not grounded within specific cultural contexts, as represented by Goffman (1967) and Brown and Levinson (1978). Ting-Toomey (1994) and Tracy and Baratz (1994) tried hard to get rid of the shackles of universalism in facework research, with limited success. The second part of this section offers a critical review of the cultural studies of face. The third part critiques the study of face in light of the grounded practical theory. The fourth part offers a critical review of ethnocultural studies of face within a given cultural context—the Chinese contexts. Here, I confine my critical review to some of the best-known studies grounded within the Chinese cultural contexts. Finally, I draw a comparison and contrast among the four.

## A Critical Review of Allegedly Universal Theories of Face

Research on theories of face is characterized by its overt tendency to privilege generality over particularity. Goffman (1967) and Brown and Levinson (1987) represent this tendency. These scholars tend to be most interested in discovering a general theory of face without taking cultural particularity into consideration. Against their own original intention, they produced theories largely characteristic of their own cultures.

Goffman defines face as "the positive social value a person effectively claims for himself" (1967, p. 5). He defines facework as "the actions taken by a person to make whatever he is doing consistent with face" (1967, p. 12) or "to counteract 'incidents'—that is, events whose effective symbolic implications threaten face" (1967, p. 12), which is an expression of face (1967, p. 44). Although Goffman's theory is intended to be generalizable to all human societies, it is implicitly grounded in Euro-American middle-class social contexts. His definition centers around self, suggesting that face is an individual's end value; facework is just a set of rational strategies to help an individual overcome barriers in order to achieve the end value. Although Goffman acknowledges that face is lodged in social interaction (1967, p. 7), he does not seem to be aware that while it can be an individual value in some societies such as the West, face is not a significant individual value in all societies. In many other societies such as the Chinese, face is a primary group value, which means one's face belongs not only to oneself but more importantly, belongs to one's significant others, such as one's family, community, or organization.

Goffman's discourse on facework was originally inspired by writings on the Chinese concepts of face, as is evidenced in his notes (1967, pp. 4-5). However, he clearly Americanizes this concept, the opposite of his intention to develop a general theory of facework. His cultural imagination must have been limited by his own cultural experience and cultural upbringing which is primarily Euro-American. No evidence shows that he did any ethnographic work outside the American society or that he did ethnographic work in his own society. As a result, his theory of facework, while intended for all cultures, does not apply to any culture well. This might be a common problem for all modern social theories that are not grounded in specific cultural contexts. Another problem with Goffman's theory is that it equates facework with interaction ritual. Goffman is not aware that his equation of facework with ritual is a description informed by the American social scene, in which facework is merely a cluster of observable rules and etiquettes executed by rational individuals for their own good. Such social actors would not execute such rituals or facework at the sacrifice of their own individual space or their individual autonomy and individual worth. In other words, facework is just the observable social surface, which does not affect how the social actors feel (emotions), who the social actors are (being or concept of humanity), the social institutions that protect the social actors (the social order), and what kind of society and person-hood the social actors are going to have (change). At least, Goffman does not seem to be acutely aware of intimate connections between facework or social rituals and these fundamental issues of the society and does not attempt to draw such connections in his study. Goffman's facework is not an accurate description of facework in other cultures such as the Chinese, in which facework is a central metaphor for the Chinese form of humanity-cohumanity (*ren*) and a dynamic form of government/institution responsible for cultivating social harmony and maintaining the hierarchical social order.

Goffman states at the end of his paper "On Face-work", "Throughout this paper, it has been implied that underneath their differences in culture, people everywhere are the same" (1967, p. 44). This quote suggests that Goffman intended his theory of facework to transcend cultural differences and to be generalizable to all peoples, even though he had not made any significant field-based studies of cultural differences in facework. He also seems to suggest that humanity is every-where the same and has little to do with cultural differences. This is where Goffman and the social constructionist view of face differ. Social constructionism holds that cultural differences are the very constituents of different forms and substances of humanity, for there is no pure humanity devoid of culture and humanity is always culturally/socially constructed; wherever there are different cultures, there are different configurations of humanity. As discussed in Chapters 2 and 3, social constructionism allows us to conceptualize face especially in the Chinese context as a central mechanism of culturally afforded and con-strained emotions and moral behaviors in shaping a given personhood and a given social order. Such a dynamic mechanism has been transfor-mative because of historical changes of personhood and the social order and can be changed through communicative interventions. All these social constructionist insights into face dynamics are not visible to Goffman because of his modernist vision about social interaction, which is primarily masculine, rational, and strategic (failing to account for emotions), acultural, ahistorical, asystemic, and static.

Brown and Levinson's politeness theory is a mere expansion and elaboration of Goffman's facework theory, with no fundamental critique or revision. The two studies have much in common. Like Goffman, Brown and Levinson also have a modernist view of social interaction that is masculine, rational, strategic, acultural, ahistorical, asystemic, and static. Methodologically, they also use cultural imaginations primarily based on their own social experience and upbringing in their own modern Anglo-Saxon culture, while intending their theory to apply to all peoples in all contexts. The modern Anglo-Saxon culture is widely acknowledged to be in close affinity to the middle-class Euro-American culture in which Goffman was brought up. Building upon Goffman's theory of face and facework, Brown and Levinson argue that a much larger concept, "politeness," encompasses the core of face. They define face as follows: "By 'face' we mean something quite specific again: our MP ["model person" by authors' explanation] is endowed with two particular wants—roughly, the want to be unimpeded and the want to be approved of in certain respects" (1978, p. 58). They further dichotomize face into negative face, which means "freedom of action and freedom from imposition" (p. 61), and positive face, which means "the positive consistent self-image or 'personality'" (p. 61). They further classify politeness into positive and negative. They classify strategies for doing face-threatening acts as either those on record that can be without redressive action or with redressive action, which can be further classified as positive politeness and negative politeness, and those off record (1978, p. 69).

Brown and Levinson also emphasize generality or "convergence" in their version of facework-politeness theory (1978). What they are most interested in is to discover face and politeness-related universal principles underlying different cultures, which they term "superficial diversities" (1978, p. 56). They make a general statement that all humans, regardless of "superficial diversities," share a common motive, "politeness," with face as its core. Like Goffman, they define face/politeness as the individual wants of their model person (MP) without seeing face/politeness as a group concept and value and without identifying the connections of face/politeness to personhood, the nature and order of society. They further argue that rationalist interpretation is the only and best approach to a better understanding of face/politeness. They conclude that "Consequently, we wish to demonstrate the role of rationality, and its mutual assumption by participants, in the derivation of inferences beyond the initial significance of words, tone and gesture. It is our belief that only a rational or logical use of strategies provides a unitary explanation of such diverse kinesic, prosodic, and linguistic usages" (p. 56) and that "the only satisfactory explanatory scheme will include a heavy dash of rationalism" (1987, p. 55). This suggests that they do not see an emotional/affective dimension in politeness. They seem to suggest that politeness/face is conducted or can be best conducted without any feelings and emotional expressions associated with it. From what they describe about their model person, one can infer that this person is exactly a moden Western white middle-class man, not a Western woman or a person of color, let alone a Chinese or Russian.

Like Goffman's, Brown and Levinson's politeness theory is insensitive to other cultures, which they feel contain "superficial diversities." For example, the core concept of their theory, "politeness," based on their definition, sounds like a conceptual offshoot of the modern Western value system made up of individual autonomy, freedom, and dignity. However, it is no equivalent of seemingly similar concepts in other cultures, such as the Chinese indigenous cultural concepts of modesty (*qianxu*) and humbleness (*qianbei*). These terms suggest an ideal personhood in the Chinese view, one which requires a member of the community to be able to overcome selfish desires and to respect authority and the hierarchical social relations by various kinesic, prosodic, and linguistic displays of ignorance, self-worthlessness, and readiness to sacrifice.

Furthermore, Brown and Levinson's work explicitly adopts modern Western rationalism as its framework. Their conceptualization of politeness as a set of rationalist strategies suggests that the use of politeness is usually highly calculated, highly voluntary, and discriminatory. It is executed on the basis of individual autonomy, freedom, and equality. It excludes politeness such as humbleness and modesty in the Chinese context as a moral and ethical imperative legislated by the elitists and as part of the deep culture, in which people take it for granted as a common social norm without which social actors can not identify and accept themselves and each other rationally. Brown and Levinson's conceptual division of face into negative face and positive face, of politeness into positive politeness and negative politeness, and of strategies of doing face-threatening acts (FTA) into on-record strategies and off-record strategies is consistently informed by dualistic thinking as found within modern Western philosophy.

## Cultural Studies of Face

According to the nine chapters in *The Challenges of Facework*, Stella Ting-Toomey defines face as "a dialectical metaphor" that represents "the civilized, balanced point of situated interaction in a given culture" (1994, p. 335). She summarizes the five themes in the chapters: face having both general and specific dimensions; face as an identity-boundary phenomenon; face having both social-emotive and social-cognitive dimensions; face as situated interaction; and face and facework operating across daily situations (1994, p. 2). While it is commendable that she has moved beyond her interpretive framework of collectivism versus individualism in this book and has moved beyond the Goffman–Brown and Levinson model, there are still many weaknesses in light of the social constructionist perspective.

Ting-Toomey's edited book takes a multiple communication perspective that attempts to be culturally sensitive. It is primarily concerned with multiple theoretical and methodological issues in face and facework research. However, it fails to systematically address face and facework within at least one culture from bottom-up multiple perspectives that are sensitive to both the synchronic and diachronic variations of face and facework within specific cultures. Defining face as a "multifaceted construct" (p. 307), the book primarily treats face as a theoretical concept and as a type of social practice only secondarily. Like Goffman and Brown and Levinson, Ting-Toomey fails to identify the practical social functions and consequences of face and facework as dynamic forces within specific cultures. Although it recognizes the centrality of face in defining an individual's identity, her book does not identify the possible role of face and facework in defining and redefining the social order and nature of the society in some cultures such as the Chinese. The book also does not explicitly recognize the dimension of emotions in the concept of face. Lacking a deeply grounded practical perspective, the book inevitably fails to explicitly address practical and conceptual changes in face and facework within specific cultures in relationship to social change and cultural transformation.

In summary, although Ting-Toomey's collection is cultural and gender conscious, it is still ahistorical, lacking a systemic and evolutionary view of face. Her aspiration seems to be to develop a general theory of face applicable to all cultures on the basis of studies of face in different cultures from many different angles with multiple methodologies. Her aspiration still reflects her modernist view of theory as primarily descriptive, rather than constructionist, keeping her from identifying the problematic of face practices, which dominate a whole way of life in a given specific historical, social, and cultural context, and from seeing the need to transform the culture of face in the context of macrosocial and economic change such as contemporary China.

## Face in Light of Grounded Practical Theory

Karen Tracy and Sarah Tracy's study, "Rudeness at 911" (1997), analyzes two telephone calls from citizens to a 911 center in a large city in the western United States. During the calls, calltakers got angry and attacked the face of the caller. Informed by grounded practical theory (Craig, 1989; Craig & Tracy, 1995), which treats practical usefulness and reflection instead of truth about communication as the objectives of inquiry and using a facework lens, Tracy and Tracy suggest a desensitizing technique to face attacks. They conclude that facework is embedded in human communication and that face attack is closely associated with negative emotions.

This study represents studies of face that have gone beyond both Goffman's and Brown and Levinson's universalist model of face (work) and Ting Toomey's quasi-cultural and quasi-universalist model of face. Its goal is to maximize usefulness—reflection and improvement of face interaction—rather than to strive for an accurate description of face (work). This study generally falls with the social constructionist paradigm. The differences between my social constructionist perspective and grounded practical theory are within-the-family differences.

Using the case study method and a theoretical perspective that is concerned about usefulness and reflectivity rather than truth about face, Tracy and Tracy's study analyzes two conversations between a caller to 911 and the calltaker. The authors identified subtle face-attack strategies and proposed that such strategies be made known in training sessions for calltakers so that face attack might be minimized. Despite their claim that the study is informed by grounded practical theory, it fails to be informed by comparative cultural/communication studies of patterns of face practices grounded within specific cultures and fails to develop a medium-range theory on the basis of such studies.

Tracy and Tracy's metaphor of face attack reminds me of the Chinese concept of face tear *(si po lian pi)* as a contrast. Such a contrast can illuminate face attack as a unique problematic American communication pattern. The concept of face attack suggests that face is treated as an object of enmity to be annihilated or to be rendered faceless with the sudden use of force, either symbolic or physical. Instead of using face attack, the Chinese have come up with the metaphor of face tear. "Tear" suggests that face is like a piece of cloth of relative elasticity. Rather than annihilating it as a whole, tear means to destroy it piece by piece. Another difference is that in Tracy and Tracy's study, the calltaker and the client are in a customer-business relationship. They are not likely to know each other. What they are doing is to make the business less professional. In the Chinese context, face tear always implies the destruction of the emotionally interdependent relationship. After face tear, the relationship is transformed from "cooked" *(shou* or familiar) to "uncooked" *(sheng* or strange), from kin to non-kin, from friend *(you)* to enemy *(chou ren)*, or the ninth/last in the relational hierarchy, as the character *chou* indicates that it is made up of two characters—the characters standing for *ren*, or person, on the left and the character standing for nine, or *jiou*, on the right side.

Tracy and Tracy's study, while abandoning the prior quest for theoretical generalization, does not connect the local and specific case with the general cultural patterns of facework in the United States and does not look at the case from a cross-cultural perspective. It illustrates the type of study that is concerned with case-specific face dynamics without drawing necessary connections between such face dynamics and larger cultural patterns inside and outside the larger American cultural context.

I would argue that a grounded analysis of face and facework as communicative action can be most usefully informed by a creative synthesis of the local scene and local logic constituted by speech acts and episode, the cultural scene and cultural logic(s) that constitute self and relationship(s), and possibly emerging translocal and transcultural logics that may constitute a new culture. The social constructionist perspective, as elaborated in Chapters 2 and 3 and illustrated by the case studies in Chapters 6 and 7, is both grounded in specific cases and informed by the larger patterns of face practices, which are formative of personhood and nature of society. The case study by Tracy and Tracy does not draw such connections. It risks seeing the tree without the forest. As a result, its usefulness may be very limited, because of its case-exclusive focus. For example, the study does not discuss if face attack is a broadly problematic American communication pattern. Recognizing the centrality of face in Chinese culture and its problematic effect upon contemporary Chinese life, the usefulness of my social constructionist perspective not only includes reflection upon face interactions but also points to the possibility of transforming Chinese personhood and the nature of Chinese society. The worth of a case study depends on the degree to which the specific case is representative of a broader problematic communication pattern in a given society.

### A Critical Review of the Ethnocultural Studies of the Chinese Concepts of Face

This line of research on the Chinese concepts of face began with Hsien Chin Hu's anthropological research at Columbia University (1944). It was continued by Leon Stover at the same university (1962) and picked up by David Ho (1976). In the 1980s, the indigenization movement of Western modern social science began in the modern industrialized regions of Taiwan and Hong Kong (Bond & Lee, 1981; Hwang, 1987; King, 1988; Chen, 1988). This indigenization movement spread to Mainland China (Zai, 1995; Yi, 1996; Lu, 1996; Zuo, 1997), overseas Chinese academic communities, and beyond in the early 1990s (Cheng, 1986;

Chen, 1991; Kipnis, 1995; Chang & Holt, 1994; Mao, 1994; Li, 1996; Reding, 1997; Jia, 1997–1998). These studies are concerned with an accurate description and interpretation of face in Chinese culture instead of an accurate description and interpretation of the face of all human beings regardless of context. From the social constructionist perspective, they are cultural in the neopositivist sense, lacking a historical dimension, an emotional dimension, and a systemic perspective; their view of face and culture seems to be highly static; their research aims to reduce uncertainty and increase control and predictability. Although they recognize the centrality of face in Chinese social interaction, they do not draw any connections of face practices and the transformation of such practices to the fundamental issues of culture such as personhood, social order, and the nature of Chinese society. These authors either implicitly or explicitly regard themselves as inside spectators instead of reflective participants who can make a change.

I call such research "ethnocultural studies of the Chinese face practices situated within Chinese culture" because they do not attempt to develop a general theory applicable to all cultures as did Goffman and Brown and Levinson. Although the ethnocultural studies contribute to a better understanding of the Chinese concepts of face than Goffman and Brown and Levinson, they are still heavily influenced by the rationalist/elitist perspectives deeply ingrained in the modern Western human sciences. Hu's study (1944) is a bit psychological as well as anthropological. Her study is primarily a quasi-indigenous interpretation or explanation of Chinese face-related folk sayings that use *lian* and *mianzi* and a differentiation of the two concepts. While her differentiation of *lian* as a moral concept and *mianzi* as a social concept and *lian/mian* concepts as more than individualistic is commendable, she did not study them in the context of social interaction among Chinese. Instead, she merely explained various face-related sayings with some psychological terms such as "ego," a Freudian term that Hu uses to refer to *"mien-tzu "* (1944, p. 45), which I spell as *mianzi*.

Ho (1976) interprets the Chinese concepts of face from a comparative perspective—face in the East and individualism or self in the West—and argues that they are not to be confused. His study is explicitly structural and ideological. He describes face as "the Chinese social ideology" (p. 868) and Western individualism as "the ideology of individualism" (p. 867). While he differentiates the Chinese concept of face from related concepts such as honor and status, dignity and prestige, he fails to treat them as family resemblances that are both similar and different. Ho does not analyze concrete communicative episodes from the East or the West to illustrate his argument, perhaps simply because his notion of face is ideological and rigid.

As the title of Cheng's paper "The Concept of Face and Its Confucian Roots" suggests, Cheng traces the origin of the Chinese concept of face in light of Confucianist philosophy, ignoring the dynamic functions of face in social interaction and its formative role in the birth of Confucianism and its mutation in the modern Chinese period (1986). In a different approach, Hwang (1987) formulates a theoretical model of face and favor in Chinese society in light of social exchange theory in the West. While it is commendable that his model incorporates *renqing*, the expressive or relational dimension of face, he primarily treats face as resources or power that can be exchanged, divided, or allocated, rationalizing and politicizing face to an extreme.

The studies of Chinese concepts of face reviewed here roughly share the following weaknesses: (1) While they all apply a more or less indigenous or emic (here Chinese) perspective, they fail to address the concepts in real-life situations, thus lacking a nuanced interpretation of how face practices are performed in daily life. (2) Because almost all these researchers tend to use modern Western social science approaches, their studies remain insensitive to a historical view of Chinese concepts of face as developmental, evolutionary, and subject to various historical forces. (3) Because of their modern social scientific commitment to the myth of objective, truthful, and neutral description and interpretation, they tend to exclude inquiries into the emotional grammar of face at the conceptual level, the social consequences of face as patterns of interactional practices, and active engagement or consultation as an effort to reduce undesirable social consequences of *lian/mian* practices. Either implicitly or explicitly, the goals of the scientific approach applied in ethnocultural studies of the Chinese concepts of face and Chinese culture are to produce an accurate and complete understanding of *lian/mian* and to enhance the ability to predict and control the Chinese *lian/mian* behavior.

While scientific analysis does not seem to be face-hurting, as the modern type of criticism is to *lian/mian*-loving Chinese, it tends to treat Chinese cultural concepts (here referring to *lian/mian* and their associated terms) and Chinese culture as almost immutable objects. The hidden assumptions of this neopositivist view are that (1) culture is atemporal and static; (2) cultural concepts such as *lian/mian* should be treated as if they were entities; and (3) philosophically, it deals with a world of object-subject dichotomy and a law of cause-effect linearity. Such studies are preoccupied with close-ended definitions. They generally lack a nuanced view of historical transformation and systemic thinking. Committed to scientific objectivity and to prediction and control of Chinese *lian/mian* behavior, the studies show little interest in investigating the possibility of enhancing Chinese self-reflexivity in a linkage of thinking and action. Their definitions of culture and views of personhood are still largely modern and Western. In conclusion, this indigenization movement in social scientific research in Chinese academic communities is far from successful, because of its inability to avoid the fundamentally modern Western bias of social scientific theories and methods applied in such studies.

## A Comparison and Contrast

The universal theories of face, while claimed to be universal, are not grounded in studies in several specific cultures. Rather, they are products of the theoretical imagination, with either intentional or unintentional reference to the theorists' own cultures (the middle-class American culture in the case of Goffman, and the British middle-class culture in the case of Brown and Levinson). The ethnocultural studies of face situated in a specifically defined cultural context (e.g., Chinese culture) draw upon and are thus indebted to the open and liberating branches of modern Western social science, such as cultural anthropology, social psychology, interpretive sociology, and social linguistics. However, constrained by hidden assumptions of modern Western culture, as previously mentioned, they generally fail to incorporate and to be informed by the fundamental assumptions of Chinese culture.

The concept of culture or *wenhua* (*wen* literally meaning "to tattoo"; *hua*, "to transform") in the Chinese linguistic and social context means to transform people into an ideal Confucianist personhood by lifelong moral and humanistic acculturation and cultivation (He, 1995, p. 130). Using pragmatism as their interpretive lens, David Hall and Roger Ames interpret *wen* as such:

> It is the creative and expansive civil side of being human (*wen*) in contrast with the destructive and delimiting yet ineluctable military occupations (*wu*). In short, *wen* encompasses those refining vocations of the human being that, in Confucian terms, make one most fully human. (1998, p. 33)

> Clearly, to the extent that the Confucian model is a project of cultivation directed at self-realization, the social and political order is derived from the participants themselves, who cannot thereby be construed as self-abnegating. (Hall & Ames, 1998, p. 28)

This is very close to a social constructionist argument in the West. But of course, the mechanism of construction and the ideal type of person to be constructed in Chinese culture are substantially different from those assumed by social constructionism in the postmodern West (for a more detailed argument on the differences, see Chapter 9). Due to the *wenhua* concept of culture, history and context are an essential dimension of the Chinese concept of culture.

The Chinese philosophical view of the world is that the world is a humancentric world carved out of the natural world; the humancentric world being made up of *ying* and *yang* and self and other, which are not dichotomous but mutually complementary; not fixed and clearly demarcated but two constantly shifting and interpenetrating dimensions, with each becoming the other at the same time (Hall and Ames, 1998, p. 26). The distinctive assumptions of Chinese culture are virtual opposites of those of modern Western culture, but they are very close to the clearly defined assumptions of social constructionism emerging out of the postmodern West. Unfortunately, most ethnocultural studies of the Chinese concept of face fail to recognize the assumptions of Chinese culture.

## INTELLECTUAL AND PRACTICAL APPROACHES TO FACE-RELATED CULTURAL CHANGE

The goal of achieving social and cultural transformation by changing *lian/mian* concepts and practices is sought by various means. Contemporary approaches to the problematic of *lian/mian* can be seen as falling within two stages. The first phase is that of discovery of face as a central characteristic of Chinese culture, a significant topic for an academic inquiry, based upon intensive observations in the field made by a Western missionary. This discovery soon spread to other parts of China and was recognized by leading Chinese social and cultural critics of the time, such as Lu Xun and Lin Yu-tang.

With the recognition of *lian/mian* and its centrality in Chinese culture, these critics' social/cultural criticisms became more specific and concrete. Thus, Smith's beginning of the interpretive approach to the Chinese *lian/mian* practices in his *Chinese Characteristics* (1894) was soon eclipsed by the negative value judgments of critics such as Lu Xun and Lin Yutang, which fall within the iconoclastic paradigm of modern Chinese cultural criticism and social movements. The way to a possible detailed understanding of the complex micro-mechanisms of *lian/mian* through the interpretive approach initiated by Smith was virtually abandoned. Smith's discovery of the Chinese face practices triggered the beginning of a second phase, which I call "the phase of criticism and revolution." My social constructionist critique of the first and second phases has generated research questions, the answers to which constitute a reflective and consultative model for *lian/mian* transformation.

## The Approach of Discovery, Criticism, and Revolution

*Discovery.* This approach began with Arthur Smith's discovery of the Chinese concept of *lian/mian* as "a key to the combination lock of many of the most important characteristics of the Chinese" (1894, p. 17). Smith was an American missionary who lived, observed, and studied various facets of Chinese life for 24 years. He first published *Chinese Characteristics*, a set of papers in *North-China Daily News* in Shanghai, in 1890. The papers were later published in book form, entitled *Chinese Characteristics*, in 1894. The first chapter of Smith's book is on face. He primarily viewed face as a dramatistic concept of Chinese social life and the balance of face as an end goal in settling a conflict, unlike Europeans who aimed for a balance of power in handling international conflicts and for ideal justice in handling interpersonal conflicts (1894, p. 17).

Although face colloquialisms had been on the lips of Chinese for the past 2,000 years, no written report or monograph on the Chinese concepts of face had been found before Smith. This discovery of the Chinese concepts of face as a topic for academic inquiry was made possible by the process of early intercultural contact and interaction between Chinese and Westerners such as Smith. By this discovery, the familiar was made strange. It triggered the reflective thinking of some well-known indigenous Chinese cultural critics, such as Lu Xun and Lin Yutang. Influenced by Smith's study, they radically critiqued the Chinese *lian/mian* practices in order to achieve cultural change.

It was a natural coincidence that the rediscovery of the same concept was also made in the context of intercultural contact and interaction in the United States in 1944, 54 years after Smith. It was made by Hsien Chin Hu, a student of Chinese origin who wrote and published the landmark study "The Chinese Concepts of Face" during her graduate studies in anthropology at Columbia University. Her study was the first social scientific study on the Chinese concepts of face. She was also the first scholar who differentiated *lian* and *mian*, interrelated concepts that had been treated as one and the same and simplistically translated as "face" by Smith and later by Goffman and by Brown and Levinson, whose theories of face moved further and further away from the Chinese view of face. There is no indication in her article that she had read Smith's, Lin's, and Lu's writings on the Chinese concept of face. Hu, through her own anthropological observations of differences between Chinese culture and Euro-American culture, noticed the uniqueness and prominence of the Chinese concepts of face in Chinese culture and in the intercultural communication between Chinese culture and the Euro-American culture. As she wrote in the beginning of her study, "In the analysis of a culture different in emphasis and basic attitudes from our own it is important to keep in mind that that society may have formed different conceptions of even the most universal aspects of human life" (1944, p. 45). Both Smith's and Hu's studies and a few other studies of Chinese social life published in the West might have helped Goffman in formulating his concept of face-work and his own very influential interactionist theory of face, as his extensive footnote recognizes (1967, p. 6).

*Modern Social Criticisms and Revolution Against Lian/Mian.* Various Chinese leaders/scholars have offered divergent criticisms of *lian/mian* in an attempt to achieve social change. Powerful political leaders with an extreme anti-tradition attitude, such as Mao Tse-tung, resorted to the Cultural Revolution to erase the Chinese *lian/mian* consciousness, "the key to the Chinese spirit" (Lu, 1934/1960, p. 129) and "the immutable laws of the Chinese universe" (Lin,1935, p. 195).

Li Zongwu (1917/1989) argues that thick face (shamelessness) plus black heart (cruelty) has been the key to success in Chinese history, whereas thin face (concern for face loss or adherence to the moral principles) and soft heart (kindness) have been obstacles to personal success; most of the people who became rulers or members of the ruling class in Chinese history were thick-faced and black-hearted while pretending to observe Confucian ethics. However, those who failed to become members of the ruling class truly believed in and practiced the Confucian doctrines. He seems to suggest that concern for loss of face is but the effect of manipulation of the common people by a small gang of the ruling class, who exploit the common people's fear of face loss; in other words, Confucian ethics and moral principles are created and used by the ruling class to cheat the common people. To Li, face is a very important political tool for Chinese rulership and other-oriented deception. Li does not see any solution to this historically grounded social problem other than to encourage people to be thick-faced and black-hearted like those powerful few in Chinese history in order to be successful. Li was obviously cynical about what he saw as the hypocrisy of Confucianism and those who claim themselves Confucianists.

Like Li, Lu Xun also recognized the double standard of face in Chinese culture. He writes: "For instance, if a rickshaw man steals a purse and is caught he loses face, but if one of the upper class makes a fine haul of gold and valuables, apparently that does not lose face for him, to say nothing of that excellent method of saving face, 'a tour of investigation abroad'" (1934/1960, p. 130). However, Lu Xun seems to emphasize the oppressive nature of face while Li seems to emphasize the hypocrisy of the *lian/mian*-related ethics. This concern for face consumes human dignity and worth beyond a minimum level, as exemplified by a case in which a poor scavenger felt that he gained face because he was talked to by his Fourth Master, although Fourth Master ordered him to "clear off." To Lu Xun, face is a tool of oppression for the ruling class and a tool of self-deception or "a means to the spiritual victory" for the oppressed class, to use Lu Xun's own words in his "The Story of a Q." Lu Xun's criticism of face seems to be informed by Marxist class theory. However, Lu does not propose a solution, although something like a Marxist revolution may have been implied in his criticism.

Lin Yutang holds that face, fate, and favor constitute a triad that acts as a major obstacle to justice and democracy. Therefore, he advocates for a revolution. He writes:

The only revolution that is real and that is worthwhile is a revolution against this female triad. The trouble is that these three women are so human and so charming. They corrupt our priests, flatter our rulers, protect the powerful, seduce the rich, hypnotize the poor, bribe the ambitious and demoralize the revolutionary camp. They paralyze justice, render ineffective all paper constitutions, scorn at democracy, condemn the law, make a laughingstock of the people's rights, violate all traffic rules and regulations, and ride roughshod over the people's home gardens. If they were tyrants, or if they were ugly, like the Furies, their reign might not endure so long; but their voices are soft, their ways are gentle, their feet tread noisily over the law courts, and their fingers move silently, expertly, putting the machinery of justice out of order while they caress the judge's cheeks. (Lin, 1935, p. 195)

By contemporary standards, I must point out that the feminization of face, fate, and favor certainly reflects Lin's deeply ingrained bias against women, which I do not agree with. However, Lin does mean that face, fate, and favor practices are pervasive among both men and women in Chinese society.

Specifically, Lin's revolution could have been capable of making everyone in China lose face. (Note that he drops the concepts of Fate and Favor in the following argument, for in his mind, Fate and Favor are part and parcel of Face itself.) He goes on to write:

So it seems that while it is impossible to define face, it is nevertheless certain that until everybody loses his face in this country China will not become a truly democratic country. The people have not much face anyway. The question is, when will the officials be willing to lose theirs? When face is lost at the police courts, then we will have safe traffic. When face is lost at the law courts, then we will have justice. And when face is lost in the ministries, and the government by face gives way to a government by law, then we will have a true republic. (1935, p. 195)

To Lin, face is an institutionalized political force in the name of *renqing* ethics, a force that is inherently nepotistic, particularistic, and favoritistic; it is antagonistic and hostile to democracy and rule by law. Obviously, the critical perspective he employs here is the modern Western rationalism characterized by truth, justice, and equality at the sacrifice of something like the Confucianist *renqing* ethics. However, Lin's resolution of this "vice" of face is a ready resort to a revolution whose goal is to eradicate face, together with those who take advantage of it. Lin's proposal for revolution smacks of something like Mao's idea of "Great Cultural Revolution."

If Lin proposes to replace face with law, Mao endeavored to eradicate it through radical political movements and to replace it with the Communist ideology. His Cultural Revolution (1966–1976) was an effort to replace face with Communist ideology. Long before the Cultural Revolution, in 1927, Mao stated in his *Report on an Investigation of the Peasant Movement in Hunan*: "A revolution is not a dinner party, or writing an essay, or painting a picture, or doing embroidery; it cannot be so refined, so leisurely and gentle, so temperate, kind, courteous, restrained and magnanimous. A revolution is an insurrection, an act of violence by which one class overthrows another" (Bantam Books, Inc., 1967, pp. 6-7). This message of Mao's guided the operation of Chinese Communist history till at least the end of the Cultural Revolution in 1976. One popular slogan used during the Cultural Revolution and after best summarizes this thought: Be Iron-Faced and Be Feelingless (*tiemian wuqing*). Here, masses and cadres are commanded to give up their own concerns about not saving their own face and not respecting others' face and *renqing* ethics and to become cruel and heartless enough to identify, criticize, torture, and mutilate their "class enemies," including their closest relatives and friends.

In the study *The Ideal Local Party Secretary and the "Model" Man*, A. S. Chen finds that the Chinese Communist Party's prescription of "direct action and initiative" (1964, p. 236) for the new citizen and cadre "naturally leaves no room for 'saving face'" (p. 238). In the stories that depict the ideal citizen, "the question of 'face'" (*mianzi, lian*), which is an elaborate network of appropriate attitudes, behavior, and emotions shaping one's relations with others, is completely absent. The traditional go-between in personal relations or in negotiating a deal is also done away with. Even when there is a difference of opinion in these stories, adversaries are faced without the middleman" (p. 238). These are merely "official efforts to overcome some important weaknesses in Chinese society" (p. 238). Chen casts doubt on the effectiveness of such a prescription for the new citizen by concluding: "The people's response to the pressure of these ideal images is conditional upon the acceptance or rejection of the overall program and ideology of the communist regime" (p. 240).

If Chen questions the consequences of official efforts to make the Maoist citizen, J. Bruce Jacobs has an answer. Jacobs finds that the very formation of Chinese Communist polity is based upon the particularistic ties (1979, p. 239) that refer to an interpersonal network of both instrumental and relational values resisting, defying, and even nullifying the general principles of equality, freedom, and individualism. Although the Chinese Communist Party pushed hard for the new citizenship, "the regime's values and undoubted penetration into society have not yet extirpated particularism" (p. 269), for "Chinese Communist cadres desiring political advancement should cultivate good *kuan-hsi*" (p. 270). Since the foundation of the Chinese Communist Party is "Face, Fate, and Favor," to use Lin's words, this Maoist top-down and radical approach to the problematic of face still leaves the system intact. To use Lu Zheng's words, "the social progress since 1949 still has not broken it. As a result, we still act within this framework of face" (1996, p. 150).

If Li's criticism targets a small number of rulers who are "thick-faced and black-hearted" hypocrites, Lu's criticism concentrates on the broken peasants and scholars from the lower class whose "means to spiritual victory" feeds into the oppressive system of *lian/mian* without awareness of their own oppression. Mao's Cultural Revolution aimed to radically transform the masses from face to faith to serve the political interests of the Chinese Communist Party, which itself was built on the triad of face, fate, and favor.

Bo Yang's sharp pen pierces the face skin of every Chinese in the world and almost every part of Chinese culture and history that form every Chinese. Bo Yang's critical ideas are taken here mainly from a book entitled *The Ugly Chinaman and the Crisis of Chinese Culture* (1991). Bo Yang calls every Chinese "an ugly Chinaman" and Chinese culture "the soy paste vat." One of the central features of this ugliness is the excessive Chinese concern for face. He characterizes the Chinese as a people of "reluctance to admit errors" (p. 14), a people who are "stuck in the mud of bragging and boasting" (p. 15). He describes the Chinese nation as "a nation of inflation" (p. 17) and "a breeding ground for the slave mentality" (p. 19) and Chinatown as "a snake pit where Chinese people devour each other alive" (p. 81). In an interview with the editorial board of *China Spring*, a New York–based liberal Chinese language journal, in 1984, Bo Yang praised Walter Mondale, who, though he lost the presidential campaign, was still open-minded enough to make a public announcement that Reagan would serve as the new president of the United States. However, he laments about Chinese politicians:

Chinese people are overly concerned about losing face, so they never surrender or admit to making mistakes. To err is human; only animals are perfect. When a Chinese person fails at something, all he can do is curse and shout. It will take another 300 years before Chinese officials start acting like Fritz Mondale. (1991, p. 29)

Bo Yang has a very specific and detailed root image in mind when he talks about Chinese culture.

Every culture flows on unceasingly like a great river. But as the centuries go by, cultures accumulate all sorts of flotsam and jetsam, such as dead fish, dead cats, and dead rats. When this detritus piles up on the river bed, the river ceases to flow and turns stagnant. The deeper the river, the thicker the layer of sludge; the older the river, the more thoroughly the sludge rots, until the river turns into one fermentation vat, a stinking repository of everything filthy and disgusting under the sun. (pp. 41-42)

What is the goal of Bo Yang's biting criticism of every Chinese and Chinese culture? Instead of aiming to discourage, downgrade, humiliate, and make Chinese readers lose face, Bo Yang's goal in this biting satire, to use his own words, is as follows:

This should remind us that China's problems are complex, and call for a high level of awareness on the part of each and every Chinese. Every one of us must become a discriminating judge and use our ability to examine and appraise ourselves, our friends and our country's leaders. This is our hope. (p. 23)

Has Bo Yang achieved his goal? From the written responses by the Chinese readers, not at all. Instead, his criticism stirred up waves of anger and drew severe counterattacks from a lot of Chinese readers. As an editorial in *The North American Daily News* predicted, "Bo Yang risks mockery and condemnation from all sides" (p. 118) with his barbs. The editorial's prediction turned out to be right. Huixuan Chu, from the *Hong Kong Economic Journal*, records that a Chinese whose last name is Liang, having read Bo Yang's *The Ugly Chinaman*, became sad, then depressed, and finally broke down in tears (p. 128). Wang Yiling, from *Pai Hsing Semi-Monthly* in Hong Kong, angered by Bo Yang's criticism of the Chinese, called Bo Yang "the contemptible Chinaman" (p. 122) who "has no right to insult others" (p. 123); who "has unwittingly been misled by his own personal 'soy paste vat,' and that his nervous system has been paralyzed by 'germs' he has bred within himself." "From this, one can see how deeply Bo Yang hates the Chinese people," he exclaims (p. 124).

Liu Qianmin, from *Luntan Bao (Forum Daily)* in Los Angeles, responded to Bo Yang's criticism much more emotionally. He writes:

With the exception of Bo Yang and his like, I can think of no other examples in world history when the citizens of a poor country have displayed such outright sycophancy and resentment in their condemnation of their own countrymen and the very culture that they depend upon for a living. . .; Bo Yang wants everybody to join in his vilification campaign and to trample Chinese culture into the ground. . . .[his] uglification campaign against Chinese culture has had a negative influence on the average Chinese. . . . Bo Yang is an intellectual hooligan. (pp. 138-140)

Compared with other examples, the response of Xu Qin, from *Huaqiao Daily (Overseas Chinese Daily)* in New York, seems less emotional but points to the heart of the problem emanating from such social criticisms as Bo Yang's in the Chinese cultural context characterized by the unique Chinese concern for face or *lian/mian* . In his article entitled "We must sweep our faults under the rug and parade our virtues in order not to demean ourselves: Some criticism and suggestions for Bo Yang," he counter-criticizes Bo Yang:

Bo Yang took 5,000 years of Chinese culture, including the great civiliza-tion created by the emperors of the Tang and Song, and in a single dismissive gesture flushed it all down the toilet. By doing so, Bo Yang makes us lose all our faith and pride in our culture. (Bo, 1991, p. 119)

Xu Qin then moves to the all-positive approach from Bo Yang's all-neg-ative approach by stating:

Only Chinese culture itself can lead the 800 million Chinese down the path of civilization and fill their lives with happiness. The Japanese people have drawn upon Chinese culture and have benefited from it greatly. Western people are studying it. As for us, the Chinese people, the last thing we should do is to denigrate or disparage what is essen-tially ours. By doing so, we not only threaten the survival of the Chinese people, we also become the unworthy descendants of those who created this culture. (1991, p. 121)

From these emotional responses, one finds that Bo Yang's modern Western type of criticism, characterized by impersonal and adversarial, violates (either intentionally or unintentionally) the Chinese *lian/mian* principles, the core value of Chinese culture.

The TV documentary *The Deathsong of the Yellow River* (Su & Wang, 1988) (subsequently referred to as *He shang*) is the most recent, "the most thorough, most complete and the most absurd negation of all the glorious traditions, histories and civilizations of the Chinese nation" (Yu,1990, p. 75). It is more extreme than Bo Yang in its iconoclasm (Bai, 1988, p. 18). The televised political narrative declares that Chinese culture, symbolized by the Yellow River, the Great Wall, and the Dragon, is declining and dying and thus becoming unsuitable for the upcoming modernization; the only alternative to the dying Yellow Culture is to let the Blue Culture—the Western democratic culture— baptize or transform the Yellow Culture. *He shang* narrates:

> This piece of yellow land has not been able to teach us what is the real scientific spirit.
> This reckless Yellow River has failed to teach us what is the real democratic consciousness.
> This piece of yellow land and this Yellow River have already proven themselves incapable of upbringing this growing population and incapable of creating a new culture out of itself. . . (p. 103)

The authors are aware of the issue of face or identity in their advocacy for a Western-style transformation of Chinese culture, but they resort to a simplistic solution—the complete and radical transformation—and fail to understand the complexity of the issue of cultural transformation. *He shang* writes further:

> The reason why reform has been so difficult is perhaps because we always have this fear: "Will Chinese still be Chinese?" We do not seem to know that during the past 200-300 years, whether it was during the Renaissance, the Religious Reform or the Enlightenment, no West Europeans whatsoever feared that after the reform Italians would become non-Italians, Germans non-Germans and the French non-French. It has been the biggest taboo only in China. This is perhaps the most burdensome part of the Yellow Civilization and the most superficial area. (p. 102)

The authors ask Chinese people not to worry that they will no longer be Chinese by urging that the culture of the yellow earth (Chinese culture) merge itself completely within the culture of the blue seas (the modern Western culture) as the waters of the Yellow River flow into the sea. To them, Chineseness is something to be overcome, not to be maintained; Chinese should give up their concern for loss of face and loss of identity and be bold enough to become un-Chinese or Westernized with a reconstructed cultural-psychological structure (Yu,1990, p. 73) and to become a modern Western type of people.

Like Bo Yang's *The Ugly Chinaman*, *He shang* ignited waves of emotional and defensive responses from hurt Chinese readers/viewers. Zhang holds that *He Shang* is "degrading and demeaning," an attempt to "thoroughly deprive Chinese people's genuine sense of patriotism and national dignity" (1989, p. 10). Instead of helping Chinese enhance their ability to be critical of their traditional culture, the documentary reinforces some Chinese people's identification with their traditional culture. For example, Huang Yuan retorts, "This ancient yellow land has been the ultimate source of lifeblood of our Chinese nation; the long Chinese tradition has been the fountainhead of our national spirit" (1990, p. 68).

Some high-quality criticisms responded rationally to the "downgrading" TV documentary. Zhong (1989, p. 11) points out that the problem with He shang is that it has elevated the partial anti-tradition to the holistic and systematic negation of the Chinese tradition. The authors have inherited the iconoclastic attitude of Chinese modern criticism and the superficial comparative perspective and have failed to reflect upon their own habitual modes of cognition and thinking in writing the script of He shang (p. 15). Shao Yumin (1988, p. 50) points out that while it outshines all other criticisms of the Chinese tradition in its emotional intensity, the documentary perpetuates the same critical approach developed in the May 4th Movement—a movement to modernize Chinese culture that started on May 4, 1919; it lacks conceptual and methodological originality. Shao also points out that while attributing the origins of the backwardness of China to Chinese history, tradition, and political system, the documentary fails to address the issue of every Chinese individual's self-reflexivity, self-cultivation, and self-independence (p. 52).

Zhao Luming (1988) calls for a creation of new symbols in our systematic reflection upon the tradition in terms of thought, spirit, morality, and institution (p. 59). He suggests that there is no real reflection conducive of creating new meanings in He shang. An editorial comment in the China Times of Taiwan (Editorial Board of China Times, 1988, p. 69) calls He shang an echoing of John Fairbank's biased perspective on Chinese culture. It urges Chinese scholars to go beyond Fairbank's perspective and think about how to reinvigorate a culture that belongs to the Chinese and that will contribute to the remaking of global civilization.

What is problematic with such cultural/social criticisms of Chinese culture in general and of the Chinese concept of face in particular as represented by Li Zongwu, Lu Xun, Lin Yutang, Bo Yang, the authors of He shang, and Mao's Cultural Revolution? Why has none of these criticisms achieved desirable social effects? I argue that it is due to the major flaws within such criticisms: They all tend to view culture as a static object; they all attack Chinese culture as if it were an object external to us; they all view change as a break from tradition, not as evolution and transformation. In sum, these modern criticisms constitute iconoclastic ideas that formulate an unrealistic plan for radical action. They seldom take identity, emotions, and feelings in association with face into serious account.

### A Social Constructionist Critique of the Iconoclastic Criticisms and Revolution

What is intellectually and practically problematic with the cultural/social criticisms and revolution that negate the Chinese *lian/mian* practices and Chinese culture in general? First, while these criticisms and social movements share the same goal—to achieve a sudden awakening of the Chinese to their own weaknesses and to effect social and cultural change in China—their social impact has been minimal during the past hundred years. Instead, fundamental Chinese cultural practices such as *lian/mian, guanxi,* and *renqing* have become more active during the current Chinese free-market economy. To use Luo Xiaolan's ideas, such indigenous cultural practices still constitute the primary form of identity of Mainland Chinese; the Communist or socialist belief of the Chinese Communist Party and the Western type of individualism have only a superficial or marginal effect upon Mainland Chinese, contrary to some naive Western scholars' and politicians' predictions on the basis of the emergent free-market economy in China (1996, p. 28). Moreover, these practices "have opened up new colonial space" (Luo, 1997, p. 25). As Lu Zeng puts it, instead of uprooting the *lian/mian* practices in Chinese culture, *lian/mian* as a deep cultural practice is still powerful and integral, is "still sustaining and developing, picking up new features" (1996, p. 140).

Generally, there are three reasons that the iconoclastic criticisms and revolutions of Chinese culture have failed to produce positive social and cultural change. First of all, the definition of culture underlying such criticisms and the proposed/implemented revolution is that culture is viewed as a closed-ended material entity that can be thrown away when necessary; and the concept of cultural change as a linear process and a sharp break. This is especially true with Mao, who attempted to get rid of Chinese people's face consciousness, and Lin, who proposed a revolution to get rid of face, fate, and favor. All these are implicated by the concept of progress along an arrow-like temporal dimension. Philosophically, their metaphor for culture is informed by Newtonian physics. Second, the attitude of the iconoclasts can be characterized as elitist, adversarial, and absolute, without any contextual qualifications. This is true of all the face/culture critics mentioned earlier who attacked and destroyed Chinese culture rather than transforming it into a more resourceful and more powerful, open-ended, and pluralist culture. Finally, the very form of such criticism borrowed from the modern West violates the conventional Chinese form of communication (which is indirect), accented patterns of emotions, and the harmony/hierarchy-oriented personhood that constitute the Chinese concepts of *lian/mian*. This is true of all these critics, especially of Mao, who used physical violence to destroy the *lian/mian* system in rural China, and Bo Yang, who used an extreme form of verbal violence to destroy the minimal identity, confidence, and dignity of Chinese people.

Theoretically, the view of culture embedded in these criticisms and in the revolution is that culture is a close-ended and single unitary entity, mass, or object that is external to researchers/critics and that can be attacked, broken, and removed. In the cases of Lu, Mao, and Lin, orthodox Marxist class theory informs their criticism in varying degrees. In the Chinese context, the Marxist definition of culture is structural and binary, with class as an inviolable concept. In the cases of Bo Yang, the authors of *He shang*, and Lin Yutang, the primary critical resource drawn from is the Western Enlightenment tradition, which treats culture as a universal value system that inherently delegitimizes all the other cultures. Both these theoretical perspectives on culture lose sight of the workings of common sense and everyday practice as the very fountainhead and essence of culture. Thus, *lian/mian* is viewed fundamentally as an institution rather than as the everyday communication, feeling, and acting that are formative of the institution.

Furthermore, underlying all these criticisms is the concept of change as a sharp break from tradition of the relationship between tradition and modernity as linear and causal. This is true with almost every case featured earlier. In arguing for change, the iconoclasts to propose a mechanical replacement of the Chinese *lian/mian* with the Western concept of law, as in the argument by Lin; the replacement of love with hatred, as in the case of Mao's Cultural Revolution, which called for a transformation from *lian/mian* to a state of hatred that is iron-faced and without feelings; and the replacement of Chinese culture, with the modern Western culture as in the cases of Bo Yang and the authors of *He shang*. All these above fail to see change as a circular, systemic, and evolutionary process closely related to the issue of emotions and feelings, which are intimately connected to identity; to see change as a reconstruction or reinvention of tradition by drawing upon various other cultural resources; and to see change as made possible by the creative use of the old and new.

The concept of criticism as a form of modern Western tool for creating, sustaining, and expanding democracy is inherently resisted by Chinese culture, which values *lian/mian*, *renqing*, and *guanxi* almost free of the conception of opposition or adversariness, which are viewed as an inherently dangerous threat to harmony, the god-term of Chinese culture. Therefore, modern criticism as a tool has, in most cases, provoked Chinese face sensitivity. Instead of nurturing Chinese self-reflexivity and producing change, modern criticism has become something Chinese tend to be culturally incapable of tolerating, let alone accepting and appreciating. Modern Chinese social/cultural criticism as illustrated by the case of *He shang*, the case of *The Ugly Chinese*, Mao' revolutions, Lin Yutang and Lu Xun's criticisms, and a series of Chinese prodemocracy social movements such as the 1989 Chinese prodemocracy movement best prove this point. Instead of eliminating the social practices of *lian/mian*, such criticisms have unintentionally reinforced them. As a result, the *lian/mian* practices become inflated and remain powerful and integral, still "sustaining and developing, picking up new features" (Lu, 1996, p. 140), still corrupting the society as well as harmonizing human relationships in some contexts.

I am not suggesting that Chinese do not need criticism, but rather I raise a series of questions: What type of criticism would best fit Chinese culture and best empower Chinese people? In other words, what type of criticism would work effectively towards necessary social change in China while its form did not violate Chinese cultural *lian/mian* norms and would still maintain a sufficient level of respect toward Chinese culture and Chinese identity? I am suggesting that we need to develop a tool for cultural change in China is culturally sensitive and participatory, that is, a tool in connection with, in engagement with, but not against or in adversarial relationship with the grammar of the Chinese communication as the modern form of criticism has been—a tool that is able to selectively wed the old and the new, the native and the foreign, into a better and more sustainable system of practices. Such an instrument, theoretically suggested in Chapters 2 and 3, is blueprinted in the following.

### The Approach of Reflexivity and Transformation of Face Practices

Four models of change are applicable to the Chinese *lian/mian* practices. The first one is the humanistic/social-critical model represented by Lin Yutang, Bo Yang, and the authors of *He shang*. The second model is the Maoist collectivist/communist model of institutionalized criticism and self-criticism meetings which Mao initiated in 1937 in Yenan, the northern part of China. The third model can be termed as the individual-based therapeutic model, as generated in the 1980s in Taiwan with the publication of the book *Chinese Renqing and Mianzi* (Editorial Board of *Teacher Zhang Monthly*, 1990). The fourth model can be called the social constructionist model, which I attempt to sketch here for the first time.

*The Humanistic/Social-Critical Model.* The first model is a humanistic/social-critical approach represented by Lin Yutang, Bo Yang, and the authors of *He shang*, an intellectual approach to cultural change in modern Chinese history. It is characterized by opposition and an adversarial relationship between the critics and the object of criticisms. This approach has its roots in the modern Western intellectual tradition because it relies on Western democracy and the rule of law as its major resource for change. However, as my analysis shows, the instrument of modern criticism adopted by modern Chinese intellectuals against *lian/mian* practices proves countereffective for its inherent violation of the deeply Chinese communication patterns.

*The Maoist Revolutionary Model.* The second model is the Maoist revolutionary model, with communist roots in Marxism-Leninism-Maoism. Its primary form is the institutionalized criticism-self–criticism meeting, which converts *lian/mian*, *renqing*, and *guanxi* into the "us versus enemy" type of relationship. Through criticism and self-criticism, masses cultivated loyalty to communism, the Party, and Mao himself at the sacrifice of making both self and others lose face and giving up all good personal networks, both voluntary and blood relations. Several strategies have been used to achieve and to maintain the power of the Chinese Communist Party. These include institutionalizing face-giving, deinstitutionalizing face-giving, and the consequences. Laid-off workers in Beijing are unwilling to accept offers to work as food vendors, street cleaners, and other manual work although these jobs are much better paid than their original posts. The reason is that they view themselves as originally *guojia ganbu* (the state cadres), a real face-giving entitlement. Doing the manual labor would not fit their status and would be face-losing.

The Chinese Communist Party's (CCP's) face-giving strategies to maintain its own rule can be understood as follows: Recognizing that Chinese are very much concerned about face, the CCP cadre system gives face to many people of all backgrounds by (1) the rule of equivalency or approximation (*xiangdang*), which rates professionals, such as teachers, doctors, scientists, or engineers as equivalent to certain scales of the cadre system, (2) a change of status or promotion (from peasant to city resident, from worker to cadre, from a lower scale to a higher scale.) so that as many capable people as possible feel recognized, and (3) the creation of more bureaucratic offices or positions; for example, the CCP recently created 31 vice-chairmanships in the P.R.C. Political Consultative Committee, perhaps a historical record for vice-chairmanships among all the political organizations in the history of the world. (This seems to be a new strategy of the CCP to win the support of many powerful people who are not CCP members.)

Remember that such promotions and the rule of equivalency do not mean a big salary raise or other material rewards, but predominantly a sheerly nominal and symbolic reward. There are promotions in the

West, but these promotions mean first and foremost a salary raise or a reward of material benefits. There are symbolic dimensions, but they are minor. In contrast, in the CCP system of promotion, the symbolic dimension is primary. However, a majority of Chinese people buy into this system. There are stories, for example, about some associate professors in China who, on hearing that they have not been promoted to a full professorship, draw their last breath or even commit suicide because of their loss of face. Through institutionalizing the face-giving strategy, CCP remains in the supreme power position.

The strategy of face-threat is another major strategy to achieve the goal of the Cultural Revolution by uprooting the social basis of hierarchy. Selecting the "five black kinds" of people (*hei wu lei*) such as the landlords (*di*), the rich peasants (*fu*), the reactionaries (*fan*), the bad elements (*huai*), and the rightists (*yiou*) and criticizing them or exposing their immoral or politically or ideologically incorrect doings so that these people lose face in front of the members of their permanent communities, Mao and his followers made sure that these five kinds of people would no longer be respected. Instead, these five kinds would be sneered at and ostracized in their daily life. Eventually, unable to tolerate the pain and loneliness from being treated as almost a nonhuman entity disassociated from the rest of the community, many of the five black kinds committed suicide and many others suffered from depression.

The Maoist revolution model had been applied within the Chinese Communist Party system and beyond ever since Mao came to power in Yenan in the 1930s. The model has been widely institutionalized. The Confucian ideal of social harmony was abandoned in favor of loyalty to Mao and the CCP ideology. Instead of giving face to each other, everyone would give face to Mao through a belief in class struggle and the utopia of communism. The goal of this model was to transform the clan or family-based face system into the political class-based face system.

*The Therapeutic Model.* The third model is a therapeutic one, with its roots in modern Western individual-based therapy and psychoanalysis originated by Sigmund Freud. While it has not been applied extensively, to my knowledge, it was proposed in Taiwan in the beginning of 1990s (Editorial Board of *Teacher Zhang Monthly*, 1990). In this model, face concerns are reconceptualized as individual anxieties. These are anxieities about expressing love, talking with authoritative figures, talking about sex, exposing one's shortcomings, and expressing oneself. A modern Western type of individualistic alternative is charted in this model. Chinese are encouraged to defeat these individual anxieties by revealing themselves (p. 125) and by being true to oneself and being authentic (p. 142). The individual-based therapeutic model as described in *Chinese renqing and mianzi* (Editorial Board of *Teacher Zhang Monthly*, 1990) locates the force to overcome apprehension over face loss and the force of face transformation within the individual psyche. Social harmony, social good, and respect for hierarchy are marginalized in favor of self-confidence, self-assertion, self-comfort, and equality between self and other. In a word, self-centered face as described in Brown and Levinson's work on politeness is favored over the other-oriented face. The goal of this model is to transform the group-based face system into a modern Western type of individual-based face system.

*A Critique.* These three models do not work very well. The first two run sharply against their goals of cultural transformation, for, because of their simplistic assumptions of an adversarial relationship between critics and their objects of criticism, cause-effect notion of transformation or radical revolution, and the misreplacement of culture with ideology (particularly in the Maoist model), indigenous cultural practices such as *lian/mian* become reinforced instead of minimized or uprooted. In other words, they have created defensiveness on the part of the Chinese for indigenous cultural practices such as *lian/mian* instead of creating more reflective thinking about these practices. This is particularly true of the Maoist model, which has left a lot of wounded relationships among people who made one another lose face during the Cultural Revolution.

The third model, by reconceptualizing face concerns as the psychological problems of individuals, relies solely on individual therapy or individual autonomy for a solution. There are at least two problems with this model. First, it is culturally biased to reduce face concerns to individual concerns. By treating the individual as the explanatory and therapeutic framework, it loses sight of the locus of face concerns as the very processes of social interaction, and interpersonal and group communication. Furthermore, in suggesting that face concerns originate within the individual, it denies their cultural, historical, and power dimensions. By relying solely on the individual as the agent for change, it pits the liberated and awakening individual against authority and the social hierarchy, closing the route to a possible coordinated effort and group alliance in social transformation.

I am proposing an alternative model—a model guided by social constructionism and instrumentalized by circular questioning, a model that aims to enable reflective individuals to perform reflective action in relation to others.

*The Social Constructionist Model.* Here I provide a theoretical outline of the social constructionist model on the basis of my theoretical reconceptualization of *lian/mian* and the social constructionist critique. The full model is elaborated in Chapter 8.

The social constructionist model, the fourth model considered in this book, is a practical extension of the social constructionist perspective on the Chinese concept of face (Penman,1994; Chen, 1990-1991; Kipnis, 1995). Chen, for example, concludes on the basis of real-life interaction data that "face is not a psychological concept or image to be cherished"; it "is located in the flow of events and is continually being constructed, negotiated, and accomplished via the course of interaction" (p. 136). Chen suggests that face in the Chinese context is within and part and parcel of social interaction itself and is never an entity on its own, separable from interaction. This casts a definition of face that is very dynamic, unlike the generalist definition, which is mechanical and analytical, and unlike the static ethnocultural definitions.

Kipnis describes a modern socialist transformation of *lian* and *mian* in China during the 50 years since Hu's first social-scientific study of the Chinese *lian/mian* practices. He identifies four variations of *mianzi* that are most prevalent, because of the Chinese Communist Party's social revolutions. These variations are (1) the administrative *mianzi*, which is a task-oriented instrument of utility that deemphasizes the moral dimension; (2) the "cellurized *mianzi*," which heightens the state's gaze and merges *lian* and *mian* through widespread implementation of the work units—cells—(*gong zou dan wei*)—a very important structural change in Chinese society (1995); (3) a mixture of morality and power-based *mianzi* of the leaders and the leadership in a nationalized political imagery due to the state's and the party's utilization of mass media such as TV; and finally (4) the vain *mianzi* endemic to Chinese intellectuals, which is impractical and opposite to the administrative *mianzi*. Treating the Chinese *lian/mian* as a complex social discourse, Kipnis offers an evolutionary perspective on *lian/mian* in the context of political, social, and technological change meshed with tradition. However, while both of them provide a social constructionist description of *lian/mian*, neither Chen nor Kipnis explores the possibility of creative engagement with or intervention in the Chinese *lian/mian* practices in the context of cultural adaptation to and creative and selective merger with modern and postmodern Western culture, so that the transformed Chinese *lian/mian* culture becomes healthier, more productive, and more sustainable. While built upon Kipnis and Chen, my social constructionist model goes beyond them.

The social constructionist model is a micropractical approach, joining the very workings of the *lian/mian* practices that embrace the emotions and feelings of Chinese social actors in real life. Creatively constructed out of circular questioning (CQ) and appreciative inquiry

(AI) and tailored to the particularities of the contemporary Chinese context, the purpose of this consultative model is to enhance grounded self-reflexivity and the ability to pro-actively facilitate and invent the self-transformation of everyday life in the environment of great social change, to attend to and learn to feel secure with emergent and contingent identities, being aware that what is lost may be rediscovered in a new and different form. Unlike the goals of the other three models, which aim for either a class-dominant face system or an individual-dominant face model, the goal of this social constructionist model aims to transform the group-dominant face system into a group-based and self-agency face system. While this model recognizes the group as the source of face, it emphasizes individual self-reflexivity and self-initiative in transforming the group-dominant face culture in a group context.

The objective of the social constructionist model is to enhance the ability of the Chinese to transform themselves and their society. Harmony and *lian/mian* are redefined and broadened. They are to merge constructively with the forces of capital, law, and technology in forging a new type of Chinese personhood that transforms and integrates constructive sources of Chinese tradition and Western modernity, both as substance and form. Thus, *zhong ti xi jong* (the principle of Chinese tradition as substance and modern Western tradition as instrument) is not applicable because *zhong* and *xi* have lost their original identities in the new Chinese personhood; but both have found a shared life in the new Chinese personhood hopefully achievable through my social constructionist model.

### Research Questions

The core question this book attempts to answer is this: What would be an acceptable and effective analytical and practical mechanism to best facilitate a continuum of micro-mezzo-macrosocial transformations for the betterment of China and its citizens, while they confront unprecedented social, political, economic, interpersonal, and individual choices and confusions in communication, relationships, and their individual, cultural, and national identities during an unprecedented transition? I have selected for study the Chinese *lian/mian* practices central to Chinese communication and identity. I want to operationalize a social constructionist perspective on *lian/mian* on the basis of a social constructionist critique of divergent lines of research on facework. What dimensions of *lian/mian* does the social constructionist theory highlight, and what unique theoretical/practical advantages does this view have that other theories lack? This big question divides into six specific questions.

1. Since social constructionism emphasizes the historicity of social interaction and the historicity of concepts of social interaction, what does a historical-cum-social constructionist perspective on *lian/mian* as patterns and concepts of social interaction/action look like? (See the first part of Chapter 3.)

2. Since social constructionism highlights action and interaction as the processes during which the human world is constantly constructed and reconstructed, what roles do/did/will *lian/mian* practices play in the Chinese world and in its formation and reformation? This question can be answered in the following two dimensions:

   a. Specifically, do/did/will *lian/mian* as a practical cultural concept occupy a central position, a typical position, or a marginal position in Chinese culture?

   b. What specific practical/social/cultural functions or malfunctions did/does/will *lian/mian* play in the Chinese society? (See the second part of Chapter 3.)

3. Since social constructionism is particularly interested in the consequentiality of communication, what consequences have *lian/mian* practices brought upon Chinese society, which has been yearning for change and undergoing change? (See the fifth part of Chapter 3 and parts of Chapters 6 and 7.)

4. Since social constructionism regards emotion as an inseparable dimension of communication, which is also constructed socially, what did/does/will the emotional dimension of the *lian/mian* practices look like? Specifically, to what extent are the concepts of *lian/mian* inseparable from certain emotions and feelings? What "feel rules" are associated with the concepts of *lian/mian* in different historical contexts? (See the third part of Chapter 3 and parts of Chapters 6 and 7.)

5. Since social constructionism emphasizes conceptual linkages (such as Wittgenstein's concept of "family resemblances") as well as conceptual differentiation, what concepts help define *lian/mian*? What other terms belong to the conceptual cluster that has *lian/mian* as its center? How are they similar to and how are they different from *lian/mian*? (See the fourth part of Chapter 3.)

6. Since social constructionism regards engagement in ongoing social cultural practices (communication) as not only inevitable but also as an ethically responsible act of researchers whose goal is to improve or enrich human lives, what does the social constructionist engagement with the *lian/mian* practices look like? What new forms of life can emerge in which new sources and forces of identification are made more accessible and more acceptable; in which unwanted social consequences and malfunctions of *lian/mian*

practices such as individual, interpersonal, and intergroup ten-
sions, sufferings, uncertainties, conflicts, and fear of change are
better managed and reduced; in which a more self-reflective,
healthier, and happier living is made possible with the synergy of
new tradition (the transformed *lian/mian*) and old modernity (the
sources useful for the transformation of *lianmian*)? (See Chapters
5, 6, 7, and 8.)

By creatively using CQ and AI, which have been used and tested both
in labs and in the field and which are theoretically informed by social
constructionism, I hope to operationalize my *lian/mian* transformation
project and to invent and illustrate my model of social constructionist
transformation of *lian/mian* practices, thus achieving the goals and
objectives of the study reported in this book.

## CONCLUSION

This chapter reviews various theoretical and methodological approaches to face or the Chinese concepts of face. At one end of the
continuum are the universal theories of face and ethnocultural studies
of face whose goal is to describe and interpret face or Chinese face
practices without an awareness of the need to transform face practices
in order to transform society. At the other end of the continuum are
critical and revolutionary approaches whose goal is to get rid of face
practices in order to achieve the radical transformation of society without a nuanced understanding of face dynamics and mechanism. Both
these extremes, according to the social constructionist perspective, are
faulty or incomplete.

The social constructionist perspective and its methodology are the
middle-ground approach, attempting to develop a more open-ended,
complete, and nuanced understanding of Chinese face practices and
attempting to create a mechanism of micro-engagement with and mild
intervention into Chinese face practices, as illustrated in specific cases.
This approach aims to enhance reflexivity on and possibly to transform
(not completely remove, which is theoretically impossible and ethically
unacceptable) Chinese face practices so that Chinese persons will selectively absorb the nutrients of other cultures such as the modern Western
culture in their communications and identity transformation. The social
constructionist perspective and methodology form a creative instrument, built upon social constructionism and its critique of the two
extremes.

# 5

# Research Methodologies

Research methodologies in this book consist of six parts:

1. The historical method, primarily informed by R. G. Collingwood (1946), whose ideas of history share an affinity with social constructionism.
2. The methods of social constructionist reading and critique.
3. The method of consultation called Circular Questioning (CQ), with Appreciative Inquiry (AI).
4. A list of questions, circular in nature, that constitute the instrument for consultation used during two consultation sessions for the case studies reported in Chapters 6 and 7.
5. The case study method, as used in chapters 6 and 7. This consultation instrument can be described as an effort to operationalize the theory of social constructionism and to apply the method of CQ in the Chinese context.
6. Drawing a conclusion.

The combination of these methods is an attempt to formulate a methodological orientation consisting of a continuum of situatedness-historicity-culturality. Cronen suggests such an orientation when he argues, "To study communication from the orientation I have suggested is to inquire—in a situated, historical-cultural way—into how we are cocreating who we are and what we are doing, and with a view as to how we might do better" (1996, p. 61).

## THE HISTORICAL METHOD

The first method used in this book is historical and could be called social constructionist in nature (see Chapter 3). This method is primarily informed by R. G. Collingwood's view of history in his book *Ideas of History* (1946). Briefly, he holds that history is a process or becoming (p. 210) that is constituted by human activity of relative freedom and that historical progress is but a chain of human acts, with each arising out of the last (p. 324). He states:

> The disappearance of historical naturalism, however, entails the further conclusion that the activity by which man builds his own constantly changing historical world is a free activity. There are no forces other than this activity which control it or modify it or compel it to behave in this way or that, to build one kind of world rather than another. (1946, p. 315)

History, historical objects, and the alleged historical laws are but what humans create through symbolic interaction or "language-games" (Wittgenstein, 1958, p. 5e), rather than the end results of natural forces.

With this method, I view the *lian/mian* practices, instead of ideas, as a major constituent of and a major agent for the making of Chinese history. Thus, I do not draw upon classical texts written by philosophical sages such as Confucius and Laozi. Rather, I draw upon a variety of historical records such as old dictionaries of Chinese characters with etymological accounts, folk songs such as *The Book of Songs*, and some relevant anthropological and sociological accounts of uses of language or "language-games," a blend of language and social action. These resources record a very complex and dynamic historical process or a social becoming that has been incessantly pushed by human interaction in the Chinese historical/social/cultural contexts. Classical Chinese philosophical texts alone are incapable of forging and accounting for such a historical or social becoming.

### The Methods of the Social Constructionist Reading and Critique

According to the social constructionist theory outlined in Chapter 2, communication is central in the formation and transformation of a culture at both the practical and conceptual levels. For example, Dewey, one of the major founders of pragmatism, argues that communication is prior to and formative of consciousness (1929/1960, p. 187). "Society not only continues to exist by transmission, by communication, but it may fairly be said to exist in transmission, in communication" (Dewey, 1916/1966, p. 4). Central to communication in a given culture are some cultural communication concepts. The understanding, analysis, and transformation of these concepts are crucial in the improvement of communication, in the transformation of a culture, and in the betterment of the human condition. For example, Cronen, John Shotter, Kenneth Gergen (1991), Rom Harré (1991), Barnett Pearce (1994), and Donal Carbaugh (1988, 1996) have all consensually identified the concept of self as central in shaping modern Western communication and culture, and all have attempted to redefine self from a given communication perspective in order to improve communication and human relations in the contemporary Western context, with signs of good results. Inspired by these scholars, I have searched and identified the concept of *lian/mian* as a central indigenous cultural communication concept and as a central patterned social practice in Chinese culture. The centrality of *lian/mian* is amply documented in the second part of Chapter 3.

Social constructionism gives increasing recognition to the role of emotions in communicative accomplishments and recognizes emotions as a hidden but powerful dimension of communication. In addition, it argues that emotions are socially achieved, socially formative, and transformative. This is discussed in Chapter 3.

Around the concept of *lian/mian* are a host of indigenous Chinese interpersonal concepts that are both similar to and different from one another. These other concepts are variants of *lian/mian*. Wittgenstein's social constructionist notions of language-games and family resemblances and David L. Hall's "cluster concept" encourage the exploration of cultural meanings and uses of each face-related concept, how these concepts differ and how they are interrelated, and how each contributes to the whole of the *lian/mian* practices that function as the cultural grammar for social interaction in the Chinese context.

Since communication is central in the formation and transformation of a culture, it is also consequential. In other words, communication points beyond itself. Cronen speaks clearly about this point: "Communication is consequential because it is intrinsic to being human" (1995a, p. 61). In extension, I would argue that communication is consequential because a given grammar of communication is most likely to perpetuate a given form of being human, which, in time, is no longer fully self-fulfilling and self-sustainable without self-reflection, critique, transformation, and the enrichment of this grammar. An attempt to highlight this urgency to reconstitute and expand the given form of being human by borrowing from other communication grammars and creating new communication grammars is presented in Chapter 3.

## CIRCULAR QUESTIONING

Circular questioning (CQ) is an unconventional approach to family therapy and organizational and community consultation. Recently it has been used in communication (Cronen & Lang, 1994; Chong, 1997). It was first formulated by the Milan Team in Italy in the 1970s. It was significantly developed by Karl Tomm (1987a, 1987b, 1988; Fleuridas, Nelson & Rosenthal, 1986) and expanded by Kingsington Consultation International in Britain, with heavy reference to the Coordinated Management of Meaning—a social constructionist theory spearheaded by Cronen and Pearce.

## A Summary of CQ

Here, circular questioning (CQ) is summarized on three levels: the philosophical, conceptual, and content.

Philosophically, CQ is formulated on the basis of a series of syntheses or mergers of sets of dichotomies constituting modern Western philosophy and social sciences. The following list displays ten of these mergers:

- the merger of objectivity and subjectivity into intersubjectivity;
- the merger of theory and practice into practical theory
- the merger of social and individual into a type of interdependence
- the merger of rationality and emotions (as in the term "social uses of emotions" or emotions as social judgments)
- the merger of representation and construction
- the merger of linearity and circularity (as in the term "circular causality")
- the merger of interviewer and interviewee/researcher and subject/consultant and consultee/therapist and client (as in the terms "co-researcher" and "researcher/practitioner"
- the merger of structure and process (as in the argument that structure is but the product of process)
- the merger of past, present, and future (as in the social constructionist saying that the past lives in the present and the future is in the hands of the present)
- the merger of macroanalysis and microanalysis

On the basis of its philosophical assumptions, CQ has come up with eight unique concepts—circularity, reflexivity, neutrality, emergency, story, grammar, context, and structure.

*Circularity* is a systemic view of the world and society. It holds that reality is constituted by a totality of circularity. It views communication as an interconnected process that is constitutive or transformative of an emergent reality. In terms of interviewing, it refers to "the dynamic structural coupling" (Tomm, 1987, p. 8).

*Reflexivity* means the ability to see things in a systemic perspective and the ability to identify interconnections, interdependence, and open-endedness among seemingly discrete parts. In CQ, a consultant or interviewer should be able to ask questions of reflexivity that may help clients to make clearer a complete cycle of behaviors or patterns of interaction and to bridge conceptual and perceptual gaps in the cycle and reconnect the missing links.

*Neutrality* here means active but equal engagement with the clients or subjects in terms of distribution of interactional resources such as attention, without taking sides with any one member or any subgroup, without being allied to anyone but accepting everyone at the same time (Fleuridas et al., 1986, p. 115), and allowing multiple positionings instead of a single positioning (Lang, 1996).

*Emergency* means indeterminacy, uncertainty, the process of coming into being, the breathtaking scene in which death and life, status quo, and change intermix, the nexus between what is and what is to be. It is a moment of reappearance as well as disappearance. It takes an acute awareness to spot opportunities to create change.

*Story* suggests that researchers or consultants are not looking for a definitive answer, because that is impossible, but that they accept and value indefiniteness. Treating data as stories suggests a constructionist bent of language and communication. Different stories about the same event may implicate different positions, which may shed light upon one another.

*Grammar* refers to rules, norms, conventions, and patterns of interaction that are not prescribed but come into being through and emerge out of communication. Grammar is in contrast with value. While value suggests eternity and unchangeability, grammar suggests unboundedness, tentativeness, and the possibility that rules, norms, conventions, and patterns of communication can be transformed in and through communication.

*Context* in CQ is not a static term. It is, rather, an interactive notion. According to Cronen and Lang, it is better to view context as a verb, meaning "weave together" in the Latin sense of the word (Cronen & Lang, 1994, p. 8). Since context is a product of communication and lives in communication, context should never be taken for granted. It has to be constantly "redescribed."

*Structure*, in the constructionist sense, is but a collection of stories that have been mistakenly regarded as the manifestation of truth. Structure can crumble when different stories are told. In this sense, structure is but a comma among stories within stories, not a full stop.

CQ, a product of the intellectual transformation of modern knowledge in the West, is committed to social transformation. It is a tool for change, which in turn changes the context of CQ. It is intended to create opportunities to reintegrate human relationships and cultural identities. Used effectively, it may help in reconstituting and reinventing new forms and stories of human experience that may eventually benefit a majority of people.

Selvini Palazzoli and associates define CQ as the "capacity of the therapist to conduct his/her investigation on the basis of feedback from the family in response to the information he (or she) solicits about relationships, and therefore, about difference and change" (1980, p. 8). Karl Tomm states: "Circular questions tend to be characterized by a general curiosity about possible connectedness of events that include the problem, rather than a specific need to know the precise origins of the problems" (1988, p. 8).

Ways of asking in CQ center around the notion of circularity. Circularity is meant in the following senses:

1. Circularity between interviewer and interviewee. Each comment made by the interviewer is clearly connected to the last comment by the interviewee. A significant technique to maintain such circularity is for the interviewer to use the same key words the interviewee uses in commenting on a prior comment by the interviewee. This is a useful way to join the grammar of the interviewee. According to Peter Lang, a consultant or researcher, instead of saying to clients, "Can I help you?", can say to them something like "Can you help me?", thus reconstituting the traditional helper-helpee relationship into a mutual helper-helpee relationship. It can also be useful to conduct consultation sessions at the client's home or office instead of always having clients come to the consultant's office.

2. Circularity in terms of connecting the members of the family or organization who are receiving consultation. The interviewer is interested in how each member is connected to each of the others. Such questions should solicit details of real life rather than variables or value constructs. One technique to help members of the group develop a systemic view of the family or organization is called "gossiping in the presence of others." For example, parents are asked to comment on grandparents' responses to a child's misbehavior at school.

3. Circularity in terms of time. Past, present, and future do not exist on a straight line, but rather coexist. They are but different perspectives on the same event. The past lives in the present, and the present is a moment of reinventing the future. It also makes sense when Peter Lang says, "The moment you start conversation, you recreate the present by the future talk" (Lang, 1996, in a workshop on CQ). I would argue that emergency could be a synonym of time since it is an active interaction of past, present, and future.

4. Circularity with respect to positions. Systemic ways of asking can create new cultural opportunities with which one is hopefully able

to do the following: to free oneself from one position into another position without losing one's agency, to take multiple positions with ease at the same time, and to be aware of a maximum of alternatives and to be able to choose.

With circularity embedded within it, CQ has several unique ways of inquiry—joining the grammar of the person(s) you are interviewing, questions of elaboration, positive reformulating, and appreciative inquiry:

1. Joining the grammar of the client. The consultant should be keen enough to pick up key terms used by the client in making a comment or asking a question instead of using professional jargon. In this way, the client experiences empathy in a different way. Furthermore, questions using the client's key terms should be able to link the client's words to specific moments of the client's experience. For example, when the client says, "I feel depressed," the consultant might ask, "When did you feel depressed? If there were not such a word, what words would you like to use to describe that feeling?" Here, the consultant joins the grammar by repeating the key term, "depressed," used by the client.

2. Questions of elaboration. Questions should tap into the details of action, thinking, feelings, and emotions of the client in an actual moment of life, asking about things people do not usually question. It has a potential to render multiple stories about an event that are both contradictory and complementary, stories, for instance, that depict the son as both a villain and a hero instead of a mere villain. For example, one might ask a son the following questions about his hitting his mother: "Why did you choose the area you hit?" The answer might be, "I did not want to hurt her although I wanted to hit her." "How did you hit her while you did not intend to hurt her?"

3. Positive reformulating. The consultant transforms a negative comment one client has made about another client into a positive comment. The purpose is to highlight a positive perspective that has been hidden from the first client so that the first client will be exposed to the possibility of reconceptualizing the relationship. For example, after the first client says, "My Dad [the second client] always shouts at me angrily when I get bad grades; he is such a tyrant," the consultant might say, "So your Dad is so much concerned about you as to sacrifice his democratic image."

4. Appreciative inquiry (AI). AI opposes solution talk and problem talk that suggest a set of endorsed norms and prevent new forms from emerging. AI is intended to dissolve the problem-solution

polarity. It affirms stories that create life and hope, and it helps nurture the fragile stories so that the future will be affirmative. It changes the language of deficit into the language of affirmation. The following are questions that exemplify AI: What are your strengths? In what situations do you feel a sense of belonging? How do others talk about you affirmatively? What do people enjoy about you? What is your explanation of what makes it possible?

## CQ AS THE INSTRUMENT FOR CONSULTATION IN THE CHINESE CONTEXT

Here, the discussion of the implications and uses of CQ in the Chinese context consists of five parts: (1) the rationale for selecting CQ, (2) a critique of CQ in reference to Chinese culture, (3) a discussion of CQ as a potential resource for cultural change in China, (4) strategic uses of CQ in the Chinese context, and (5) a layout of the specific instrument for consultation in the Chinese context, as employed in the case studies of Chapters 6 and 7.

### Rationale for Selecting CQ

While Hyon Sook Chong uses CQ as a data-collecting method for CMM, which she treats as both a theory and an analytical tool for description, interpretation, and critique (1997, p. 44), CQ and AI I use here serve as a tool for engagement with and transformation of the *lian/mian* practices, with CMM/practical theory/social constructionism forming the theoretical perspective. The *lian/mian* practices are described, interpreted, and critiqued in light of relevant theoretical dimensions of CMM/practical theory/social constructionism. This description, interpretation, and critique of the *lian/mian* practices are a fusion of the micro-mezzo-macro levels, which seems more inclusive than the CMM analytical machinery. The CMM machinery does not prepare for engagement and transformation. In the most recent research on CMM, the description, interpretation, and critique achievable by the CMM analytical machinery no longer seem to be at the top of the research agenda of leading CMM scholars such as Cronen and Pearce.

Cronen's research agenda in the past several years has been the development of Practical Theory (see Chapter 4). The core concern of this theory is engagement and transformation. On the other hand, he has been consistently doing projects of engagement and change in a variety of different forms, such as conducting workshops in collaboration with Kingsington Consultation International in London (a social constructionist group of theorists/practitioners using CQ and AI) and organizational consultations using CQ and AI. Barnett Pearce has set up his own organization, called the Public Dialogue Consortium in California to be fully engaged with social change in light of traditional CMM theory. In a sense, he has become an activist/practitioner/researcher with CQ and possibly AI as major tools.

To engage with change and transformation is not just a choice for social constructionists, but an ethical responsibility or even a historical mission. Cronen best summarizes the social constructionist credo: "For ethical reasons, enabling creative evolution has precedence over description" (1996, p. 17). While the CMM analytical machinery is in conceptual detachment from engagement—or is preengagement and may be pro-engagement and pro-transformation—CQ and AI can be said to be the working hands of engagement and an engine for transformation or quiet revolution. Thus, an intelligent and creative use of CQ and AI could constitute the very process of transforming a problematic culture.

### A Critique of CQ in Light of Chinese Culture

Comparatively, there are cultural differences between CQ and Chinese culture, as there are differences between CQ and modern Western culture. However, many of the cultural uniquenesses can be regarded as affordances for Chinese culture as well as affordances for modern Western culture, although different aspects of CQ may be useful for each culture. Practitioners/researchers should be aware of the following differences between the "culture" of CQ and Chinese culture.

Deeply embedded in CQ are its view of human beings as equal and its view of culture, self, and social institutions as dynamic and interactive. This is in sharp contrast with the Confucian view of the human world as a natural hierarchy and its belief in an ideal form of social harmony.

According to CQ, communication is construction of social reality, whereas the Confucian notion of communication is but a way to respect the hierarchy and to cultivate and maintain social harmony. Communication that threatens social hierarchy and breaks harmony is discouraged and even penalized.

On the basis of these differences, to actively join the grammar of a Chinese client who speaks a hierarchical language would pose some difficulty for a change agent not familiar with the culture. To adhere to the principle of neutrality in joining the grammar of Chinese participants means to distribute the change agent's symbolic resources among the clients who occupy different positions of the social hierarchy on an equal basis. This may create grievances against the change agent among senior members of the group. Faced with this situation, the change agent should use some techniques to save the face of senior members. Otherwise, the change agent may lose the clients too early because of the disruption of the hierarchy.

Hypothesizing obviously originates from natural sciences in the West. It carries the Western value of creativity and exploration for truth. Although Western natural sciences and social sciences introduced to China have produced some good results, such scientific discourse has failed to penetrate Chinese social life, which is so much engaged with mundane living as hardly to have room for thinking about what may happen next. The change agent, therefore, has to learn how to explain a hypothetical statement with Chinese examples, especially when faced with clients with little education.

Positive reframing is interventionist in nature. It seems to run against the principle of neutrality. If the change agent positively reframes the comment made by the first client about a second client who is senior to the first client, that is permissible because the junior client expects it. If the senior client's comment is reframed, the senior client will feel that the change agent is making the senior lose face in front of the junior. To the senior, the change agent's positive reframing of a comment about the junior would be a message of disrespect that would invite or encourage the junior to disrespect the senior. The senior would  be likely to think that the consultant is ganging up with the junior against the senior. Thus, positive reframing can produce disruption when used too early during the session. A culturally forceful way of positive reframing in the Chinese cultural context would be for the change agent to travel between the two persons to consult with each separately.

AI runs against the Chinese virtue of modesty. In order to maintain social harmony, Chinese are socialized to be modest. But this does not mean that Chinese do not accept appreciation and praise, but that they accept appreciation by a ritual of self-denial or self-deprecation. The change agent does not have to give up AI, but should not take the client's self-denial and self-deprecation at face value. The agent should emphasize the sincerity of the appreciation. However, direct or highly exaggerated questions should be modified to become more acceptable. For example, the question "What are your strengths?" is too direct to Chinese. The client is most likely to answer, "Oh, sorry! I do not have any strengths." The question can be reframed as something like, "What did you do that others thought successful?" If the client still appears to be too modest to give a positive reply, the consultant may ask other members of the group to say something appreciative about this client. After positive comments made by other members, the consultant does not have to confirm the comments with this client, who may still be afraid of being viewed as content.

Questions of elaboration fit very well with Chinese culture. Both CQ and Chinese culture value mundane living. Chinese love to ask each other situationally based questions about each other's everyday life, without any concern for privacy. Questions of elaboration would be a very useful way to establish rapport and trust with Chinese. But the change agents should also expect that they can be asked the same questions of elaboration, to show concern or good feelings in return.

Identifying missing links among human relations seems to be a predominant theme only in contemporary Western society, due to its institutionally endorsed individualism. Chinese society seems to have quite an opposite theme—how to trim too many burdensome links in human relations to reduce emotional dependency and to strengthen individual agency to a sufficient level. As Ping He's citation of Xiao Shafu testifies about the Chinese need for individual agency:

He criticized the Confucian emphasis on moral cultivation and the idea that the harmony of social relationship reduced the individual to a mere element of social hierarchy. Moral nature was regarded by Confucius as the essence of the individual. Other aspects of individual life, especially the rights of the individual, were thereby overlooked. The individual was therefore not considered as an independent entity possessing cognitive and aesthetic capacities, but merely as a vehicle for the maintenance of abstract ethical norms. Moral norms were so alienated as to become a tyranny suppressing and enslaving the individual. (1995, p. 145)

Can CQ in its original form help construct a moderate amount of individuality for Chinese and help them reduce the emotional strains and undesirable social consequences due to the *lian/mian* practices so that they will gain sufficient agency without losing necessary community? If not, how can the original form of CQ be transformed to best facilitate transformation of the Chinese *lian/mian* practices?

### CQ as a Resource for Cultural Change in China

Hyon Sook Chong critiques CQ with reference to the Korean cultural context (1997). Chong's major argument against the blind use of CQ in the Korean context is the Western cultural biases that CQ carries. These biases include a Western concept of self as higher than the cultural norms, neutrality against the Korean social hierarchy, and so on. Problems with her critique seem to be as follows: First, Chong fails to recognize the transformative nature of CQ, blaming it as intrusive. Instead, she treats CQ merely as a data-collecting method that should be free of cultural messages. She fails to differentiate between the culture embodied by CQ and modern Western culture, labeling them the monolithic Western culture. She seems to be a cultural nativist and protectionist, almost labeling every cultural assumption within CQ that does not fit the Korean culture as biased.

As a matter of fact, the culture embodied and championed by CQ has many major differences from modern Western culture. These differences are intentionally created and synthesized by reflexive and liberal Western intellectuals such as the CMM group in order to transform the problematic modern Western culture. Can we say that CQ is culturally biased against modern Western culture? I would not think so. Therefore, to remain at the level of identifying the cultural biases of CQ against another culture, such as an East Asian culture, is xenophobic and unreflective. I would treat those uniquenesses of CQ as having potentially transformative potential for a problematic culture such as the Chinese.

The goal of the *lian/mian* transformation in China is to develop a healthy and creative form of life capable of surviving in this world of unprecedented change. Instead of focusing on CQ's cultural biases against and constraints on Chinese culture, I am going to discuss what new affordances CQ and AI may create and how we can take advantage of such affordances to achieve a healthier and more sustainable *lian/mian* transformation in contemporary China.

I think that CQ consists of the following cultural resources useful for social transformation in China. First, CQ's deep respect for equality could help transform social hierarchy. Second, CQ's ingrained penchant for change could derigidify the status quo and enhance social mobility. Third, CQ's redefinition of self as a process of social construction offers a moderate model of personhood between the promotion of the extreme of individualism in the modern West and the strong endorsement of selflessness in China. Fourth, CQ's belief in communication in constituting and reconstituting a type of relationship could challenge the Confucianist presumption of pan-human relationships (*fan guanxi*), which tends to dictate fixed forms of communication. Finally, CQ's respect for multiple positions and diversity could help transform the Chinese identity of racial and cultural homogeneity to be more open-ended and more receptive of diversity, which Confucianism tends to regard as chaos or disorder (*luan*), and to be more appreciative of self-reflexivity.

China is currently undergoing a transition from a planned economy to a free-market economy. All the preexistent social, cultural, and political norms and institutions are undergoing transformation. In reference to the current situation in China, I see CQ as a heuristic tool for facilitating transformation in the following areas:

1. Various radical approaches such as a blind quest for money, a blind quest for power, and radical nationalism have been employed at

both individual and group levels. CQ may help develop citizens' self-reflexivity on such radical approaches.
2. The contradiction between tradition and modernity has become more acute than ever before. A social constructionist view and CQ may help generate an alternative that would be neither traditional nor modern and at the same time both traditional and modern.
3. CQ attempts to cure the ills of modernity in the contemporary West. A transformed version of CQ would also help China's modernization minimize both modern and traditional social ills.
4. CQ and its social constructionist theory would offer a reconceptualization of transition in China. Instead of looking for models derived from the modern West, social constructionism would attend to transition as emergence. Indeed, the concept of transition implies a linear view, which suggests that the society will eventually reach a stable and mature state after a temporary period called "transition." This would mislead researchers' attention to models of the past and away from attending to transition itself to spot opportunities for change and away from nurturing a grassroots social constructionist model. Social constructionist theory and CQ would help correct a linear search for a stable and ideal state after transition and help cope with a new contingency. As a matter of fact, there is nothing nontransitory, according to the assumptions of CQ.

## Cultural Strategies for Using CQ in the Chinese Context

CQ is a tool for strategic, purposeful, and mutually beneficial engagement with social interaction and transformation of the impoverishing forms of life. In the Chinese context, the following CQ strategies could be used to achieve a better result.

1. Learn to join in the Chinese cultural grammar. In other words, try to create and affirm cultural identification or try to fit and get accepted into the system first. Specifically, learn to enact *lian/mian*, *renqing*, and *guanxi* practices. Also learn to speak some Chinese and the language of the Chinese cultural grammar. Having been accepted into the system, you may gradually induce change by using CQ. This strategy might be called "within-system transformation" or *ti nei gai ge*. Otherwise, even cultural insiders would not be accepted as change agents. This can be called "to give *lian/mian* first." After acceptance, start gradually peeling off the *lian/mian* or help clients develop self-reflexivity on their own *lian/mian* practices or those of others.
2. Create a *guanxi* network in which you are regarded as an insider so that members do not reject your request to give a consultation

session. Start at least half a year beforehand. It takes a long time for Chinese to develop a relationship. However, once it is developed, it is very hard to sever. Therefore, do not start doing consultation until a trusting relationship has been developed.

3. For consultation, identify a typical face-related case about other people in real life. This way, participants will talk more freely. Chinese tend to like to chat about others in groups, without the concern about privacy shown by people in the West.

4. Gossip in the presence of others can be postponed until after you find out if the participants relate to each other hierarchically or equally. You may use the technique of gossip behind the back first on a one-on-one basis. This might avoid causing participants at higher levels of the hierarchy to lose face.

## POSSIBLE USES OF CQ IN THE ANALYSIS OF THE CHINESE *LIAN/MIAN* PRACTICES

CQ is a tool used to help enhance reflexivity. Originally, CQ was a tool used to help highly individualized people in modern industrial societies, especially in the West, to enable themselves to view things in connection to one another; it institutes a systemic worldview of interdependence that differs from the modern scientific, analytical worldview of departmentalization. There may be cultural constraints to using CQ in the Chinese context, in which social practices are too undifferentiated at the conceptual level and function as a closed system. One certainly needs to modify CQ or transform CQ to fit in the Chinese context. It should be able to "put human reflection at the core as a constitutive social phenomenon" (Maturana and Varela, 1987, p. 245) for Chinese and be able to compel Chinese to become constantly vigilant against their/our own weaknesses and to see the possibility of creating a different and new, more lovely and livable world with an enhanced reflexivity.

The modern Western type of social criticism generated by Bo Yang and the authors of *He shang*, assumed to enhance reflexivity *(fan si)*, run counter to the most basic face needs of Chinese. As a result, they injure the Chinese readers'/viewers' face sensitivity and spur their counterattacks against the *lian/mian* of the critics. Thus, the goal of cultural transformation aimed for by such criticisms has not been reached. Instead, the criticisms have helped affirm the values of Chinese *lian/mian*.

It seems to me that in order to transform the Chinese *lian/mian* practices, one has to learn not to make explicit value judgments about them. CQ is more analytical, reflective, and proactive than critical. Instead of making Chinese lose face, CQ is inherently respectful of *lian/mian*. Therefore, it can help enhance the Chinese participants' self-reflexivity on their *lian/mian* practices and help them comfortably transform themselves, with few side effects.

A new CQ might help Chinese untangle, differentiate, and resynthesize their issues of face on the basis of respecting the most basic face needs of the people and adapt to the emergent modern society, which is not quite receptive of their traditional persona. For example, laid-off workers refuse to accept new jobs selling lunchboxes and cleaning streets for fear of face loss, although they could earn more than with their former jobs. They are still carrying their traditional *lian/mian* persona, while the changing Chinese society requires a new persona that is less rigid and more open and flexible and pragmatic. This new persona can allow for the separation of a professional role from a private way of life.

"We tend to live in a world of certainty, of undoubted, rock-ribbed perceptions: our convictions prove that things are the way we see them and there is no alternative to what we hold as true. This is our daily situation, our cultural condition, our common way of being human" (Maturana and Varela, 1987, p. 16). This seems to be also an insightful description of many Chinese who are also "keyed to action, not to reflection" (Maturana and Varela, 1987, p. 24). CQ, as a tool for reflection, may help Chinese turn back upon themselves to discover the areas that they have been culturally unprepared to examine. It should be able to generate an alternative to the taken-for-granted way of being human that is confined by the *lian/mian* practices. With these possible uses of CQ in mind, I developed the following instrument for consultation on the Chinese *lian/mian* transformation.

### Types of Questions Asked During the Consultation Session

Consistent with the preceding discussions of CQ at its philosophical, conceptual, and instrumental levels and CQ's potential uses and drawbacks, I formulated the following questionnaire, which was used in the case studies reported in Chapters 6 and 7.

1. Questions about the cultural representativeness of the case:
   a. Does this type of case happen often?
   b. How often?
   c. Could you give me similar examples?
   d. Are the behaviors of the major characters in each case typical in Chinese communities?
2. Questions of cultural/historical elaboration:
   a. How would you describe the kinds of cultural norms or rules that inform the way the persons in the case interact with each other?

     b. How would you describe the emotions and feelings of the persons in the case?

     c. What do you think has made them who they are?

     d. Where and how do you think they might have acquired *lian/mian* practices primarily?

3. Questions about legitimacy for concerns:

     a. Is this a concern for you as an observer? Please elaborate.

     b. Would this constitute a concern for the actors themselves in the story?

     c. Do you think that they would regret what they did later on?

4. Questions about consequences of *lian/mian* practices in the case:

     a. In your opinion, what socially or personally desirable consequences have the persons' *lian/mian* practices in the case brought about?

     b. In your opinion, what socially or personally undesirable consequences have the persons' *lian/mian* practices in the case brought about?

     c. How could they have enacted their *lian/mian* so that the socially or personally undesirable consequences could have been minimized?

5. Questions about change:

     a. How do you think that the persons in the case should have communicated to avoid or manage the conflict?

     b. If you were in a similar situation like any of the actors in the case, what would you do? Please elaborate.

     c. What do you think we should do to help persons like them deal with such cases more constructively?

     d. Do you have any additional comment about the case?

6. Reflective questions:

     a. Can you infer what the goals of my interview are?

     b. What do you think of the goals of my interview?

     c. Do you agree with each other's answers to my questions so far?

     d. What is most memorable about my interview to you?

     e. What questions did you not expect from me today?

     f. What questions do you think pushed you to think or feel in ways you have not thought or felt before?

     g. How would you act differently if or when you encountered a similar situation in the future?

     h. Do you have any additional comment related to the questions above?

7. Meta-Interview questions

     a. What suggestions do you have about the way I conducted my interviews?

     b. Have my questions restricted your thinking about the case?

    c. Do you find my questions easily comprehensible?

    d. Do you have any additional comment about today's interview?

Before my interviews, I provided my participants the culturally relevant following information about the way I would conduct the interviews. (Subsequently I call participants "consultants" because they help me further validate my own insights into the *lian/mian* practices as a native Chinese myself, while I help them reflect upon the *lian/mian* practices.)

> My interviews are for my research in Chinese communication and culture, not about Chinese politics. So, please feel relaxed. I will record my interviews with your written permission to help me accurately remember what we have said for the sake of my analysis. But I will destroy the tapes after my research is done. Since we have been friends, let us trust each other. Friends help instead of betraying each other. I would not have asked you to answer my questions had you not been my friends. Please also try to observe how I am conducting my interviews since I will ask your feedback about the effectiveness of my interviews [I read the meta-interview questions to my consultants here]. Please also be informal. Let us make it like a small talk we have had before.

I interviewed my consultants in groups. This enabled me to use CQ in a group context. For example, I asked them to comment on each other's answers or to "gossip in the presence of others," a technique of circularity in CQ. The questions listed earlier are the generic questions I used in the case studies presented in Chapters 6 and 7—not word-for-word, but in roughly the same order. I interviewed for each case separately, making my interview structure open-ended and rephrasing these questions. I added some case-specific and interview context–specific questions when necessary. Whichever additional questions I asked and however I rearranged the order of questions and rephrased the questions, I was persistently mindful of the general principles of CQ and its limited but valuable heuristics for my social constructionist study of *lian/mian* practices in the Chinese context. In Chapters 6 and 7, I recount how I planned and conducted these interviews consistent with what is laid out here.

## THE CASE STUDY METHOD

Traditional case studies in general and of facework in particular are characterized by description, understanding, and explanation (Tracy and Baratz, 1994; Chen and Pearce, 1995). The case study method referred to is philosophically consistent with social constructionism

(Chen and Pearce, 1995). It is concrete, specific, and in-depth, unlike the ethnographic approach, which is concerned only with descriptions of cultural patterns across situations. However, cases should be taken from real life and be typical of the culture, or "recursive" (Chen and Pearce, 1995, p. 149). They should also constitute a pragmatic problematic for the researcher or the cultural insiders, or both, who have a genuine concern for the betterment of lives.

The goal of my case studies is to initiate the discursive engagement of communication scholars of social constructionism with ordinary Chinese or to initiate a long but mindful, reflective, and creative conversation with ordinary Chinese about their *lian/mian* practices in their daily social interactions, unlike Tu Wei-ming's elitist notion of dialogue (Tu and Leung, 1995). This would be a conversation about their hopes and worries, their joys and sufferings, their dilemmas and confusions, in association with their *lian/mian* practices; a conversation about how to create a new way to transform the traditional *lian/mian* practices into a new type of *lian/mian* that is free of near-absolute hierarchy, status quo, rule-governed communication, homogeneity, lack of agency, and thoughtless action; a conversation about a new type of *lian/mian* that is inspirited with equality, change, open-ended communication, multiplicity, a strong sense of individual agency, and self-reflexivity. To use Chen and Pearce's words, the goal of my case studies "is not a search for factual and theoretical information about an event but is a way of understanding or approaching practical wisdom of life's experiences that enables us to engage creatively in the process of communication" (p. 143).

"We are in the midst of rediscovery that social reality is constructed by human agents—even by social scientists!—using cultural categories and language in specific situations or contexts of meaning" (Altheide and Johnson 1994, p. 493–494). In this study, I view myself as a facilitator or catalyst for change who uses CQ and the social constructionist case study method informed by the social constructionist perspective.

## CONCLUSION

Incorporated into my use of the methodologies described is a comparative perspective espoused by some modern Sinologists in the contemporary West, such as D. L. Hall and R. T. Ames (1998, 1995, 1987). These scholars study cultural differences between the East and West in light of American pragmatism, which is a major intellectual fountain of social constructionism. They prefer to view culture as primarily a lifeworld and to view Chinese culture and modern Western culture as different forms of life, each shaped by a different communication system rather than a different pure philosophical system.

While the methods I have incorporated have their major uses in certain chapters (the historical method in Chapter 3, the method of social constructionist reading and critique in Chapters 3 and 4, and CQ in Chapters 6 and 7), all the other chapters are more or less informed by a mixture of these methods plus the comparative method espoused by Hall and Ames.

In its application in the Chinese context, CQ in the original form gets transformed. As a tool for transformation, CQ transforms itself in the very process of transforming the other. This is perhaps the heart of transformation, in the social constructionist view. Let us see how the following two case studies illustrate how CQ can help enhance reflexivity on and transform Chinese culture and how CQ itself is transformed in its use in the Chinese context.

# 6

# Case Study 1

## Kneeling Down to Save Face

The case analyzed here is a social scene in an urban area in contemporary China. A female employee in a bowling alley accidently provides one of her clients unsatisfactory service. The client, a low-ranking official from a local government internal revenue bureau, feels that this female employee does not respect his face. He wants to save face by having her kneel down in front of him, his fellow players, and the bowling alley staff.

After describing the case in detail, I report the results of my CQ-based consultation on the case with a group of Chinese consultants. I then reflect upon the usefulness of CQ and social constructionism in the engagement with *lian/mian* change in China.

My goals are to illustrate an application of social constructionism and CQ in Chinese culture and to identify the transformative potential of CQ. This method is useful in sensitizing Chinese consultants' self-awareness of their own and their compatriots' face-oriented culture and in enhancing their self-reflectivity upon their own and their compatriots' *lian/mian*-centered cultural communication practice. It helps to them and their compatriots to proactively transform themselves from *lian/mian*-centered beings into a new type of Chinese, who emerges out of the creative interplay of the Chinese *lian/mian* culture and other cultures such as the modern Western culture.

Using the generic questionnaire shown in Chapter 5, I interviewed my Chinese consultants after my application to use human subjects was approved. Before the interviews, I briefed my consultants on the interview protocols and asked them to read the following case in Chinese, as described in a Chinese newspaper (Zi, 1998). I conducted one interview with six Chinese consultants. The following case description is my own translation of the newspaper article from Chinese to English. As a professional translator and a translation theorist with a strong publication record in translation theory and practice, I tried my best to follow the three principles of translation widely accepted in the field of Chinese-English translation studies—faithfulness, expressiveness, and elegance in both the linguistic and the cultural dimensions.

## CASE DESCRIPTION

The following is my translation of the newspaper article originally in Chinese:

### Why did Ms. Huang kneel down so sadly?—An episode which behooves our deep reflection

In a bowling alley in Shenzhen Special Economic Zone of Southern China, on the evening of December 18, 1998, Ms. Huang, a department manager, was pressured to kneel down. This farce occurred as follows:

That evening, there was a lot of business in the bowling palace. Ms. Huang, manager of Customer Service, was very busy. At about 9:00 P.M., something minor went wrong with a machine in the bowling track. A man about 50 years old threw the ball, knocking down nine pins. Just as the scoreboard showed "9," the tenth pin also fell down. He shouted happily: "Full score!" But the scoreboard still showed "9." This happens often. But the man insisted that a service representative change the score from "9" to "10." At that time, all service representatives were busy. So a good-willed repair man came up and changed it to "10" on the scoreboard. Unexpectedly, the man became outraged that no service representative showed up. He shouted to the repair man: "Who are you? How dare you change it? Ask your manager to come over!"

Ms. Huang was hurried over by a service representative; she asked in a professionally polite manner what had happened. The man ignored her question and asked her: "Can you make this decision? Can you allow me to start afresh?" Ms. Huang replied: "I can make this decision and you have a right to make this demand. But allow me to find out what happened and where we were wrong?" The man said arrogantly: "You can not make this decision. Send your general manager over!" Ms. Huang felt that he was overreacting, but she went ahead for the general manager. On her way, she met new customers and stopped to greet them. This time, a service representative hurried up and told Ms. Huang that the man was even fiercer.

When she came back, the man said to Ms. Huang insultingly: "What shit do you think you are made of?" At this point, his two male and six female companions joined him. The man patted her on the shoulder and asked her to sit down. He kept patting her even after she sat down. Though in a nervous state, Ms. Huang controlled herself and protested mildly: "Please stop patting me." The man rolled his eyes and flirted: "So what? I am just patting you on the shoulder. I am not patting you on the private parts!" Hearing this, his female companions burst into laughter. Ms. Huang defended herself twice by blocking his patting with her elbow, but he rudely continued patting her. She elbowed him again indignantly, only to hit him on one of the knees. The man hit her hard on the left cheek, triggering her anger. She hit him on his face in defense. Like a herd, the man's companions shouted at Ms. Huang. The man threw a bowling ball at Ms. Huang, who was fleeing. On the sixth floor, Ms. Huang heard the man's thunderous voice from down the stairs: "Come down! Do not just wait till you get caught! Otherwise, you will be dead tonight!" He was about to call the police station with his cellular phone to have his police friends come over and arrest her when Xiao Wang, a security person in the bowling alley, advised him not to call the police. The man rudely reacted to him: "You little security person! Shut up! Go and get your general manager. Otherwise, I will not pay!"

Xiao Wang got the General Manager, who asked Ms. Huang to come down. The man told the General Manager his version of the story and demanded that he be allowed to strike her on the face to settle this case on the spot; otherwise, he would not let the issue go. Ms. Huang asked the General Manager to listen to her side of the story, too. The Manager did not seem to hear Ms. Huang's request and said to the man: "Let Xiao Huang apologize to you." The man's female companions retorted: "Merely apologize?" Ms. Huang did not want to have this incident negatively affect the business and the reputation of her bowling alley, but she did not want to apologize to the man, either, for she felt that whatever she had done to him was justified. She said to the Manager: "Fire me, Boss!" "Fire you?" the man said, "Firing you does not dissipate my anger. Today, you have beaten me on the face in front of my colleagues. How can I continue to lead them? How can I have my *mianzi* back?" One of the man's companions said emphatically: "Unless you kneel down for him and make a cup of tea, (he will not let it go)." Hearing this, Ms. Huang felt that all the blood in her body rushed into her head. She became extremely angry.

She heard her Boss say, introducing the man to her quickly and indistinctly, something like "He is a department director of the Bureau of Revenue Services." (Or, a vice-director of the Bureau. Her Boss said it too quickly for Ms. Huang to understand.) It was clear to her that man was a director of some sort from the Bureau of Revenue Services. Although she did not know which bureau of revenue services, he must be a real official with power. Ms. Huang did not need to think further: You can ignore a hooligan. You can also offend an official. But can you offend a hooligan-official? Should you negatively affect more than a hundred employees of the bowling alley just because you do not want to bow down?

Ms. Huang almost rushed to the bar and made a cup of tea, returned, knelt down and held the cup of tea with her two hands above her head for the man. This demonstrated that she apologized to the man, admitted her mistake and asked this revenue official to pardon her. The man was startled with Ms. Huang's sudden change of attitude and gesture. He asked to pay for his and his companions' uses of the bowling services immediately. But she heard her Boss say "No, unnecessary, unnecessary!" The man replied generously: "I will pay you! Why should I not pay you?"

It is said that the next morning, the General Manager invited this revenue official for a feast, but the man declined it. The interpersonal atmosphere was quite harmonious.

On the afternoon of December 30, when the journalist heard about this incident, he contacted the bowling alley. Suddenly, the journalist encountered a series of obstacles in his investigation. He could not find the man. He did not know if the General Manager refused to be interviewed for fear that the incident would be exposed to the public or for fear that "the official" would be offended again. Even though the journalistic investigation was conducted using all available sources, the whereabouts of "the official of the Bureau of Revenue Services" have not been identified. (Zi, 1998, p. 4)

## CASE-SPECIFC METHOD

I developed my case-specific and Chinese culture-specific interview method with CQ as a heuristic tool. I recruited my fellow Chinese consultants only after we became good friends. I had six consultants altogether. Four of them were female and two were male. Five of them were in their thirties and one is in her fifties. Five of them had undergraduate education in China and had or were having graduate education in the United States. The two men were working in an American midwestern university. The three young women were either homemakers or half-time students in the same university. The senior woman was visiting her son and her daughter-in-law, who were also consultants.

Since we moved to this small college town with a small Chinese community July 1998, I had been in frequent interaction with the Chinese community. I had helped one another do many things such as shopping for Chinese groceries in another town, babysitting, inviting one another to parties during the holidays, and so on. This had been far more than just rapport-building. It had been part of my family's and my consultants' sources of enjoyment. By agreeing to provide consultation for case studies, they agreed to help me as we had been doing for one another in the passing year. Rapport-building as commonly adopted in traditional social science research in the West is direct, short-term, instrumental, and time-saving. This type of endeavor is contrary to the Chinese cultural orientation for indirectness, long-term relations, and a mix of instrument and end in dealing with other people. My use of friendship-building fits very well with the cultural preferences of my Chinese consultants. My interactions with them in 1998 allowed me access to their heart felt comments in 1999.

Unlike conventional interviews, which ask about personal information, my interviews centered on *lian/mian* cases of other Chinese whom my consultants do not personally know. The present case is based on a story reported by a Chinese journalist in a popular regional Chinese newspaper, as just translated. I made this choice for several reasons. First of all, to ask my Chinese consultants about their personal experiences of *lian/mian* loss would risk disrupting our friendship. On the other hand, Chinese seem to enjoy talking a lot about the *lian/mian* loss of other Chinese they may or may not know. My choice seemed to fulfill their need. Furthermore, to ask them to comment on the case meant to give them face, for I asked for advice, suggestions, or insights. Still further, in their comments on and answers to my questions about this case of *lian/mian* loss, they unavoidably related their own experiences of face loss. Through their comments and answers, I could also understand their views of face and identify their potential for transforming their own *lian/mian* practices and those of other Chinese. This is consistent with my Chinese consultants' cultural preference for indirectness in asking for personal information. Most importantly, I hoped to find out tentatively whether or not the CQ employed here made my consultants more aware of the undesirable social consequences of *lian/mian* practices, more reflective on them, and more creative in transforming them. To use some of my consultants' own words, I was able to help Chinese *danhua* or dilute Chinese *lian/mian* consciousness. Interviewing my consultants this way proved to be a very good means of engagement, a major research goal espoused by social constructionism in communication.

## INTERVIEW DATA

### Cultural Representativeness of the Case

After the consultants read the case in Chinese, clipped from the Chinese newspaper *The Liberation Daily*, I asked, "After reading the case, do you think that the story is typical of the Chinese society, Chinese culture, or the Chinese people as a whole?" They all answered that the face practices in this case were typical of Chinese communication. One of the male consultants said, "The case is relatively typical, for it is a real-life case reported and published in the newspaper. *Lian/mian* is connected to people of different levels. The case involves a female employee in the bowling alley who either intentionally or unintentionally slapped a man of a very important position in front of his inferiors. From the man's perspective, this constitutes a very serious *lian/mian* concern." I shifted my sitting position to indicate that I was interested in having other consultants' feedback, too. One consultant said, "This case is about the loss of *mianzi*. Before one loses *mianzi*, one earns or competes for *mianzi*. This loss of *mianzi* occurs between two persons in an unequal relationship. I do not know how they would have managed this loss of *mianzi* when they were of an equal relationship." The third consultant said that there were many similar scenarios in Chinese society.

Another consultant commented that the *lian/mian* practices as reported in this case had been common throughout Chinese history. He cited popular stories from Chinese history to support his point. He referred to Xiang Yu, a Chinese general in the Han Dynasty (206 B.C.) who committed suicide near his hometown due to his loss of face in front of his relatives and senior members of his hometown. He had vowed to become emperor but had been defeated by his opponent Liu Bang, who became the founding emperor of the Han Dynasty. He alluded to Mu Lan, a female patriotic hero during the Song Dynasty (960-1279 A.D.), who won many battles against foreign invaders and earned face for her relatives. Again during the Song Dynasty, Li Qingzhao, a well-known Songtsi poet, wrote to urge her countrymen to keep to this motto: "When alive, try to stand out as a hero among human beings; when dead, try to be a hero even among ghosts."

One consultant went into greater detail. She said that the director was typical in that when employees did not behave respectfully toward their boss, the boss would take revenge; but a typical boss would not ask the "disrespectful" employee to kneel down in front of him for fear that he would be viewed negatively by the community. The director complained first, according to a Chinese popular saying that the evil person reports the case first to put the innocent party in the wrong. Ms. Huang knelt down in front of the director as she felt that she had already been wronged; she let herself be further wronged to win more sympathy from the public.

## A Cultural/Historical Elaboration of *Lian/Mian*

I asked my consultants, "How would you explain in simple and easily understood language to someone who does not know anything about the Chinese *lian/mian* practices what happens in this case?" First, all of the consultants thought that face is closely linked with group. Chinese feel a most intolerable loss of face in front of a crowd or the public. Loss of face is not so serious in the family environment. Face would be meaningless if one were alone. Ms. Huang knelt down in front of the director and gave up her face to save his face to benefit her bowling alley and her superiors and subordinates. To quote one consultant, "In China and in the East, a person is either consciously or unconsciously indoctrinated with the idea that the the individual is of less significance than the collective. It might be for the principle that the interest of her company is larger than hers that Mrs. Huang kneels down."

Furthermore, most of the consultants told me that, in this case, face is linked with power. The more power one has, the more face one needs and the more desperately one reclaims the face that someone with less power has made one lose. In other words, a superior's face is more important than the face of subordinates. The power imbalance makes the people in the game unequal in relationship. If there were less disparity in power, the more powerful ones, such as the director, would not seek to reclaim their lost face with extreme measures. This is characteristic of Eastern society. The director has more power than Ms. Huang in that he is a government official who has power to punish Ms. Huang and her company. One consultant said that if the director were an ordinary citizen, he would not even have felt that Mrs. Huang's delayed response to his dissatisfaction constituted a loss of face. Another consultant added, "The case reflects the cultural norm of our Eastern society that there is an intricate relationship between power/position and *mianzi*. The person with power would refuse to apologize to the public even if he or she feels conscientiously that he or she is wrong, for apology equals loss of face and in extension loss of power, which constitutes the sole identity of this person. No apology means no substantial loss of face and power; in the West, no apology means more trouble from the public and more loss of face and power." President Bill Clinton apologized to the American people for lying to the grand jury about his sexual misconduct with Monica Lewinsky and benefited from it. His apology dissipated the public anger, saved his face, and maintained his power. The director might have felt that it was wrong to have threatened the life of Ms. Huang and to have had Ms. Huang kneel down in front of him, but he would still refuse to back down. It was further explained that the director's behavior toward Ms. Huang and other employees in the bowling alley is "the result of a social pattern of hegemony and oppression."

I asked, "Why did the director seek this symbolic measure to address his concern instead of other measures, such as legal and economic measures?" Most of the consultants said that the director is not even aware of alternative measures. His only concern is that he would lose his face in front of his subordinates if he did not reclaim his face. His subordinates would not respect him and would no longer obey his governance. Even if they did not think so, he thought so. Before this incident, his subordinates would hold him in awe for his power. But the news of his loss of face would spread among more people in the Internal Revenue Bureau. Many people would dare to talk back to him by saying, "Come on! You were slapped in the face in the bowling alley last time but you did not fight back. How come you are governing me?" Therefore, he reclaimed his face and restored his power.

One should not lose one's face, especially in front of one's subordinates. The same is true with a teacher, who should not lose face in front of students. Although the director got what he wanted from the bowling alley, he would act like an obedient dog toward his own superior. In front of his superior, he does not need his face. If his superior had been with him in the bowling alley, he would have acted like an obedient dog. Without his superior, the director's subordinates acted like a pack of dogs loyal to the director. When Ms. Huang defended herself against the director's arrogant behavior, his subordinates barked against her. They were helping their director in order to curry favor from him in the future.

"Why did Ms. Huang kneel down in front of the director?" I asked. The consultants shared the answer that Huang knelt down not to protect herself but to save the face of the director and to protect the face of the bowling alley or the face of her superiors and colleagues. One consultant added that Huang did so not out of her own heart-felt willingness, but out of self-perceived pressure from her collective, her superiors, and her customers. She was afraid of being cursed behind her back even if she quit her job.

Another female consultant said, "But I think that she knelt down purely out of *du qi*." (I define *du qi* as an obstruction of air in the chest—an unarticulated self-destructive move to attract attention from the public and win more sympathy.) When I heard this consultant use the phrase *du qi* to describe Ms. Huang's kneeling down, I was pleasantly startled. I picked up the phrase *du qi* from this consultant and probed, "You have used a very interesting phrase to interpret Ms. Huang's kneeling down. Why is it that Ms. Huang's *du qi* is actually doing something harmful to herself?" There was a pause. I then further probed, "How can we let Americans understand the Chinese *du qi* behavior?" "It is very hard," said one consultant, "for *du qi* means first and foremost not to verbally express oneself." Another consultant added: "What is more important about *du qi* is that the result of the *du qi* behavior does not bring any benefit to the person who uses *du qi*; instead, it brings harm to him or her. But *du qi* is a way to compete for *mianzi*."

This discussion provoked me to think further along that line: *Du qi* is just the opposite of *chu qi*. *Chu qi* means the release of the excessive air that constitutes built-in anger—an other-oriented destructive or aggressive move of revenge. There are many examples of *du qi* in Chinese society. Having been wronged and victimized but without hope of having justice restored after many efforts, many people have resorted to suicide instead of homicide in order to garner attention and win sympathy from the public. The assumption is that they will prove with their loss of life that they are innocent or morally decent and that the people who have harmed them will feel shameful and be punished in the unknown future.

"How can each character's emotions be described?" I queried. The consultants said the following: Ms. Huang felt very angry and shamed. The longer she was kneeling down, the more intensely she must have felt that she no longer had face to meet other people in the future. She felt angry when she was insulted and was treated as a lesser human being by the director. She knelt down out of extreme anger. She must have hated to kneel down. The director must have felt angry with the loss of his face when he felt that he was slighted by the bowling alley. He must have felt surprised when he saw Ms. Huang kneel down in front of him. He suddenly felt that he had overreacted and that Ms. Huang gave him too much face. But he still did not back down. He won the game. Ms. Huang powdered his face, but too much of his face was saved.

One consultant pointed out that people in the East and the West express different emotions toward the same event. For example, the three American soldiers who were caught and released by the Serb Army during NATO's military campaign against the Yugoslav President's ethnic cleansing policy and practice felt proud, and their relatives felt honored for them. However, if they were Chinese, they and their relatives would have felt ashamed or loss of face. If they were Japanese, they might have committed suicide out of an extreme sense of shame due to their captivity. In 1998, an American soldier stationed on the Japanese island of Okinawa raped a teenage Japanese girl. When interviewed, his American mother said, "I am proud of my son." A Chinese mother would have felt too ashamed even to be interviewed about her son's crime.

"What are the roots of *lian/mian*?" I asked. They said consistently that the patterns of face practices have been shaped in the society and the family and derived from the long history of the cultural norms. For example, one consultant said: "*Lian/mian* has a composite origin. Americans are concerned about *mianzi*, too. Otherwise, they would not have a grading scale. For instance, some American kids fail to be on top for the math exam and weep. All cultures seem to have shared characteristics such as honor or *mianzi*. But our society has its own characteristics. One is the family. A Chinese person is instructed from childhood not to cause the loss of face of his or her parents and the family. In the past, he or she would be instructed not to cause his or her ancestors to lose their faces. This is the connection between *mianzi* and family. Second, as the case reveals, the face of the superior is more important than that of the inferior. This is the relationship between *mianzi* and the social hierarchy. Third, *mianzi* is related to Chinese education. In China as well as in Japan, but not in the United States, students are supposed to follow teachers (*shi dao zun yan*). Teachers need *mianzi*, and students are not to challenge teachers. *Shi dao zun yan* is not a big issue in the West." Other consultants added that babies do not have any such face concepts and that children have less face consciousness such as reflected in the case. Our face patterns anchor in the public context. One female consultant said, "To *lose mianzi* in front of a group is the most unbearable for Chinese persons." "Teachers cannot afford to lose face in front of their students," one male consultant added. One consultant pointed out that such face practices occur not only in public contexts but also in the context of unequal competition.

### Legitimacy for Concerns

"How do you feel about the characters in the case?" I asked. Most of the consultants expressed sympathy with Ms. Huang and anger and even hatred toward the director, whom they found unbearable. They hoped that such practices would gradually improve. One consultant answered, " I feel that this is a problem. I feel frustrated with the scenario only when the issue which has never happened before suddenly occurs. I am relatively sympathetic with Ms. Huang. I feel angry, too, but not too angry because our society and culture make this kind of thing happen. Not only has it happened in the past, but also it happened this time and will happen again in the future." Another consultant felt that he had two kinds of frustrations over the issue. He felt frustrated over the issue when Ms. Huang seemed to choose to kneel down, and he felt frustrated over the inequality between Ms. Huang, her company, and the director. The discussion brought up another case in a Korean company in China in which a Chinese employee refused his Korean boss's demand to kneel down to apologize for his errors. In South Korea, according to one consultant, to kneel down to extend an apology is still a widely practiced ritual for punishment, which originated in China. This Chinese employee's refusal to kneel down, according to the consultants, constitutes "a different kind of *mianzi*—the nationalist *mianzi*."

I cut the discussion short by asking another related question, "Do you think that the director and Ms. Huang would feel regretful of what they did?" Several consultants answered that they would. One added, "Even though the director is corrupt, he still has latent conscience. . . . However, he may regret it but will not admit that he has done something wrong."

### Consequences of *Lian/Mian* Practices

"Have the dynamics in the case brought any consequences?" One consultant replied, "I think that positive *lian/mian* makes people uplifted whereas negative *lian/mian* pushes people down. This case clearly belongs to the latter." Some of the consultants answered that the *lian/mian* practices in this case bring negative consequences. The senior consultant said, "Ms. Huang saved both the director's *mianzi* and the bowling alley's *mianzi*. But she herself was insulted and felt miserable. She was also a human being and had her friends. She also needed her face. She gave face to the director but had none to herself. This would cost her own life." They demonstrated a lot of sympathy with Ms. Huang and hatred against the director. They hoped that law and regulations would be adopted to alleviate this unfairness. They also hoped that the director would learn a lesson in the future.

Other consultants seemed to be ambivalent or confused about the consequences of this case, particularly when they compared this *lian/mian* conflict management/resolution to the legal approach to a similar conflict in the West. For example, one consultant said: "I do not hope that Ms. Huang and the director resolved this conflict in court. It was better to solve it by giving face, which transforms big issues into small matters (*da shi hua xia* ). Americans tend to make fuss over conflicts as small as sesames by relying on the court. . . . But perhaps giving face is better in solving conflicts in China than law, and litigation is better at solving conflicts in the United States than giving each other face. But I personally prefer the individualistic approach." He implied that since he is living in the United States, he favors the legal approach, as Americans tend to do; this may be advantageous to him.

### How to Make a Change

I asked, "What might be a better way to manage or resolve the conflict?" One consultant replied rhetorically: "Is a better way available? In that cultural context and with that social structure, they could not determine their alternative way. If the director encounters a similar case in a different context, he will do the same. So long as the soil of the culture does not change, such behavioral patterns will not change." I further asked, "Where is the soil of the culture?" He answered: "It is in the society, history, family, and education. It is also in our knowledge of power and social relations." Another consultant seemed to point to the American culture of politeness as a resource for making a change. He said, "The scenario in this case would not be an issue in the United States. Although we just discussed that Americans tend to resort to litigation in dealing with conflicts, they speak more pleasant remarks such as 'I am sorry,' 'Excuse me,' and 'Thank you' more frequently than Chinese. Chinese would feel loss of face if they made such remarks, whereas Americans do not feel so while speaking such polite language." He then explained that Chinese these days are feeling unsettled in their own home country and are prone to lose their temper because economic reform and quick social change have created many uncertainties. He quoted an old Chinese proverb, "People are polite when their basic needs are fulfilled." He was echoed by several other consultants.

Since they expressed great concern about the *lian/mian* practices in the case, I asked the consultants what can be done to change such practices. I asked, "What might you have done in the same case at the time?" The consultants had mixed answers. One answered: "If I were Ms. Huang, I would have refused to admit that I was wrong and would have refused to kneel down. If I were the director, I might have misbehaved in the same way as the director in the case because I had to maintain my relationship with my subordinates." The second consultant said that if she were Ms. Huang, she would have poured the cup of hot tea onto the director to see what he might do to her further. The third consultant responded that he might have asked Ms. Huang to apologize to him verbally instead of asking her to kneel down in front of him. The fourth consultant said that individual personality might also help determine how to behave in the situation. The fifth consultant said that Ms. Huang might have knelt down out of her immediate concerns. She wanted to maintain her job. If she had had several job interviews scheduled, she might not have knelt down. She obviously had no alternative but to kneel down. "In China, in most cases, you do not have many career choices. You cannot be your own master. Everything is arranged for you by the Party," she said.

I asked, "What could you do now to persuade the persons in the case to deal with the conflict more constructively?" They all said that they would ask the director to be rational and sympathetic. It was irrationality that made *mianzi* rampant. The case showed that there would be chaos without using law. Using *mianzi* as the substitute for law failed to create social harmony. But in this case, *mianzi* was playing the function of the law. One consultant suggested that the director try to save face through the court instead of trying to save his face by insulting, humiliating, and even intimidating Ms. Huang. Another consultant even suggested that the law be used to curtail the director's hegemonic behavior. "In *lian/mian* practices, everything is connected with everything else; one part changed alters the whole scene," he said.

My interview now triggered a discussion on the differences between *lian/mian* and law. Their consensus was that law is not concerned about face, but with truth and equality. One consultant illustrated, "However old you are and however powerful you are, you are equal to everyone else before law. If the dish is too salty, most Americans will say truthfully that it is too salty. Chinese can not cover up their face and say so." When asked if law and face are opposites, they answered that law can be used to save face, ensure justice, and remove all the mess that affection/emotion-based face brings. In a word, law is more sacred than face. When asked how to make law work, the consultants said that everyone should study law and implement it. In China, everyone has face consciousness but not legal consciousness. "Is there any way to let both law and face function?" I asked. They shared the view that *qingmian* (affection-face) should be secondary to law. If law is secondary to *qingmian*, things will go badly. Inequality will abound. Some people will benefit unjustly and be happy, and others will lose and suffer. One consultant illustrated the general point: "For example, within a family, between husband and wife, between adult sons, daughters and parents, finances should be managed individually. This will secure good relationships because everyone is treated equally. There is a Chinese proverb that goes, Good friends should clear accounts. However, Chinese practice it far too little. If we practice it, we are afraid that we will hurt each other's face and feelings and destroy the good relationship."

When asked which should dominate family life, law or face, most of the consultants were presented with a dilemma. They said that when law rules family life, there will be no affection, which leads to loss of face, which in turn leads to loss of everything. If we let *mianzi* rule family life, some people will be treated unequally. One consultant added, "The American law is too cruel *(tai wu qing)*. Once you grow up, you abandon your parents. In China, grown-up kids still live with their parents. They live an enjoyable life. But the American law generates much better justice."

Since their answers seemed to suggest that the director and Ms. Huang should be equal in front of the law, I asked, "Is it possible to persuade the director to treat his subordinates and Ms. Huang equally?" One consultant replied, "It is difficult because a director is always a director wherever he goes in China." Another one said, "Wherever a director goes, he feels himself as a director." The third consultant said, "In China, even an actor or actress is addressed as 'teacher.'" The fourth consultant commented, "This ego is built not just by the person in question himself, but by the society which either pretentiously or sincerely recognizes him as a person of special significance wherever he goes."

On the other hand, subordinates look up to their boss even in social occasions such as this one. When the director felt slighted by the personnel of the bowling alley, his six subordinates demonstrated against the alleged slight, stimulating the director to build up his need for face. With their support, he had to reclaim his face even if he did not want to do so personally. This answer triggered a discussion on differences in superior-subordinate relationships between the United States and China. Some thought that while the superior-subordinate relationship does not exist after work in American universities, it does exist in American companies, to a lesser degree than in China. In American universities, tenure and promotion are based on one's job performance instead of on how much respect you show to your boss. However, in the American corporate world, promotions are more arbitrary. It is hard to say if American corporate promotions are even more unfair than Chinese ones. But there are alternatives in the United States, where you can change your job whenever you want to. In China, you cannot afford to change your job, because to do so means much more than the mere job change—change of child care, housing, health care, and even your meal tickets to the canteen.

I explained to them, "My challenge is how to make the undesirable features of *lian/mian* dissipate while retaining the positive aspects of *lian/mian*." One of the consultants said, "One way is to add new resources to Chinese culture through cross-cultural studies like those you are doing now."

### Reflective Questions

For the first set of questions, I asked the consultants to infer the goals of my interview and to comment on my research goals and each other's answers to my questions so far. The consultants had the following to say about my goals: (1) I wanted to find out if *lian/mian* practices bring undesirable consequences upon interpersonal communication and upon solutions to social problems. (2) I wanted to compare and contrast Chinese culture and American culture. (3) I wanted to keep the good aspects of of *lian/mian* practices and get rid of the bad aspects. (4) I wanted to explore the good and bad aspects of law in regulating social behavior. (5) My ultimate goal in this study is to transform Chinese society.

After saying that their inferences were correct, I asked for their comments on my goals. Four comments were given by the consultants: (1) "We need to change our *lian/mian* practices for the good of the society; your research goal fulfills this need." (2) "It is difficult to transform the Chinese *lian/mian* practices through interviewing people, but it is worth trying." (3) "While it is necessary to change them, it is impossible to do so, for the *lian/mian* practices have been around for thousands of years of Chinese history." (4) It is not necessary to change *lian/mian*, for, according to one consultant, "generally, *lian/mian* works well. It maintains the social relations. This might be an extreme case." One added that *lian/mian* is of significant cultural continuity even within a Chinese family living in the United States. She said, "Since we came in the United States, we have been more or less influenced by the American culture. Our children may be slightly different from us. But they will be generally similar to us in terms of tradition, cultural conceptions, and *mianzi*."

When I asked: "Did you have any substantial disagreements on your answers to my questions so far?" some said that they did not have any, for they had many things in common—the same ethnicity (all *Han* Chinese), similar age, and similar social/cultural experience and educational backgrounds. "We are all Chinese," one explained. None of them felt surprised by this case, since such cases occur so often in China. Of special note, however, was a consultant who is perhaps the oldest but received the least education. She said that while she and her daughter had similar opinions, her daughter expressed them better. When asked to comment on her mother's answers, the daughter critiqued them by saying that her mother should not have displayed a hot temper and hatred toward the director in answering my questions because this was not rational. To use the daughter's words, "Mom, you should not say that you are going to pour a cup of hot tea on the director to ventilate your anger. This is not rational." Her mother smiled at her daughter and nodded her head to express agreement.

For the second set of reflective questions, I asked, "Would you please talk about what is most memorable about my interview, if there is something? Or ask questions out of your expectations, things which made you think and feel differently now than before the interview, and things which might make you act differently in the future?" One consultant said, "I probably will not forget our discussions today." Several consultants felt that my interview questions were "provocative." One of the female consultants answered, "I feel that your questions are deepening my thinking, since I have never thought of some of your questions." "Could you give me an example?" I asked. "Questions like 'what would you have done if you were the director or Ms. Huang in his or her situation?'" she replied; she was echoed by several others. Such questions were difficult to answer but, she said, "I felt compelled to answer them." She said further, "When I heard you ask how I might have acted in that cultural context, I immediately asked myself: Given my personality, to what extent would I have felt the loss of face and with what intensity would I have reclaimed my face or saved someone else's face? I still remember other questions you have asked me. But I will never forget this question." Saying that she had never realized that *lian/mian* practices would have social consequences until after this interview, she added, "I would do whatever seemed natural to do. I have never thought that *lian/mian* practices influence the society." I further probed, "Do you think that *lian/mian* practices really influence the society?" She answered, " Now I think they do." She was echoed by the two male consultants. Another consultant said that there were many questions that she had not expected. Some are: What did the director and Ms. Huang do to get out of this *mianzi* game, respectively? What are some of the advantages and disadvantages of *lian/mian* practices? Should law dominate over *lian/mian* or vice versa? She said: "These questions made me tongue-tied, but they made me think."

One of the male consultants said that he would never forget this interview because this was the first interview he had ever had and he found it very interesting. Another consultant said that the questions I asked will eventually fade away, "because the consultants shared many similarities, which did not provoke any debates and arguments. Another reason might be that the issues are Chinese issues, which are so common to us who share the Chinese cultural background and belong to the same generation. If some younger Chinese youths were interviewed, their answers might have been quite different from ours."

Most consultants said that they would think, feel, and act differently than they did before my interview. For example, one consultant said, "If I were the director before the interview, I would have been like the director and would have given the bowling alley a hard time. If I were him after the interview, I would be cool-headed. I would feel responsible for whatever I did. I would ask myself: Am I right to have Ms. Huang kneel down in front of me to save my face? What consequences would follow from asking her to kneel down? I would be aware of law and its role in reclaiming my lost face instead of intimidating her and shaming her. With reason/wisdom (*lizhi*) and the legal consciousness, I would not try to reclaim my face by any irrational means. If I were Ms. Huang before the interview, I would not have knelt down; instead, I would have had a physical fight with the director and further embarrassed him. I would have thought: I am a department director, too, in the bowling alley. I need *mianzi*, too. The more desperately the Internal Revenue Director needed face, the more strongly I would refuse to give it to him. After the interview, if I were Ms. Huang, I would have reason/wisdom (*lizhi*) and even more strongly refuse to kneel down; I would be cool-headed; I would confront him face-to-face assertively but not aggressively. I would use the law to argue with him. I might still feel wronged and feel hurt inside without the personal ventilation of my anger. But, the problem would be solved. To sum up, if I were Ms. Huang, after the interview, I would be assertive instead of submissive or aggressive." She went on to illustrate her point by referring to the Chinese government's response towards NATO's bombing of the Chinese Embassy in Yugoslavia in 1999. In the past, Beijing would have taken a military revenge against any aggressor to ventilate its outrage regardless of consequences. But present-day Beijing weighed consequences and responded to the bombing with a cool head so that World War III was averted.

Another consultant said that while he thought that my interview helped him reflect upon *lian/mian* practices, he also thought that such a journalistic report on this case and the to-be-published research on this *lian/mian* case definitely put social pressure on people like the director to curtail their petty but rampant *lian/mian* behavior. Before I moved to meta-interview questions, one consultant added that this interview helped her become aware that she had become more realistic. She said: "Ever since we came to the States, we have learned to become more pragmatic." This was echoed by her husband, who added, "We are neither like Chinese back in our home country nor like Americans in terms of *lian/mian* behavior due to the fact that we have been influenced by the two cultures."

I asked further, "How would you act differently if or when you encountered a similar case in the future?" "At least we would not act like the director or Ms. Huang," one consultant answered, and he was echoed by several others. Another consultant added, "Such an interview will have a positive impact on us." "It will be of help. . . . Chinese should change themselves," added the third consultant. "But how can we change, since both the Eastern culture and the Western culture are self-contented?" lamented another.

### Meta-Interview Questions

The meta-interview consisted of the questions from me to them and questions that they asked me. First, I asked, "What suggestions do you have about the way I have conducted my interviews with you on the case so far?" In summary, the consultants had the following suggestions.

1. "This type of research can be most effectively done only outside China. Among Chinese in China, Chinese culture will never be talked about in realistic terms. If you must do it in China, you have to criticize Western culture and praise Chinese culture. Otherwise, you will be cursed as a national nihilist and other people will attack you," said one consultant.
2. "I hope that cultural exchange between China and the United States will be promoted on peaceful terms. Unfortunately, the East

and West are demonizing each other now. The only successful result of the East-West cultural exchange is Japan," said another consultant.

3. I should interview as many people as possible to understand their psychologies. People are different.

4. If I interview Chinese who are ten years younger than my consultants, I may get different answers because they grew up in an environment that has been open to the West and they are more active in thinking.

5. One consultant said that he was for random selection of subjects and suggested that I call Chinese in the local Chinese community directory. This way, I might get more reliable results.

6. Several consultants wished that I had given them the case description a day before my interview. That way, they could have given the case more thought.

7. Some also wished that I had read all the questions to them before I began my interview. This way, they would have remembered more of my provocative questions and been better prepared to answer them. Without having heard the questions prior to the interview, they had not been able to come up with quick answers.

8. I might include two versions of my questionnaire—one Chinese and one English.

9. If I decide to interview more people, I should continue to give each person equal opportunity to speak, for each person may have something different to say. I should also continue to be informal instead of formal so that people will be free of constraint. Finally, I should continue not to encourage people to talk about Chinese politics, for Chinese here in the United States are still afraid that their political remarks will bring them trouble when they go back to China.

Second, I asked, "Did my questions restrict your thinking or answers?" "No, we felt at home and felt free to say whatever was on our minds because we knew each other before your interviews. However, people randomly selected from the directory whom you did not know might have felt differently," said one consultant, who was echoed by several other consultants. I said that I would fear that I would not have good cooperation with Chinese persons I did not know at the personal level. Several consultants agreed.

Third, I asked, "Did you find my questions easily comprehensible?" The consultants had the following to say: (1) Did I translate my questions from English to Chinese? My questions were a bit Westernized in structure and wording and were not as easily understood as the Chinese newscast. But the questions were not that difficult to comprehend. If they did not understand me, they would always ask me for clarification. But if they did not know each other, they might not have asked me for clarification. (2) My questions did not sound colloquial enough.

The consultants asked me the following questions, which I answered. (1) "Have you interviewed Americans in the way you have just done with us?" "No, I have not. I may interview them in the future to ask Americans with Chinese cultural experience about their observations of this case. But this will be a separate study," I answered. (2) "Do you know if there is any counseling service in China that deals with similar issues?" "I think there might be. But counseling is a modern Western psychological service that treats all issues from a perspective of individual psychology. It also regards many social issues as individual pathologies. I regard my interview as a consultative model, which aims to enable people to reflect upon and improve interpersonal and social communication. In my model, the behaviors of the characters that raise your deep concerns are problems not rooted within themselves but rooted within the society in which they have grown up and within the culture with which has made who they are."

Finally, I asked them for additional comments about my interview. One consultant said that she would use reason/wisdom *(lizhi)* in dealing with everything in the future. Another consultant said, "I will be somewhat between *lian/mian* and pragmatism. I will treat face neither too seriously nor too lightly. It is hard to change, though. We all grew up in China and we still speak Chinese." The third consultant commented: "To change *lian/mian* practices through interviewing will have both positive and negative impacts. For example, Americans can learn our cultural ways to communicate. We can learn their cultural ways to dilute our *mianzi* consciousness and use their ways to solve the problems we have been trying to solve with *mianzi*." The fourth consultant said: "Interviewing should be helpful. Through comparing and contrasting the American and Chinese cultures, your interview has made us reflect *(fansi)* upon ourselves. It reminded me of a book on *mianzi* I read that also talks about changing *mianzi*. I agree with you that China should be changed."

## Interpretation of the Data

On the basis of the case-specific data, I can now discuss to what extent the consultants' answers have legitimized or possibly answered the research questions set forth in Chapter 5. Specifically, I intend to elaborate, justify, and explain the consultants' native view of the Chinese *lian/mian* practices, as expressed in the consultation. This is done in comparison to the social scientists' and humanistic scholars' (largely

Chinese) views of the Chinese *lian/mian* practices, which I have elaborated both in discussing the *lian/mian* practices and in reviewing the scholarly literature. I also explain the rationale for the interview questions and the unique points of the consultants' answers.

### The Cultural Representativeness

The questions about the cultural representativeness of the case were intended to find out if such a case is widely accessible in Chinese society both synchronically and diachronically. The consultants' answers repeatedly affirm the existence of present and historically discernible Chinese *lian/mian*-centered communication patterns by referring to many similar cases in contemporary Chinese society and by citing many popular allusions in Chinese history.

The consultants' answers confirm the consensual view of the synchronic existence of the *lian/mian* practices in Chinese society included in the literature review in Chapter 4. They also confirm the historical view of the Chinese *lian/mian* practices specified in Chapter 3.

## A Cultural/Historical Elaboration

The questions concerning a cultural/historical elaboration of *lian/mian*—the nature of face, the emotional dimension of face in the case, and the origins of face—were intended to help understand *lian/mian* in its more specific details. The consultants' answers and comments include many insights and also confirm many of the observations about face described in Chapters 2, 3, and 4.

My consultants' answers confirm my argument elsewhere that face is communal (Jia, 1997/1998). They all agreed that face always functions in front of a "cooked" or familiar audience or within a familiar group, as the case of Ms. Huang and the director illustrates. However, I emphasize in the present study that the excessively communal nature means that social actors virtually lose their own sufficient agency. The director might not have so rudely demanded that Ms. Huang save his face if none of his subordinates were on the spot. If Ms. Huang had a strong sense of self-agency and a weaker consciousness of her superiors and subordinates and had been a little bit more concerned about herself and a little bit less concerned about the management and staff of her bowling alley, she might not have knelt down. Another interesting point about face that the consultants brought up is that face is based on power. Here, power can be understood to be synonymous with social status and social hierarchy. The higher one's position or status in the hierarchy, the more face one needs and the more aggressively one tries to get it back once it is lost. In this sense, the director needs to save his face because he thinks that he has more power than Ms. Huang does, and Ms. Huang may feel so, too.

The major source of face, according to the consultants, is socialization in the Chinese social context of "unequal competition." Chinese children have much less face consciousness than Chinese adults. This is consistent with the social constructionist perspective on *lian/mian*. While the practical concepts of face have evolved over Chinese history (see Chapter 3), the consultants' argument that a Chinese may have different levels of face consciousness points to the existence of another kind of history of face—a life history of how members of Chinese society have acquired the grammar of face practices. The concept of "unequal competition" seems to suggest that, in the Chinese context, people are socialized into and and generally adapt to the social context of rigid hierarchy, while they all need face. People like Ms. Huang seem to defeat themselves before battling hard and wisely. This knowledge highlights the undesirable social consequences of pervasive *lian/mian* practices in the Chinese hierarchical context.

During this episode, one consultant offered a very interesting interpretation on why Ms. Huang knelt down in front of the director: Ms. Huang practiced *du qi*, literally meaning "to be further suffocated with anger," instead of *chu qi*, literally meaning "to release one's anger." *Du qi* is a common practice of a subordinate who has been wronged in Chinese social interaction. Instead of directly seeking to restore justice, such as by asking the wrongdoer to apologize or compensate, the wronged one usually harms himself or herself to indirectly tell the wrongdoer and the community that he or she has been wronged. Furthermore, *du qi* is used to alert them to the wrongdoer's wrongdoing or to embarrass the wrongdoer, and to make the community sympathize with the wronged one and morally sanction the wrongdoer. The classic story of *du qi* often heard in traditional society and occasionally heard today tells of a daughter-in-law who is extremely wronged by her mother-in-law and hangs herself in her mother-in-law's bedroom. Here, suicide is her ultimate protest against her all-powerful mother-in-law, who is culturally assigned to strictly govern the everyday life of her daughter-in-law. The daughter-in-law's assumption is: I will be the martyr so that the wrongdoer will learn a lesson and stop doing other people wrong in the future. This assumption is based on Chinese culture.

In Chinese culture, selflessness is inculcated as a paramount moral ideal. Tolerance is the first principle in dealing with conflicts and aggression. On the other hand, self-defense, assertion, and the pursuit of justice through legal means are generally discouraged. If one employed any of these strategies, one would be frowned upon by the public and lose the high moral ground. Therefore, in order to win, one has to lose more. Hence, although Ms. Huang was harassed by the director, she knelt down in front of the harasser under no external coercion. She felt that she had already been wronged, so she let herself be wronged more seriously. She seemed to be successful. Her kneeling down caused so much sympathy for her and so much criticism for the director from the public that a journalist investigated the incident. I have to point out that *du qi* is not a strategy calculated out of a strong sense of self-agency but a culturally preprogrammed, thoughtless act by a person with a vague sense of self-agency.

The consultants also pointed out that the Eastern (here specifically Chinese) pattern to refuse to apologize when wrong is also associated with the concept of face; this is in sharp contrast with the Western pattern of ready apology when one has done something wrong. Their explanation is that in the East, apology brings more trouble, whereas apology gets rid of trouble in the West. I agree with their observation, and here is my interpretation. This pattern seems to be confirmed by the director, who hid himself to avoid the journalist's interview. To refuse to apologize means to be afraid of losing face, one's power and social status. Since to apologize means to admit immoral deeds, one loses one's legitimacy to enjoy privileged status. Therefore, to refuse to apologize and to be afraid of losing face is to strive for a cultural ideal—the man of perfection, or *junzi*hood (gentlemanhood), a Confucian creation on the basis of the assumption that to err is inhuman. This is in stark contrast to the popular Western proverb, To err is human. The Chinese concept of face shapes itself out of this Confucian ideal. One has to appear to be right even if one feels that one is wrong. The present Chinese government's continuous refusal to correct the wrongs inflicted upon the 1989 Chinese Prodemocracy Movement during the past ten years is another good example. Thus, the Chinese pattern to refuse to apologize suggests that the Chinese concept of face is deeply inflexible, close-ended, and unrealistic. Within it, there is little room to negotiate, to compromise, and to begin anew. It seems to lack the democratic seed that allows negotiation, compromise, amendment, and the cultivation of flexibility, open-endedness, and pragmatism.

Their answers also included a very interesting *lian/mian* phrase not mentioned in Chapter 3—*ge* somebody's face *muo fen*. This literally means to powder another's face, another Chinese way to say "to give someone face" or "to save someone's face." The phrase "to powder one's face," originally a term of female beautification, was used by a female consultant metaphorically to mean "to give face." This addition to the list of *lian/mian* terms also suggests a yet-to-be-developed hypothesis that there may be gender differences in the use of Chinese *lian/mian* vocabulary and face practices.

The consultants described the emotions of the characters as well as constructs of face in the case. From the case description, they inferred that the director must have felt anger associated with his loss of face. But when he saw that Ms. Huang knelt down to give him face, he felt surprised. Ms. Huang was angry with and then hated the director when she was harassed and intimidated by him. But when she knelt down, she must have felt a strong sense of shame. The consultants' observations about the characters' changing emotions cast doubts on the single emotional dimension of the Chinese concepts of face popularly held and accepted. They also challenge Potter's argument that the Chinese social order has nothing to do with emotions (1988, p. 186). As Chapter 3 suggests, different emotions can be associated with different degrees of intensity of face consciousness in response to changing social acts in the ever-changing context even within a single event. What we need to do is not to identify one major kind of emotion and to pretend not to see other kinds of lesser emotions in interplay within an actor, but to try to identify as many emotions associated with the actor's face consciousness as we can and to analyze how these emotions are in interplay with each other and how they are in interplay with the face consciousness of the actor. In this light, it would be advisable to understand the characters' emotions from a social constructionist perspective. From this perspective, we can see that the director's emotional experience and that of Ms. Huang are always open to change in terms of both quantity and quality in constant response to communicative acts from other parties.

In the director's case, anger arises out of the incongruities between reality and his commonsense expectations. The director began to be annoyed by the first incongruity, between the fact that ten bottles fell and the number "9" appeared on the scoreboard. He was further annoyed by a second incongruity. He became angry when he saw a repairman change the score, instead of the customer representative, who was of a higher status than the repairman. This was the third incongruity—the one between his expectation that a customer representative should be helping and apologizing and the fact that a repairman fixed the score without apology. This is where the director must have felt a sense of face loss latently associated with a sense of shame in front of his subordinates, who were observing what was happening. The director experienced a fourth incongruity when Ms. Huang came over, inquiring what had happened instead of apologizing first. Here, while the director became more angry, he must have felt a deep sense of shame, too, in front of his subordinates. He experienced a fifth incongruity when Ms. Huang promised to send the general manager over but stopped first to greet new customers. This was where his anger and his shame reached their climax. These five incongruities constituted a serious neglect of his legitimate complaint and of his face needs as a customer and, most importantly as a director. He felt that the bowling alley did not give him face; on the contrary, it caused him to lose his face.

Once his face was lost, the director must have felt confused about himself. He turned his anger and shame into verbal insults and physical aggression against Ms. Huang. Incidentally slapped by Ms. Huang in her own defense, he became enraged and chased after her, not even caring to maintain his demeanor. Ms. Huang's kneeling down and serving him a cup of tea was such a dramatic gesture to give him face that the director felt startled. Coupled with his surprise might have been a fleeting sense of guilt within himself. But with her gesture, to demonstrate that Ms. Huang was a lowly servant serving him tea obediently, he did feel that his anger was released and his face was restored. He felt superior again over Ms. Huang and over the personnel at the bowling alley, and he felt that his face was expanded. He felt spiritually compensated by Ms. Huang's kneeling down and insisted upon paying the bill, which the general manager had wanted to credit to please the director.

According to the consultants, three kinds of emotions are associated with Ms. Huang—anger, hatred, and shame. While I agree with them, I would add that she also felt more intense pain than the director. She appeared to be not accommodating but a little confrontational in response to the director's confrontation when she first came up to him. She sounded as if she was also a manager in front of her customer. Here I can infer that Ms. Huang might have felt and appeared dignified. All this made the director feel his face loss. He wanted to make and must have made Ms. Huang lose her face by rejecting her for her low position as a middle manager, not the general manager of the bowling alley. Given his superior status, the director needed to have the general manager deal with his complaint. Ms. Huang might have felt the director's face threat toward her. Stopping to greet her new customers on her way to the general manager might have been a symbolic in response to the director's face threat toward her. The director might have interpreted Ms. Huang's delay as revenge, which would further tear his face. He began to insult Ms. Huang and to physically harass her. During this episode, Ms. Huang must have felt ashamed in front of her audience and angry with the director. In kneeling, she must have controlled her anger or *du qi* to let herself be further humiliated.

The emotional paths of the director and Ms. Huang seem to be zigzagging and open-ended, unlike the popular belief that only shame is associated with Chinese *lian/mian* and that thus Chinese culture is a shame culture whereas Western culture is a guilt culture. Instead, an emotional perspective and the face perspective seem, from the preceding analysis, to have a partial overlap. I am inclined to argue that face practices are a visible part of the emotions more or less regulated by a given culture. Like the waves of the sea, which can be reshaped by external factors as well as by the dynamics of the water in the deep sea, face practices are constantly reshaped by both the emotion work of human actors and their interactions with society. Approaching face practices in light of emotions creates an opportunity to understand face practices in a much more elaborate manner than approaching them merely from perspectives that do not incorporate emotions. It may also help us to identify the emotional mechanism against change and to create an emotional mechanism for change.

The consultants also talked about their own observations about the differences in face-based emotions between the East and the West. While the American people and their relatives felt proud of the three American soldiers caught by the Serb Army and later released, Chinese or Japanese people might have felt ashamed or lost their face for relatives in a similar situation, who also would have felt ashamed or even committed suicide because of their captivity. While the mother of the American soldier said in an interview in an American TV station that she felt proud of her son even though her son had raped a Japanese girl, a Chinese or Japanese mother in a similar situation would have felt too ashamed of her son to be interviewed by a TV network, let alone saying that she felt proud of her rapist son. These examples tell us how deeply face-based emotions such as sense of shame are culturally constructed and how differently the East and the West are in constructing and expressing emotions. They also tell us that Americans tend to value positive emotions so much so that even minimal negative emotions are masked to present an assertive stance to avoid legal trouble. The rapist's mother dared not say that she felt ashamed since saying so would cause her son legal trouble. Her "excessive" concern for legal problems may have masked or even erased her sense of shame and loss of face. What may be more important is that a mother in the Western culture is supposed to love her children unconditionally. However, in the Eastern context, if an Eastern mother expresses shame about her son, she participates in the moral sanction of the community to make her son change his behavior in the future as part of her parental responsibility. Even if she does not feel ashamed, she has to demonstrate that she feels ashamed to order to avoid the moral sanction of the community. Given the case of the American mother's behavior, cultural change seems necessary to restore the moral court as a complement to the legal court in American society. In the case of the captured soldiers, Easterners seem to focus on past failures and to link them with the moral character of the soldiers, whereas the Americans seem to focus on the future and to view past failures as accidental in comparison to the personality and personhood of the soldiers.

The American view accords unconditional dignity and open-endedness to a person, whereas the Chinese or Japanese view of a person assumes an ideal moral personhood, which can be lost by one immoral deed. Cultural change seems to be necessary for Chinese or Japanese to treat individuals' moral failures more liberally or openly so that individuals will be encouraged to take another chance. I must point out also that the consultants' comments about the general patterns of communication of Americans and Chinese may risk perpetuating cultural stereotypes. However, the consultants' answers help to legitimize the project of *lian/mian* transformation undertaken in the present study.

### Legitimacy for Concerns

The question of legitimacy for concerns sought to find out if the *lian/mian* practice shown in this case to brings a better result for parties involved. The word "concerns" may imply that although there is nothing wrong with *lian/mian* practices, they could be transformed to empower people. The consultants all expressed sympathy toward Ms. Huang and anger and even hatred toward the director. They expressed their hope that *lian/mian* practice would improve in the future. This attitude legitimizes my argument that the Chinese *lian/mian* practices should be transformed to embrace some modern Western communicative values such as equality, relative agency, and choice within a systemic view. The concerns the consultants showed about the *lian/mian* practices in the case are very important because these are native concerns from within Chinese culture or personal concerns of insiders such as the director and Ms. Huang. One hundred years ago, such a case would have been very common, and no one would have agreed that this was a concern. Because of social and cultural changes in the past century in China, such concerns seem to have become more and more acute.

However, it seems to me that the more Chinese culture changes, the more difficult it is for Chinese culture to change. The past changes, as Chapter 3 documents, seem to be structural macro-changes, achieved by macro-structural approaches such as revolution and the modern Western type of social criticism. The deeply cultural Chinese communication dynamics, with *lian/mian* as their core, while becoming increasingly incongruent with the increasingly sophisticated Chinese market economy, remain largely untouched and poorly understood, let alone transformed. A micro-detailed and incrementally transformative approach such as the social constructionist communication perspective used here is expected to facilitate the needed micro-change. The consultants also brought up a different type of *mianzi*—the nationalized *mianzi* enacted when a Chinese employee refuses to kneel down in front of his Korean boss in a Korean-owned company in China.

## Consequences of *Lian/Mian* Practices

These questions are closely related to the discussion in Chapter 3 of the consequentiality of *lian/mian* practices for contemporary Chinese life. While that discussion documents the social consequences of *lian/mian* practices from the scholarly literature, these questions elicited anwers from native informants grounded in a real *lian/mian* case. Consensus among the consultants, the scholarly literature, and my own scholarly observations would most powerfully prove the hypothesis that unbalanced *lian/mian* practices bring many undesirable social consequences upon contemporary Chinese life.

In this case, the *lian/mian* mechanism between the director and Ms. Huang is unbalanced. This imbalance escalates a triviality into an interpersonal conflict and then into an intergroup conflict, which is ended by Ms. Huang's ritualistic kneeling down. To kneel down is a traditional Chinese ritual performed by lowly servants or slaves for their masters to indicate their own humble position and to express respect toward their master. This demeaning and dehumanizing ritual was outcast as feudal half a century ago in China. However, Ms. Huang had no choice except to enact this ritual to save the director's face—to symbolically restore his status as a master in front of Ms. Huang. The consequence of this face drama is the recovery and perpetuation of social inequality. While she gave face to the director, his subordinates, and her colleagues, she had no face left to herself. But, she is also a human being. She needs face in front of her friends, too. However, due to the hierarchical nature of *lian/mian* practices, the weak and the powerless at the bottom of the hierarchy only become even weaker.

## How to Make a Change

The question of how to make a change was intended to find out what proposals for change the consultants could come up with, as native members of Chinese culture who are not students of *lian/mian* and cultural change. Their remarks identified three proposals for change: (1) Teach people like the director and Ms. Huang about rationality, for *lian/mian* practices are often irrational and bring chaos. (2) Persuade them to be equal with each other in interaction; this is difficult, but it can be done, bit by bit. (3) Use the law or the court, which is based on rationality, to negotiate face needs. This way, disputants will get fair results because everyone is equal before the law. Although *lian/mian* often plays constructive functions in human relations when it is in balance, to use it as a substitute for law breeds injustice and inequality. Therefore, law or the court should dominate over *lian/mian* in handling human affairs.

The first two suggestions overlap with part of the social constructionist methodology for change, in that they rely on gradual persuasion. The last idea is primarily an institutional solution. This is quite different from the revolutionary model of change and the social criticism model of change documented in Chapter 4. But some of the consultants have a dilemma over *lian/mian* and law. They seem to be emotionally attached to *lian/mian* practices while being rationally attached to law.

### Reflective Questions

The reflective questions are primarily content questions that aim to look back over the discussion and identify what changes have occurred in the consultants' view of *lian/mian* practices. The questions are intended to find out to what extent the consultants have understood the goals of the interview and have agreed with one another in their answers, and to determine how effective the interview has been so far in helping them reflect upon *lian/mian* practices in general.

In general I was pleasantly surprised with the quite obvious effectiveness of my interview so far. The consultants described the effectiveness of the interview with words such as "provocative," "made me think," and "felt compelled to answer." One said that she had never linked social consequences with what she does naturally—*lian/mian* practices—until this interview. Some questions first made another consultant "tongue-tied" and then pushed her to think. Other comments presage good prospects for the consultants' own behavioral change in the future. For example, one consultant said, "If I were the director before the interview, I would have acted like the director; if I were him after the interview, I would be cool-headed." She continued, "If I were Ms. Huang before the interview, I would have had a physical fight with the director. If I were Ms. Huang after the interview, I would be assertive instead of submissive or aggressive." One consultant even suggested that reporting such a *lian/mian* case through news media would also add to the public pressure to change. One consultant concluded this interview episode by saying, "China should really be changed."

### Meta-Interview Questions

The meta-interview questions are primarily designed to encourage the consultants' feedback on possible improvements to the interview method. Such feedback seems necessary when CQ is used for the first time in the Chinese context. These questions are also consistent with CQ practice. In this interview episode, the consultants provided very important consultations. This step of CQ also helped to equalize my relationship as a researcher with the consultants, who are usually called "subjects" in modern social science research. Since *lian/mian* practices are a profound group pattern, it takes a group to transform them. Interviewing this way is two-way; consultation this way is two-way; and reflection and transformation are also two-way, unlike the traditional interview, which is one-way and top-down.

Many of the consultants' comments on the interview method confirm my own observations about the cultural rules of recruiting and interviewing Chinese informants. For example, one of my rules for interviewing Chinese informants is to recruit and interview them only after they and the researcher have come to know each other and have become friends. This is confirmed by the consultants' comments that "we felt free to say whatever was on our minds because we knew each other before the interview" and "we felt free to clarify our questions whenever we did not understand your questions because of our 'cooked' relationship." Their contributions included suggestions that I should give informants my questionnaire a day in advance to give them more time to think; I should introduce the different episodes of the interview to them before the interview so that they would feel more certain about the process; I should avoid talking about Chinese politics with Mainland Chinese in such interviews. They also suggested that I phrase questions more colloquially instead of following a written questionnaire. Finally, they suggested that I stay informal and keep interviewing consultants I know at the personal level. These suggestions, based on their immediate concerns, are very legitimate.

## EVALUATION OF THE INTERVIEW

Here, I summarize how I used CQ in the interview and discuss its effectiveness. I then identify the limitations of CQ as used in this case and discuss future implications for using CQ in the Chinese context. The case study presented in Chapter 7 was conducted on the basis of these lessons from the present case study.

## THE PROCESS OF MY USE OF CQ

I used the CQ technique of joining the grammar a lot. For example, I picked the term *"du qi"* in one consultant's answer and asked her to elaborate on that. This led to a breakthrough in our understanding of

Ms. Huang's sudden kneeling down and to the consultants' new insights into the *lian/mian* behavior of their own culture. *Lian/mian* can be earned by *du qi* or self-harming nonverbals, a dialectical practice that neither the generalist literature on face nor the Chinese ethnocultural literature on the Chinese concept of face has covered.

I also used the technique of circularity—having consultants comment on each other's answers and having the consultants comment on my questions. For example, among the consultants, two have a mother-daughter relationship. When I asked the consultants if they agreed with each other, the daughter's criticism that her mother sounded too irrational in her critique of the director did not seem to make her mother feel challenged and embarrassed. Instead, the mother seemed to happily accept her daughter's criticism. The daughter-mother relationship seemed to be very equal during the interview. This is probably due to the consultants' effective socialization into the American cultural pattern of interactive equality. It may also correlate to the way I administered the interview—in an atmosphere of informality, freedom, and equality. CQ as I used it allowed the consultants and the researcher to interact as true equals within a system of interdependence. This encouraged us to learn from each other and empower each other. While I "enlightened" them, their answers also "enlightened" me.

I also used the technique of circularity with respect to positions, asking the consultants what they would do if they were characters in the case. They said this had pushed them to think hard.

I used the technique of reflexivity as well. How one designs and administers an interview can be an inseparable and effective part of the mechanism that aims for transformation. In other words, the engine for change or transformation can be built into the very shape, manner, and process of an interview. I took the opportunity of the interview to ensure that the consultants were equal to me and equal among themselves, which was made possible by reflective thinking, a technique implied but not explicitly articulated in the current CQ literature.

I used the technique of elaboration when I asked the consultants to define or explain terms they take for granted, such as "*du qi*" and "*liang zhi*" and "to powder one's face." This helped the consultants reflect on these terms and understand their meanings.

I also used the technique of appreciative inquiry. During my interview, I did try to avoid problem talk, emphasizing that I was not trying to Westernize Chinese culture. I recognized *lian/mian*'s positive functions in interpersonal relations while trying to let the consultants see the consequences of *lian/mian* practices for the society. When one consultant mistook my consultation as counseling, I responded that consultation does not assume that people involved have psychological problems; it aims to enhance reflexivity and expand one's horizon and enrich one's cultural resources. I stayed positive about the consultants' contributions, even though some of their remarks did not sound plausible to me.

However, I did not find positive reframing to be very useful in the interview, perhaps because we were talking about third parties. If I were interviewing Ms. Huang and the director, I might use reframing to make them feel positively connected and constructively reconceptualize their conflict.

In Chapter 5, on methodology, I discuss at the theoretical level the possible cultural resistance CQ may encounter from Chinese culture, such as the belief in hierarchy. I did not encounter such resistance during my interview, probably because the consultants have adapted to the American culture of equality and may have enjoyed equality. This is evidenced by the fact that when one consultant criticized her mother, another consultant, the mother seemed to be at ease with her daughter's criticism. This lack of resistance may also be due to the fact that most of the consultants were of a similar age and a similar level of education and experience. I hypothesize that if Chinese consultants of prominent differences in education, position, gender, age, region, and family background had not been exposed to and socialized into the Western culture of equality, they would resist the built-in force of CQ to break down social hierarchy.

## The Effectiveness of My Use of CQ

By effectiveness in this context, I refer to the practical and conceptual impact of CQ on the consultants, although that was not its central purpose. Analysis in the traditional sense aims to break down data into conceptual categories. Researchers come up with findings "objectively" according to the categories. My analysis here has a moderate purpose—to gauge and interpret change via the interactions between the consultants and me in light of the questions I asked and the answers the consultants came up with during the interview. Here, I conceptualize change as a concept consisting of practical and conceptual/attitudinal dimensions. I will identify these aspects of change in the data generated out of my interview.

The evidence for conceptual change in the interview is perhaps more voluminous than that for practical change. Since I have elaborated the conceptual change, under "Reflective Questions," I will not repeat the points here.

Practically, the consultants seemed to feel at ease with my emphasis on equal status and equal opportunity between male and female consultants and between mother and daughter. These scenarios do not conform with the hierarchical pattern of Chinese social interaction shown in the literature, the scene in the case, and the received view. Male consultants did not seem to dominate the conversation. During my interview, I tried at every moment to give equal attention and equal acknowledgment to the responses both from female and male consultants, both verbally and nonverbally. I made it possible by seating everyone at a round table. I sat in a position that allowed me to be face-to-face with everyone. When I sensed that a male consultant seemed about to dominate the discussion, I nonverbally signaled that I would like to hear a female voice, too. The way one conducts an interview is not neutral, but cultural and even axiological. I tried to maintain my awareness of it during my interview.

## Limitations and Implications

When asked reflective questions, the consultants expressed mixed views about the possibility of change through interviewing. While quite a few reported serious change, a couple expressed a pessimistic view of change. One said that it is very difficult to change *lian/mian* practices through interviewing. The other one said that *lian/mian* practices have been around for several thousand years in Chinese history; while it is necessary to change these practices, it is impossible to do so. While I do not agree to the latter idea, I do think that this is a gigantic project. It took several hundred years for Western Europe to acquire its modernity out of the iron hand of theocracy. Confucian societies like Japan, Taiwan, and South Korea, unlike China, have been economically and politically modernized. However, the cultural persona at the individual level has been predominantly Confucianist.

I am not suggesting here that the *lian/mian*-based cultural persona in East Asian societies, including China, should be completely Westernized. Rather, this Confucianist persona should be transformed to integrate the constructive elements of Western culture so that the transformed *lian/mian* persona becomes more resourceful, more synergy-generative, more adaptable, and more powerful. China began its economic modernization several decades later than Japan, Taiwan, and South Korea. Its political modernization has barely started. Added to its complexity is China's political heritage of communist institutions, if not communist ideology. The *lian/mian*-based persona in China should be more difficult to transform than that in Japan, Taiwan and South Korea.

CQ seems to focus on enhancing clients' self-reflexivity by means of systemic conversations and seems unprepared to go beyond that. Complementary to CQ should obviously be an instrument that enables clients to act creatively and helps build their problem-solving ability. While CQ is reflection-oriented, its complementary method should be action-oriented. One should also be aware that *lian/mian* practices are both systemic and hierarchical. In fact, such practices form a close-ended system that often constrains the freedom of action. Therefore, CQ faces multiple tasks: to deconstruct *lian/mian* by getting rid of hierarchy and reducing the excess of the systemic view; to reconstruct *lian/mian* by building equality, communicative rationality, and relative agency, and by retaining a constructive mechanism of systemic functioning that allows both useful group ethics and freedom of action. The Western version of CQ has its own agenda. It was invented to curtail an excess of individualism in the West by injecting a group sense. Its challenging task is to retain equality, build a group sense, and transform rugged individualism into relational individualism.

The original version of CQ is not fully equipped to deal with a new agenda of change in a non-Western cultural context such as China. Since this is my first attempt to apply and adapt CQ to the Chinese context, unforeseeable issues in China may demand further adaptations of CQ itself. Future researchers along this line are advised to be cautious and to be proactive in dealing with new issues CQ encounters in the attempt to transform the *lian/mian* practices.

Although the interview seems to have been quite successful from my professional view and the views of most of the consultants, several consultants pointed out that it targeted only people of similar age and similar backgrounds. I agree with them. In addition, the consultants also share similar age and educational background with me. We are all in our mid-thirties (except one consultant more than 50 years old), grew up during the Cultural Revolution, were educated through K-12 and college, learned English in China, came to the United States, and finished or are finishing graduate degrees in social sciences; we are all working in the United States. To use CQ in helping these people reflect upon *lian/mian* practices seems to have been relatively easy, as they have confronted themselves both personally and academically in their daily intercultural interactions and are ready to be "enlightened."

However, to apply CQ to Chinese who lack a substantial amount of intercultural encounters may not be this easy. Future researchers need to be ready to overcome resistance to reflection or change from their consultants by the questions they ask and the way they administer interview sessions. They are also advised to adapt to different gender groups, age groups, and class groups such as the rich and the poor and the more educated and the less educated and to consultants in different regions, such as urban areas and rural areas or coastal areas and inland areas.

If interviews occur in China, researchers from abroad, including both Chinese expatriates and international professionals, should learn to be shrewd, patient, and good-tempered since they will have to go through a series of security and ideological screenings from various Chinese government bureaucracies. They should at least phrase their research goals in neutral or mutually beneficial terms. This was suggested by a consultant, who said that only research projects that praise Chinese culture and criticize Western culture are allowed in China. Finally, Chinese-speaking researchers without Chinese language assistants should be ready to speak and understand given Chinese regional dialects, for many consultants can speak only their own dialect, although they understand the standardized Chinese or *pu tong hua*. English-speaking-only researchers will have to hire assistants who can speak both *pu tong hua* and the given regional dialects.

It would sound naive if I aimed to change the *lian/mian* behavior of a group of Chinese consultants through an hour-long consultation such as this. To my knowledge, since CQ has not been applied to the Chinese context and has rarely been used in a non-Western culture, I have several limited goals for using CQ here and in the next case study in the next chapter: (1) to illustrate how CQ and social constructionism might be used in the Chinese context; (2) to generate new insights on the part of consultants that may lead to long-term reflection and guidance for practical projects of social engineering; (3) to start a civic kind of conversation about cultural change; and (4) to experimentally start wedding two cultural discourses in our everyday life—the Western social constructionist discourse and the Chinese *lian/mian* discourse.

In short, I intend to illustrate two models of social engagement in sequence. One is the model of grounded reflexivity, and the other is the model of grounded transformation. These goals are already ambitious. Based on the preceding description, interpretation, and evaluation of the first case, I conclude tentatively that except for the model of grounded transformation, all the other goals are fulfilled. The next case study was undertaken with the same goals in mind.

# 7

# Case Study 2

## "I Don't Have Face to Meet My Mother"

The case analyzed here is excerpted from a popular Chinese TV play series. The excerpt is about Mi Lan, the protagonist, who has been victimized by societal corruption. It is a story of a contemporary Chinese youth's dilemma over affection versus *lian/mian*/obligation and the fight for justice versus tolerance of injustice. For this case study, I had the same goals as for the previous case study—to illustrate an application of social constructionism and CQ in Chinese culture and to identify the transformative potential of this instrument of engagement in enhancing the self-reflexivity of Chinese people.

The interview for this case was consistent with the generic questionnaire presented in Chapter 5. I interviewed the same six Chinese consultants with the same procedure. Before the interview, I briefed consultants on the interview protocols and asked them to watch episodes seven and eight of the Chinese TV play series entitled *Elder Sisters and Younger Sisters' Adventures in Beijing* (Zeng, 1997). The following case description is my own translation/summary of the relevant parts of the two episodes. The credibility of my translation lies in my professional credentials in translation studies and Chinese-English translation practices.

### CASE DESCRIPTION

The case in question is derived from episodes seven and eight of *Elder Sisters and Younger Sisters' Adventures in Beijing*, a TV play series released in China (Zeng, 1997). Mi Lan, a young female singer from Northeast China, has been striving to be a star in Chinese pop music for many years in Beijing, with meager financial support from her hard-working peasant mother for the several years since her high school graduation. Through her hard and successful work and communication skills, she has been selected to be a candidate for the Gold Medal for the Popular Singer at the Popular Music Contest, which she deserves. She is so happy that she telegraphs her mother to come to Beijing to attend the contest, to hear her sing and see her receive the gold medal. However, Mi Lan is replaced at the last minute by Xiao Dan Dan, whose fiancé donated 500,000 Chinese yuan to the executive committee for the Popular Music Contest when the contest is about to begin. Mi Lan is shocked, feeling angry and ashamed. Seeing her mother arrive at the auditorium, she hides herself. Her Beijing sisters hurry up to Mi Lan's mother and take care of her. Afraid that her mother will be unable to bear the news about Mi Lan's last-minute replacement, Mi Lan's Beijing sisters tell her that Mi Lan has just sung very successfully, won the gold medal, and left for the city of Wuhan in Hubei Province to sing at another concert. Not quite believing what they have told her, Mother wants to find her daughter in Beijing.

Feeling disappointed and ashamed, Mi Lan does not want to live any longer. She is about to commit suicide from a tall bridge when two of her Beijing sisters save her. Later in the day, Mi Lan goes back to the office of the executive committee for the night, for she knows that her mother will use her bed in her dorm. The next morning, Xiao Xue, another young woman, a roommate and close friend of Mi Lan, calls her at the office and tells her that her mother does not mind her being replaced and her failure to win the gold medal and asks her to meet her mother. "You are her daughter, after all. Why can't you tell your own mother about your anger?" Xiao Xue says to Mi Lan on the phone. Mi Lan blames Xiao Xue for calling her and hangs up. She turns to packing up and is about to leave the office, being afraid that her mother will come to the office and find her. The executive director of the committee, Ma Qi, comes back to the office and sees Mi Lan with great surprise. No sooner has Ma Qi come into the office than Mi Lan's mother comes up. Mi Lan spots her mother and immediately hides herself behind the door, gesturing to Ma Qi not to tell her mother that she is in the office. Her mother asks Ma Qi if Mi Lan is in. Ma lies that Mi Lan is not in the office, according to Mi Lan's request. Hearing her mother's footsteps fading away from the office, Mi Lan weeps, blaming Ma for replacing her with Xiao Dan Dan so that she does not have enough courage to meet her mother.

Xiao Xue looks for and finds Mi Lan's mother in the hotel lobby. Mi Lan also comes down to the lobby. Seeing her mother and Xiao

Xue, she hides again. She hurries out of the lobby and onto the street. Coincidentally, Xiao Xue and Mother walk out onto the same street where Mi Lan is walking and in the same direction. On their way, Xiao Xue sees Mi Lan inside a shop, selecting food for her mother. Xiao Xue secretly comes up and whispers to Mi Lan while her mother is at the door of the shop selecting food items, whispering that they are for Mi Lan. Mi Lan hears this and sobs again. She tells Xiao Xue to take her mother back to the dorm and then come back out to pick up a big bag of food for her mother. Knowing that her daughter feels too ashamed to meet her, the Mother hides behind a tree trunk outside the dorm when Mi Lan comes the other side of the tree, passing the bag of food for her mother to Xiao Xue. Weeping, she says to Xiao Xue: "I do not have *lianmian* to meet my mother. She is in poor health and cannot bear to hear a failure's story such as her daughter's. I vow to succeed in the future, to make her face glow and have her come back to Beijing with her face glittering in brightness!" Having overheard her daughter's words from behind the tree trunk, Mother's eyes are full of tears.

Early the next morning, Xiao Xue and another Beijing sister of Mi Lan's are accompanying Mi Lan's mother to the railway station where she will take a train back home. The third Beijing sister wakes Mi Lan in a friend's dorm, telling her that her mother is going back home. Mi Lan hurries out and rushes to find her. She sees only a note left for her by her mother on the door of the dorm. While she is reading the note, her mother is already on her way home without having seen her daughter after several thousand miles' travel to Beijing and several days and nights' effort to find her. Breaking down, Mi Lan darts in the direction of the railway station to catch her mother.

## CASE-SPECIFIC METHOD

In looking at the present case, I employed the same case-specific method described in detail in the previous chapter. I interviewed the same consultants and used the same interview strategies and techniques. To review the details of the case-specific method, see the previous chapter.

## INTERVIEW DATA

### The Cultural Representativeness of the Case

After the interview on the first case, the consultants and I watched episodes seven and eight of the TV play series (Zeng, 1997), which I purchased in Boston's Chinatown in 1998. After we were done, we moved to the dinner table and sat around it. I began my second interview by saying, "You have watched the two episodes of the TV series just now. Do you think that Mi Lan's case is common in contemporary China?" Half of the consultants thought that Mi Lan's case was special, and the other half said that the case was typical. For example, one consultant said, "This case reflects the tragedy and inequality of the society. But it is less typical than the previous case since it is fiction. The way the loss of face is handled in this case is not as typical as the previous case." Another consultant said, "To bribe for fame is very common in China." "Mi Lan is too concerned about her face to feel affection towards her mom. She wants to take the shape of a human being [*hun chu ge ren yang*, meaning "successful"] before she can meet her mom," said a third consultant. "Many people in China are like Mi Lan: They love *mianzi* to death but suffer from loving it," said a fourth. They were more or less echoed by the others.

### A Cultural/Historical Elaboration of *Lian/Mian*

I asked: "Why did Mi Lan avoid meeting her mom by all means even though she had invited her mom to come to Beijing from several thousand miles' distance to see her?" The consultants all tended to agree that Mi Lan avoided seeing her mother due to her profound affection or *qing* and strong sense of obligation (*bao en zhi qing*) toward her mother. "Mi Lan felt strongly obligated to her mom for her mom's persistent spiritual and financial support," said one consultant. Another consultant said: "Mi Lan avoided meeting her mom primarily because she could not erase her face off (*muo bu kai mianzi*)." "She did not want to have her mom know that she is suffering from her failure and did not want her mom to share the emotional burden with her," said the third consultant. These remarks were echoed by other consultants.

I probed them to elaborate their remarks by saying, "Could you say more?" The consultants provided the following elaborations: Mi Lan did all she could in order to be successful so that she could shine her mom's face. However, she was replaced by someone who was much less competent at the last minute. This made it impossible for her to meet the high expectations of her mother and people from her hometown. Not only did she lose face and lack the courage to meet her mom and her countrymen, but also her mother could not have face to provide a true account of her daughter's career for the people her mother knew. The people her mother knew would respect her more for her daughter's success and would look down upon her mother due to her daughter's failure. She avoided seeing her mother because of her own failure to win the medal, which constituted failure to earn face for herself, her mother, her relatives, and her countrymen all at once. She wanted to share her success with her mother, but when she was replaced at the last minute, she did not want to let her mother see her in the abyss of disappointment for fear that her mother could not bear to see her daughter suffer. In other words, she did not want to make her mother feel miserable with her failure and her own miserableness. All this shows that she cared about her mother very much.

If Mi Lan had been successful, she would have rushed to see her mother, for she would have thought that she had made her mother happy and brightened her face. Like General Xiang Yu in the Han Dynasty, she did not have enough courage to erase her face off (muo bu kai ta de lan) in order to see her mother. What is more, she was appealing for justice. Mi Lan's Beijing sisters understood all of this about Mi Lan. They tried to fabricate a success story (yuan chang or harmonize the scene) in front of Mi Lan's mother to save Mi Lan's face and her mother's face so that her mother would be able to provide her country-men a face-saving account for Mi Lan.

When asked for a cultural explanation, the consultants all alluded to the deeply rooted Chinese belief in success—winners are regarded as kings with a righteous cause and failures as evildoers without a righteous cause, according to a Chinese saying (cheng ze wei wang; bai ze zei). Success means having a big face that garners vast power. When I asked, "Is Chinese culture prepared for and tolerant of failures?" some consultants alluded to a Chinese saying that goes: Failure is the mother of success. But they further added that this is just from the book. In reality, very few Chinese believe it.

To answer my question, "How would you describe the emotions and feelings of the major characters such as Mi Lan in this case?" the consultants had different characterizations. One consultant said, "Mi Lan felt sorry for her mom since she had not been successful." Another consultant said, "She felt painful." The third consultant said, "Mi Lan thought that justice was on her side. So, she felt justifiably angry." The fourth consultant said, "She was emotionally reserved toward her mom." when I asked, "What do you mean by 'reserved'?" he answered, " I mean that she pent up her affection for her mom and let it self-dissipate within herself. She did not tell her mom about her emotional depression for failure, her deep affection for and feeling of indebtedness toward her mom, but she hoped that her mom would understand all of this. This kind of emotional reservedness may be hard for a non-Chinese person to understand." The fifth consultant added, "I also think that Mi Lan must have felt wronged." The last consultant compared Mi Lan with school children who do not get good grades and are unwilling to tell their parents. Mi Lan also felt guilty and painful for her mother because, in order to win the gold medal, she had sacrificed so much. She was cheated by a man and had sex with him. She had moved out of her dorm and lived separately from her Beijing sisters, running the risk of losing her friends. She invited her mother to share the joy of her success when she had a 99% possibility of success. She should have won, but she was replaced by someone who had more power but fewer qualifications at the last minute. How could she have had face to meet her mother, and how could she have expressed her affection toward her mother?! How could she not have felt painful and guilty toward her mother?! But this was out of her control. Mi Lan did not have enough power to reclaim her face, which the other, much more powerful person had made her lose. But Mi Lan regretted at the last minute that she had avoided meeting her mother.

Talking about Mi Lan's emotions in this case, my consultants picked up the general discussion on emotions in the East and the West that they had started in my previous interview. People in the East and the West have different emotions about the same event. For example, the three American soldiers who were caught and released by the Serb Army felt honored and their relatives felt proud for them. However, if they were Chinese, they and their relatives would have felt ashamed or loss of face. If they were Japanese, they might have committed suicide out of an extreme sense of shame due to their captivity.

I asked where Mi Lan got her face consciousness. "I think that she might have gotten it from the society, or from the public contexts," said one consultant, who was echoed by several others. Another consultant added, "Mi Lan might not have needed *mianzi* if she were alone." The consultants were in agreement that the patterns of face practices reflected in this case have been shaped in the society and come from the long history of the Chinese cultural norms. "Our face patterns anchor in public contexts. They often occur in the context of unequal competition," she said. One consultant's answer seems to suggest that Chinese *lian/mian* consciousness may get diluted when Chinese persons are in a different cultural context such as the American. He said, "I know some Chinese students who have to make a living by working in a Chinese restaurant in the United States. They do not seem to feel loss of face. However, if they worked in a restaurant in China, they would absolutely have felt the loss of face. This applies to myself. This is because the cultural context has changed." I asked, "Are you suggesting that face is not important in the United States?" A female consultant answered on his behalf, "Not necessarily. The reason is that a Chinese person's loss of face is of a higher emotional intensity in front of the people he or she knows than in front of a group of strangers and greater in China than in the United States." She was echoed by several others.

They also repeated the three origins of the *lian/mian* practices in China—
the family, the society, and education—one of them had brought out in
the first interview.

### Legitimacy for Concerns

"As an observer of this case, what disturbs you in this case?" I
asked. One consultant answered, "I feel sympathetic with Mi Lan,
who was a victim of the abuse of power." She was echoed by other
consultants. Another consultant said, "Mi Lan was so concerned about
her face that she forgot her relationship with her mom as a daughter."
I asked, "Do you feel disturbed by Mi Lan's effort to avoid meeting
her own mother?" "Yes, I do," a few consultants replied. I further
asked, "Which relationship do you think should be primary between
Mi Lan and her mother, the affective one or the obligatory one?"
Instead of directly answering me, one consultant said, "The desire to
meet social expectations, a strong sense of obligation and piety toward
her mom, is much stronger than Mi Lan's affection for her mom. This
is even hard for some Chinese persons to understand. Her effort to
avoid her own mom when she failed to get the gold medal is beyond
the normal practice." "What do you think?" I motioned to other
consultants to speak, too. "Her Beijing sisters also overperformed in
trying to save Mi Lan's face," another consultant said. "The effort to
deceive Mi Lan's mom for Mi Lan's good and for her mom's good
failed because Mi Lan's mom discovered it as a white lie." In their
discussion of the extreme *mianzi* behavior, one consultant told a story
of an official in the Qing Dynasty (1836-1911 A.D.) who was sentenced
to death. Before he was executed, he asked to be allowed to wear the
official uniform so that he would die as an official. Hearing this, one
consultant concluded, "We are approaching the end of the twentieth
century. Many Chinese persons still love *mianzi* to death like this
Qing official."

### Consequences of *Lian/Mian* Practices

"Did the *lian/mian* practices in Mi Lan's case bring any personal or
social consequences? What did Mi Lan get out of this *lian/mian*
game?" I asked. One consultant replied, "*Lian/Mian* practices bring
either socially desirable or undesirable consequences depending on
the situation. When functioning well, they can motivate people to
achieve." "What is your opinion?" I encouraged the other consultants. Another one added, "But in this case, *lian/mian* practices bring
negative consequences to the society such as inequality and unreal-
ism as described in the case. Mi Lan did not get what she should have

got while the briber got what she should not have got. The briber's face was brightened by becoming an instant star who attracted many fans. So long as no one publicized the bribery, the briber would continue enjoying her fame." The third consultant cut in, "Obsession with face made Mi Lan and her Beijing sisters busy with cheating themselves, Mi Lan's mom, and possibly her country fellows, instead of concentrating on exposing the briber's ugly act. As a result, real and substantial issues such as injustice, abuse of power, and bribery remain unaddressed. This is like building a luxurious gate while leaving the pollution of the backyard untreated." They were echoed by several other consultants.

When I asked how to avoid the negative social consequences of *lian/mian* practices, one of my consultants proposed giving up *lian/mian* and adopting law and regulations, which are based on truths. "If there is justice, such negative social consequences could be avoided. Laws and regulations make sure that whatever is, is; and whoever is qualified should be selected. As for Mi Lan, she should not have felt miserable and self-pitying. She should not have felt that she no longer had face. She should pluck up her courage to seek another opportunity to reclaim her face." Another consultant compared the Chinese *lian/mian* with Western law. He said that Chinese persons primarily rely on *lian/mian* to regulate Chinese social behavior, whereas Western society relies on law to regulate social behavior. Each functions on its own soil.

I asked: "Can law and *mianzi* coexist?" "It is hard to say. I prefer Western law," answered one consultant. "Although it is hard to say which is better globally, Western law is realistic and better in terms of social consequences. In China, we minimize big conflicts and make small conflicts nil. Mi Lan does not seem to try to deal with her case legally. In the States, people do the opposite." Another consultant objected, "I think that there is a way to combine Western law and the Chinese *lian/mian*. To deal with life-death and right-wrong issues, we can use Western law. To deal with unsubstantial and trivial issues, we can rely on *lian/mian*," she said. In response to this consultant's answer, another consultant lamented that it is very difficult not to primarily rely on *lian/mian* to deal with conflicts in the Chinese cultural environment. There are no better methods available in the society. Another consultant expressed pessimism about the possibility of successfully combining *lian/mian* and Western law. She said: "As the American society does not accept the Chinese *lian/mian* as a major mechanism to regulate American social behavior, I, as a Chinese person, cannot tolerate the practice that relatives and friends sue one another. However unjustly I was treated by my parents, I would never sue my parents," she said.

### How to Make a Change

Since they expressed a deep concern about the *lian/mian* practices in this case, I asked the consultants what could be done to change such practices. When I asked, "What might you have done in the same situation then?" some said that they might have done the same as Mi Lan did and some said that they might have met their mother, for one should not have a face concern that prevents one from seeing one's own mother. One consultant added, "I would be more eager to meet my mom if I had been successful. When I was treated unfairly like Mi Lan, I would meet my mom in a state of anguish. But I would also feel helpless."

When asked, "If we had someone who is very much like Mi Lan among us, how would you persuade that person to deal with the situation more effectively?" the consultants tended to suggest ways to alleviate Mi Lan's face concerns and to make room for mother-daughter affection. One consultant said, "I would try to touch her heart and persuade her to meet her mom by telling her that her mom had come to see her from thousands of miles away. I would also tell her that she was too concerned about her face to maintain an affective tie with her mom; that she should reduce her face consciousness and make her psychologically prepared for failure and to deal with failure." She also added that if an American woman were in the same situation as Mi Lan's, she would not have been so hurt by her failure that she was afraid to see her mother. Excessive face concerns do not allow for failure."

I further asked, "How can we make Chinese persons afford to fail psychologically?" Several consultants answered, "Not practicing *lian/mian* so much is the way." Another consultant added that Mi Lan had no alternative, but she would tell Mi Lan to abandon her fear of *diou ren* (loss of personhood or loss of face) in front of her own mother. The third consultant said that she would encourage Mi Lan not to feel loss of face and to get rid of depression and self-pity; she should pluck up her courage to seek other opportunities for success and for reclaiming her face. The fourth consultant suggested, "Mi Lan's loss of face was caused by the abuse of power and corruption in the society. She should try to reclaim her face by using legal means to restore justice." Other consultants echoed one or some of these suggestions.

### Reflective Questions

For the first set of reflective questions, I asked the consultants, "Can you infer the goals of my interview? Could you comment on my research goals and on each other's answers to my questions so far?" The consultants had answers that were similar to their answers in the first interview. They believed that (1) I wanted to find out if *lian/mian* practices would bring undesirable social consequences upon interpersonal communication and upon solutions to social problems in the Chinese context. (2) I wanted to compare and contrast Chinese culture and American culture. (3) I wanted to keep the good aspects of *lian/mian* practices and get rid of the bad aspects. (4) I wanted to explore the good and bad aspects of law in regulating social behavior. (5) My ultimate goal in this study was to transform Chinese society.

After I told them that their inferences about my goals were correct, I asked for their comments on my goals. There were three different kinds of comments: (1) We need to change our *lian/mian* practices for the good of society; your research goal fulfills this need. (2) It is difficult to transform the Chinese lian/*mian* practices through interviewing people, but it is worth trying. (3) While it is necessary to change them, it is impossible to change them, for the *lian/mian* practices have been around for thousands of years of Chinese history. When asked if they had any substantial disagreements on their answers so far, some said that they did not, for they had many things in common—the same ethnicity (all *Han* Chinese), similar age, and similar social/cultural experience and educational backgrounds. None of them felt surprised about this case, for such cases happen often in China.

For the second set of reflective questions, I asked, "Would you please tell me what is most memorable about my interview if there is any such as questions that you did not expect, things that made you think and feel differently now than before today's interview, and things that might make you act differently in the future?" This question seemed to make the consultants reflect on the interview. I further added, "Do not give me face when you answer this question." This made the consultants laugh.

Several consultants felt that my interview questions were as provocative as they were in the first interview. One consultant answered that the questions I asked made her think, as had the questions I asked during the first interview, for many questions went beyond her expectations. She gave a similar answer to that in the previous interview. For example, the question "What would you have done if you were Mi Lan in her situation?" is difficult to answer, but she said that she felt compelled to answer it. "When I heard the question, I started to think: How might I have done in that cultural context? Given my personality, to what extent would I have felt my loss of face? I still remember other questions you have asked me. However, I do not know if I will remember these questions within a week. But I will never forget this question." She continued that she had never realized that *lian/mian* practices would have social consequences until my interviews. She would have taken them for granted. Another consultant also said that a lot of questions went beyond her expectations. She said, "I have never thought of these questions: What did Mi Lan get out of this *mianzi* game? What advantages and disadvantages did *mianzi* bring about? If Mi Lan had deep affection for her mom, why was it that she un-affectively avoided seeing her mom who had come several thousand miles after several years' separation from Mi Lan, her daughter?"

The third consultant said, "Your question 'Can law and *mianzi* coexist?' provoked us to have a rich discussion, which has raised a lot of questions such as: Is Chinese culture prepared for failure? How can we make Chinese persons afford to fail? Should law govern *mianzi*, or vice versa? Should law or *mianzi* be used among relatives?' These questions made me feel tongue-tied. Now, I think that law should be more import-ant than *mianzi*. Law can judge everything. It ensures better justice and equality. But *mianzi* is biased. Also, when I said that Mi Lan's relation-ship with her mom can be described by affection, you asked, 'Then, why is it that Mi Lan tries not to meet her mom when her mom has come to see her?' This question has puzzled me. Should law or *mianzi* be used against relatives? This question came out of our discussion on your questions, too. I find this question of yours difficult to answer, too." These consultants' answers were echoed by other consultants.

A few consultants said that they would think, feel, and act differently than they did before the interview. Before this interview, if they were Mi Lan, they would have thought, felt, and acted like Mi Lan in the same case. For example, one consultant said: "After the interview, I would not have hidden myself from my mom when I failed. Failure is failure. So what? I can always go to a different place to seek another opportu-nity. I would be cool-headed." Another consultant answered: "After the interview, if I were Mi Lan, I would sue the corrupt official who had accepted the bribe and had replaced me with the briber." One consul-tant said, "I was as critical of *lian/mian* practices before the interview as I am now after the interview. You and I share many similar views. We might have received a similar education."

Some other consultants, instead of directly answering my questions, compared and contrasted differences between the Chinese concepts of face and the American concepts of face. They said that some issues are of serious face concern but not at all so to Americans. Things we feel as common sense might surprise them. Americans also fight for face, but they do not fight for it as much as Chinese. Chinese fight for face for the sake of face. Americans are pragmatic and realistic. One consultant said that since he came to the United States, he had become more realistic. Another consultant said, "I would be very much concerned about my face while in China. But today I am much less concerned about it. Living in the United States can dilute a Chinese person's face consciousness without one's own awareness.

This Chinese person can only discover that his or her face conscious-ness has been diluted when he or she goes back to China. When you are back in China after a few years' stay in the United States, your Chinese friends will say: How come you have been Americanized so fast? You are spending money so carefully." Hearing this, another consultant provided an example of her financially insecure mother back in China, who would always send expensive gifts to relatives and friends when she visited them.

Another consultant pointed out that Chinese expatriates like him are neither like Chinese back in China nor like Americans here in the States in terms of face and related emotions. They are in between. He told us his story to illustrate his point. A month ago, as a green-card holder with Ph.D. from a prominent university and two years' full-time teaching experience, he was interviewed by an American institution as one of three finalists. However, the position was offered to an American citizen of allegedly fewer qualifications. Given his competitiveness, he had been confident that he would get the offer. He waited for a long time with stretched tolerance, but he did not get a call from the employer. When he called the employer and found out, the chair of the search committee asked him to wait; if the first offer was turned down, the job would be offered to him. Sensing my consultant's reluctance to wait, the chair told him that she had gotten her current job because she had waited during her own job hunt. He felt too slighted to control his emotions. He had a strong emotional reaction toward the chair on the phone and released his anger. If he were an American, he would have felt good about being one of three finalists. If this American strongly alleged that the decision was unjust, he would have adopted legal measures to complain or redress it. He would not have reacted so emotionally. However, if he had socialized himself in American society, he would not have had a very strong negative emotional reaction toward the self-perceived slight much earlier. With all their answers, these consultants seemed to suggest that the American culture can be a good context in which Chinese persons can transform (dilute) their *lian/mian* practices and that the American culture can be used as a resource with which Chinese *lian/mian* practices can be transformed and the Chinese character remade.

I asked the last question as in the previous interview: "Do you have anything to add?" One consultant said, as he had said in the previous interview, "The questions you asked will eventually fade away because we share many similarities, which did not provoke any debates or arguments. Another reason might be that the issues are Chinese issues so common to us with Chinese cultural backgrounds. If some younger Chinese youths were interviewed, their answers might have been somewhat different from from ours." This was echoed by another consultant.


### Meta-Interview Questions

The meta-interview questions I asked the consultants for the present case study were mostly the same as for the previous case study. I adopted some of their suggestions from the first interview, such as avoiding politics, previewing all my interview questions at the beginning of the interview, and being more colloquial with my questions and less structured in my interview. I continued to maximize equal participation by my consultants. I also asked them a comparative question: "How do you compare this interview with the first interview?" One of them answered, "We feel more motivated to speak because you asked more provocative questions." Another one said, "I feel more certain with this interview." They were echoed by others, who added that I had employed some of their suggestions made during the first interview. However, one consultant reported that I sometimes cut in to have other consultants speak while she was answering. She said, "I did not feel comfortable with this." I explained that my goal was to ensure that all consultants had an equal opportunity. Hearing my explanation, she expressed her understanding. The consultants I encouraged to speak expressed their delight with my practice of interactive justice. One consultant said, for example, "I feel motivated to speak with your encouragement." As the final question of this interview, I asked, "Do you have any additional comments?" One consultant said, "I think that it is good to have everyone speak for a similar amount of time. I like it." "Any more?" I asked. They remained silent for a few seconds. Since the consultants did not have any additional comments, I thanked all of them for their active participation in both interviews.


## Interpretation of the Data

Here I elaborate, justify, and explain the native view of the consultants on the Chinese *lian/mian* practices relative to the view of social scientists and humanistic scholars (mostly Chinese) on the *lian/mian* practices, as reflected in both my own discussions of the *lian/mian* practices and in the review of scholarly literature. I also explain the rationale for my interview questions and the unique points of the consultants' inputs. Many general discussions on the following subtopics by the consultants are already elaborated in Chapter 6. These discussions and my interpretations are relevant to the present case, too, but I will not repeat them here.

## Cultural Representativeness

The consultants had mixed views on the representativeness of this case, unlike their unanimous consensus over the typicality of the previous case. The reason might be that the present case is drawn from a TV play series, which is not based on real life but fiction. Compared with the previous case, this case is less common. However, the consultants all agree that many Chinese are like Mi Lan in that they love *lian/mian* to death (*si yao mianzi*) only to find themselves suffer from it (*huo shou zui*). *Si yao mianzi huo shou zui* is actually a popular modern Chinese proverb that is used to sneer at those who love *lian/mian* at the cost of suppressing their own fundamental needs. There are many examples, such as Chinese couples who spend lots of money on their wedding only to find themselves in huge debt, Chinese guests who suffer from thirst and hunger at parties in American homes because they decline the hosts' first offers out of *keqi* etiquette, and a Chinese worker who boasts of a special connection with someone who controls first-class train tickets—a special commodity in China—and always accepts requests from friends in order to maintain his face, only to find himself sleeping in the open at the train station, waiting for the ticketing window to open to secretly buy tickets for his friends. Underlying the love of *lian/mian*, it seems to me, is a strong motivation to meet group/communal expectations and to win communal acclaim by any means—at the cost of losing reality, losing self, even losing integrity itself. Mi Lan wants to succeed to meet the expectations of her mom, her Beijing sisters, her countrymen, and her relatives. Since she does not succeed, she almost commits suicide and suppresses her own desire to meet her mother. While such *lian/mian* practices would be praised as virtuous in traditional Chinese society, the proverb "Love *mianzi* to death only to find yourself suffering from the love" shows that people have become critical of such practices. The consultants use this proverb to express their negative view of Mi Lan's *lian/mian* practices.

In the consultants' answers is another statement commenting on Mi Lan: She wants to take the shape of a human being (*hun chu ge ren yang*) before she can meet her mother. Here, to take the shape of a human being means to succeed as to brighten the *lian/mian* of her significant others as well as her own. In China, there is another proverb which goes that victors are the best of civilized human beings and failures are the worst of the species, below the human level. This means that humanity or non-humanity is defined by whether one has met the expectations of one's community, made a contribution to one's community or significant others. To the consultants, it seems that Mi Lan tries to avoid meeting her mother because she thinks that she has tarnished her own face and her mother's face and lost her personhood (*diou ren*) by her failure. She will not meet her mother until she succeeds, acquires her human face and her full humanity, and takes the shape of a civilized human being. She can not meet her mother as a lesser human being or a nonhuman. In contrast, with a huge bribe, Xiao Dan Dan replaces Mi Lan and "wins" the Gold Medal for Singing even though she cannot sing. She has become an icon for the youth and the focal point of the media. She has acquired her human face through unjust means. But many people who do not know her dark secret are eager to meet her and get her autograph. Xiao has lost her integrity but taken the shape of a civilized human being. What an irony!

### A Cultural/Historical Elaboration of *Lian/Mian*

When I asked the same questions on this subtopic of this case as I did for the previous case, the consultants came up with unique answers and some general discussion that applies to both cases. The following interpretation focuses on the unique answers. I first explain the phrases "to feel obligated to return the grace" or *bao en*, "to erase one's face off" *muo bu chu lian*, and "to harmonize the scene" or *yuan chang*. Then, I discuss Mi Lan's emotions.

Why does Mi Lan feel obligated to return all her mother has done for her? Why should she *bao en* to her mother? The best cultural explanation is from Lien-Sheng Yang (1957). According to Yang, *bao* means to respond, repay, or return; *en* means grace or favors. To *bao en* is to adhere to the ethical principle of reciprocity between Confucius' Five Relations within the family, which are most pervasive and especially prominent in Chinese society. In fact, they were believed by Confucius to be a foundation for social harmony. One of these relations is between father and son, and in extension between mother and daughter. "Rewards and punishments, curses and blessings, are all transferable within a family" (Yang, 1957, p. 302). Observing this principle of reciprocity in turn solidifies the family system. Filial piety or *xiao* is justified on the concept of *bao* or return. In fact, *bao* and *xiao* can go together as a verbal phrase in the Chinese language. Although the principle of reciprocity within the Five Relations was created by Confucius in 300 B.C., observation has been persistent and widespread.

Mi Lan, a Chinese youth of some 20 years of age who was brought up mostly in the increasingly free-market economy in late 1970s and 1980s China, observes this principle of reciprocity. The only difference between now and the time when Confucius invented the principle is that

Confucius concentrated on the father-son relationship; in Mi Lan's case, the reciprocal relationship Mi Lan is observing is the one between herself as daughter and her own mother. Her strong sense of obligation to repay her mother love must have motivated her to overcome all kinds of hardships in order to achieve. However, her unexpected failure made her lose the opportunity to repay her mother by shining her mom's face. This means that she has failed to observe the law-like principle of reciprocity in Chinese culture. Such a failure further makes her feel like a bad daughter who does not have face to meet her mother. In fact, according to this cultural principle, not meeting her mother in her situation would prevent her from losing more of her face. If she had met her mother without the gold medal, she would have been criticized by her relatives and countrymen for not wanting her face. Not wanting one's face is even more morally base than losing one's face after trying to maintain it, according to this cultural logic. Mi Lan seems to be deeply Confucian, acting quite consistently with this cultural logic.

Mi Lan could not erase her face off *(mu bu chu lian)* in order to see her mother. What does this mean? In order to have courage to meet her mother, Mi Lan has to be free of the sense of shame caused by her failure to fulfill her obligation to repay the love her mother has bestowed upon her. However, she is overwhelmed with her face consciousness. She might have yearned in her heart to get rid of it and even tried to do so to meet her mother, but she could not. The emotional cost and consequence of meeting her mother without fulfilling her obligation beforehand were just too big. She would run the risk of tarnishing her mother's face and this would make her mother's health deteriorate; she would also risk losing her face and losing her civilized humanity. She vowed to fulfill her obligation to repay her mother's love by making herself a victor in the future so that she and her mother could meet happily.

Another idiomatic phrase, not included in Chapter 3 but used by the consultants, is "to harmonize the scene" or *yuan chang. Yuan* means to make round. *Yuan chang* literally means to make the scene round. Its extended meaning is to mask inconsistencies so that they look consistent. A typical example of *yuan chang* is when a couple is actually having a verbal fight, but tell onlookers that they are just joking. This way, the couple's faces are saved, and the verbal fight may be ended by your effort to *yuan chang*. My consultants use it to describe Mi Lan's Beijing sisters' effort to make Mi Lan's mother happy by telling her a false success story instead of her daughter's true story of failure.

Mi Lan's emotions about her failure are mixed and complex. They seem to be simultaneously context- and relationship-dependent. They are all culturally appropriate. In other words, she follows the Chinese cultural norms of emotions and feelings. She is angry due to being wronged; reserves her affection towards her mother; feels shameful and guilty towards her mother, her Beijing sisters, and her countrymen; and suffers from pain due to anger. Her anger is directed toward corruption, injustice, unfairness, and the institutions that breed them. Her anger functions as a kind of moral protest toward the unjust society. Coupled with anger is the pain of her flesh, which consumes her inner physical strength. She represses her affection for her mother and lets it dissipate within herself due to the role-based instead of affection-based mother-daughter relationship she has been acculturated into.

As I argue in Chapter 3, in the Confucianist culture, natural emotions are regarded as wild and out of control. One has to cultivate them as if they were plants so that they will become harmless and useful. As a result of this Confucianist cultivation, Chinese emotions tend to be less spontaneous. They are primarily strictly regulated and unintendedly but consequentially burdened and suppressed by mountains of ethical norms and rules of social interaction. Because of our cultural constraint about freely expressing our emotions in everyday life, we tend to feel tired. Mi Lan is obviously one of us. Mi Lan feels shameful in front of her audience but she feels inwardly guilty *(nei jiou)*, primarily because of her failure to observe the moral principle of reciprocity. The former is public in nature and the latter is primarily moral in nature. This is evidence against the traditional argument in the Western academic world that Eastern culture is shame-based and Western culture is guilt-based, as if shame and guilt did not coexist and cofunction within the individual and the culture. The consultants' characterization of Mi Lan's emotional world further shows that emotions are multidimensional, deeply social, moral, and functional; they are also culturally different. My hypothesis, which can be further tested in another study in the future, is that shame and guilt may both exist and interact in a culture, with one dominant and the other latent.

### Legitimacy for Concerns

The consultants' concerns over the abuse of power that victimized Mi Lan, over Mi Lan's obsession with her *lian/mian* at the sacrifice of her affective tie with her mother, and over Mi Lan's Beijing sisters' effort to harmonize the situation at the sacrifice of truth helped legitimize my project of *lian/mian* transformation in the social constructionist communication perspective and methodology. These expressed concerns also act as the basis for subsequent reflection.

### Consequences of *Lian/Mian* Practices

The consultants' answers suggest that the prevalence of the *lian/mian* rules without the workings of law produced corruption, injustice, grievances, and deceptions, as this case shows. Such consequences are consistent with the scholarly documentation presented in Chapter 4 and my own observation. They have also weakened the insiders' courage and ability to battle against and uproot corruption and injustice, which have robbed people who lack special resources such as money and special opportunities for success. The tragically self-intoxicating obsession with *lian/mian* by Mi Lan, her Beijing sisters, and her mother has perpetuated the status quo and might have prevented them from concentrating on fighting for justice. This might be the reason why modern Chinese discourse argues for change but has failed to bring about real change in Chinese society.

The consultants' answers also reveal their mixed feelings towards *lian/mian* and law, as in the first interview. The consultants' mixed feelings might indicate that they have more or less given up a monolithic view of what is good and what is bad. It may be a sign of a possible deep change in the future. However, one should be alerted that the consultants view face and law as being in opposition to each other. In fact, they may be as interrelated as they are oppositional.

### How to Make a Change

In the consultants' replies, I have identified the following proposals for change: (1) to alleviate Mi Lan's face concerns and make room for mother-daughter affection; (2) to dilute her face consciousness so that she could be psychologically strong enough to deal with failure; and (3) to use legal means to restore justice. These proposals are based on the consultants' concerns over undesirable consequences of *lian/mian* practices. Their replies seem to suggest two methods: one is to change the individual; the other is to change the society. The former is a micro-change in cultural psychology, whereas the latter is a macro-change in social structure. However, structural change is not my central goal in the present study. The proposed micro-change is consistent with the objectives of change explored here.

### Reflective Questions

By asking reflective questions, I wanted to find out to what extent the interview so far had provoked the consultants to reflect upon the *lian/mian* practices in this case and hopefully their own *lian/mian* practices as well.

First of all, they all understood the objectives of my interview well. They described my questions as "provocative" but "difficult," tongue-tying but compelling, or quite interesting and unexpected. This interview episode also elicited several consultants' accounts of their own experiences of diluting their *lian/mian* consciousness and transforming their own *lian/mian* communication patterns while living, studying, and working in American society. Their account suggests that experiencing or learning from a different culture such as the American one, which has much less face consciousness than Chinese culture, might be another effective way to dilute the Chinese *lian/mian* consciousness and transform the *lian/mian* patterns. The consultants' experience shows that making Chinese culture open-ended and pluralistic seems to be the key to the transformation of Chinese *lian/mian* culture into a self-rejuvenating and powerful culture. Huddling between the Great Wall of China and the coastlines of China can only perpetuate the status quo. Their experience of neither becoming completely American nor remaining completely Chinese in the original sense also shows that transforming the Chinese *lian/mian* culture by experiencing and learning from a culture with much less face consciousness may reshape Chinese persons who are situated in healthy intercultural dynamics. This falls within the ultimate objective of my social constructionist research on the Chinese *lian/mian* practices, which tries to draw upon the two cultures creatively to reconstruct the Chinese character.

### Meta-Interview Questions

Except for asking the consultants to compare the two interviews, I asked roughly the same questions during this interview as during the first one. While their answers were essentially the same for both, they did point out that this interview seemed to be more effective because both they and I had acquired some experience through the first interview. They were pleased that I had implemented some of their suggestions, such as phrasing my questions more conversationally, previewing my questions, being less structural in my interview, ensuring equal participation, and avoiding talking about Chinese politics. This is very important, because they felt recognized for their contributions. This is also why I prefer to call them consultants. However, I did not use other suggestions such as random selection of participants, interviewing younger Chinese persons, and interviewing more people, including Americans. While I think that these suggestions are constructive, they do not fit the major research goal of the present study, which is to illustrate the use of CQ in the Chinese context. I will certainly consider these suggestions in future studies.

## EVALUATION OF THE INTERVIEW

Here I discuss the process and the effectiveness of CQ in the second interview. Then, I identify the limitations of CQ as it is used in this case and discuss future implications for using CQ in the Chinese context.

### The Process of My Use of CQ

Although I used many techniques in the previous interview, such as joining the grammar, questions of elaboration, circularity between interviewer and interviewee, and circularity among interviewees, I tried to build this second interview upon the first interview to make it more effective. This second interview is unique in that it seems less structured, more open-ended, and more provocative than the first.

Although I followed the order of the prewritten questionnaire, I did not try to repeat its questions verbatim. I tried to make the questions more colloquial. I also asked more questions after the topic questions, to have the consultants elaborate the emergent issues brought up in their answers and discussions. I characterize this interview as more semistructured than structured, and the first interview as more structured.

I tried to make the interview more open-ended, motivating the consultants to speak as much as possible. I tried to ask as many interesting questions as possible and tried to listen to them as much as possible. I also asked the consultants to make additional comments at the end of each episode. However, I did find that the goal of maximizing equal participation contradicted the goal of making my interview open-ended. One consultant said that she felt a little ill at ease when I cut in to ask someone else to speak while she was speaking. She had expressed a similar concern in the previous interview. However, once my consultants became aware of the significance of equal participation and knew how to enjoy their share of interactive justice, they took turns relatively smoothly.

I tried to make my second interview more provocative. I define provocative questions as ways of asking that push consultants to the edge of their comfort zone or push them to become aware of gaps in thinking, feeling, and perception or motivate them to challenge things that they take for granted. As a result, this interview seemed to focus more on reflexivity than the first one. However its goal still remains at attitudinal change and conceptual change instead of behavioral change and emotional change. This type of asking seems to be broader than the technique of positive reframing, which can be classified as one kind of provocative question. I did not use positive reframing here because the interview is not direct intervention.

In addition, I have used Appreciative Inquiry much more globally than in the first interview. I made more effort to maximize equal participation by all the consultants. I encouraged those who tended to speak less to speak more by directly soliciting their comments. I also used some of the consultants' suggestions to improve this second interview, such as previewing the questions before the interview started. Finally,

I listened to the consultants with more attention and appreciation. Such moves not only empowered them but also motivated their active participation and enriched the interview results. I used this technique without using words such as "thanks," "I appreciate it," and so on that explicitly express appreciation. I would call my version of Appreciative Inquiry (AI) "structural/global appreciative inquiry" rather than a verbal version of AI. During this interview, I tried to create a context in which the consultants could use opportunities I created to empower themselves. In this sense, I went beyond mere verbal and nonverbal appreciation to empower them.

To summarize, I did find that it was more effective to use the less-structured interview format for this occasion, but it was time-consuming. My consultants tended to talk in greater detail but more randomly.

## The Effectiveness of My Use of CQ

The behavioral change is hardly documentable, because of the nature of this interview. However, the conceptual, perceptual, and emotional change seems to be more obvious in this interview than in the first one. During this interview, especially in the episode of reflective questions, the consultants seemed to have been more self-reflective. Using the insights they acquired through the interview on the transformation of *lian/mian* practices, they vividly accounted for their experience of diluting their *lian/mian* consciousness and transforming their *lian/mian* practices in the Sino-American intercultural context. Their account not only shows their sophisticated self-understanding of their own transformation but also points to a possible effective strategy by which to take further advantage of the bicultural or intercultural communication experience of Chinese overseas or overseas Chinese in refining CQ as a change instrument in the Chinese context.

## Limitations and Implications

While most of the limitations of CQ identified in the previous case study apply to the present one, one major limitation seemed to be alleviated. One of the limitations of CQ is that it is reflection-oriented instead of action-oriented, which might limit its change potential. However, the consultants' accounts of their experience of diluting their *lian/mian* consciousness and transforming their *lian/mian* practices point to a possibility of formulating an action-oriented instrument of change to complement CQ as a reflection-oriented instrument of change. Future studies can use CQ to accumulate as many stories as possible of the *lian/mian* transformation of overseas Chinese, especially in Western countries such as the United States, to identify the experiential tracks of *lian/mian* transformation and the various dilemmas and difficulties, challenges, and consequences of *lian/mian* transformation along the tracks. Such real-life cases can help develop an action-oriented CQ and refine reflection-oriented CQ. The most effective models of *lian/mian* transformation can be built in reference to such real-life cases with the repeated and alternate uses of action-oriented CQ and reflection-oriented CQ. Real-life cases of *lian/mian*/identity transformation of individuals in the Four Little Dragons in East Asia can also be identified and used in helping develop effective models of *lian/mian* transformation in China.

Furthermore, the consultants' repeatedly expressed dilemma over *lian/mian* versus law reveals their emotional attachment to *lian/mian* practices, which may render their rational choice and rationality ineffective. This suggests a need to build an emotional model of change that aims to transform the emotional attachment to *lian/mian* into a rational attitude toward *lian/mian* and that aims to transform the rational attachment to law into an emotional attachment to law. This need entails a strategy to identify emotional, rational, and dialectic interconnections between *lian/mian* and law and to creatively wed the two.

Finally, the way I have used CQ in these case studies does not necessarily imply that other scholars and students of change should use CQ exactly in the same way. Other ways of using CQ are encouraged.

# 8

# A Social Constructionist Model of *Lian/Mian* Transformation

After summarizing the answers to my research questions in the previous chapters, as informed by the two case studies, I elaborate the social constructionist model of transformation on the basis of the broad theoretical outline provided in Chapter 4. In contrast to the two complementary models of the ethnocultural view of *lian/mian*, I argue that the social constructionist model is a better choice for contemporary Chinese society because of its maximum openness, which allows unlimited and creative two-way communication with other cultures.

## TENTATIVE ANSWERS TO MY RESEARCH QUESTIONS

The following integrated summary of the answers to my research questions is based on the two case studies:

*Lian/mian* practices have been shaped and reshaped by daily social interaction in Chinese contexts. They have been fundamental in constituting and maintaining the Chinese identity and the destiny of Chinese culture. The *lian/mian* concepts have many versions that variants and help configure a powerful grammar of social action and interaction. Implicit in them is a rich repertoire of emotions such as honor, shame, anger, guilt, pain, and suffering, which often simultaneously govern the *lian/mian* practices to a significant extent according to the cultural rules and norms.

Given the homogeneity, closure, and rigidity of the preexistent *lian/mian* practices in the increasingly changing social and economic environment of China, they are proving less and less able to regulate political, social, and business activities, less and less able to create long-term social order and maintain social harmony. On the contrary, they produce more and more conflicts, inequalities, and injustices. The solution seems to lie in a bottom-up, systemic, persistent, and cumulative group effort to enhance self-reflectivity on *lian/mian* practices by members of the Chinese community, to facilitate their creative interaction, to transform their grammar of action, and to reconstitute their identity—a new cultural identity of rationality, plurality, openness, and interdependence that may emerge out of the constructive interplay and synergy of Eastern culture and Western culture. The case studies in Chapters 6 and 7 are intended to illustrate this constructionist effort.

Within the answers to my research questions in general and within the case studies specifically is embedded a social constructionist model of *lian/mian* transformation better illustrated and more elaborated than the blueprint described in Chapter 4. A more detailed description of the model follows.

## THE SOCIAL CONSTRUCTIONIST MODEL

This is a consultative approach to the *lian/mian* practices. It is theoretically based on systems theory and social constructionism. Unlike the therapeutic model, CQ does not generate problem talk. It is characterized by curiosity, neutrality, and active engagement with clients (such as joining the grammar of clients). Lin's modern criticism model and the Maoist model of radical revolution both assume that cultural change is a sudden break and rupture, unlike the ethnocultural model of *lian/mian*, which is solely interested in describing the native view of *lian/mian* dynamics without any effort to account for change.

The social constructionist model is interested in joining in the grammar, attunement, and coordination with objects of change, which/who are also conceptualized as agents of self-change. It digs into the micro-details of everyday life and attempts to work into the very being, emotions, and communicative behavior of clients. Its assumption is that cultural change will consist of gradual and cumulative transformation from the bottom. Its objective is to enhance clients' ability to disentangle confusing relationships, to attune to the emergent forces, and to produce reflective action.

In other words, the social-constructionist model attempts to enhance clients' self-reflexivity and ability to proactively facilitate and invent an emergent way of life in the environment of great change, to attend to and feel secure about the emergent and contingent identity with the hope that the lost can be found in the new. Its goal is to enable clients to relate, communicate, and emote in new and more constructive ways; to enable them to build an open-ended identity and to better adjust themselves to contingencies and emergencies; and to make better use of them rather than to succumb to such contingencies and emergencies.

Techniques such as appreciative inquiry (AI), the technique of desensitization (TD), and the technique of relative individuation can be used to build a stronger agency (to reconstruct) while a level of systemic view and way of life is maintained to allow sufficient interdependence. As M. Brewster Smith says, "it still makes sense to regard self-conception as agent rather than patient as an aspect of modernity, and, indeed, as an attribute likely in the long run to be valued in a way that transcends cultures" (1985, p. 81). A stronger agency out of the *lian/mian* constraints can be instrumental in constructing Chinese modernity at an individual level.

## A CONTRAST

The following consists of sketches of three models: the social constructionist view of *lian/mian* transformation and two versions (the descriptive and the critical) of the ethnocultural view of *lian/mian* documented in Chapter 4. The goal is to highlight, by way of contrast, the uniqueness of the social constructionist model of *lian/mian* transformation.

The ethnocultural model of face can be described as a web which consists of the following:

1. Selves and others form nexuses of relationships which constitute a closed-ended web in which self is within the other and the other is within self.
2. Self is obligated to be concerned about the other.
3. Face is unidimensional, and unidirectional, and other-oriented.
4. The Maslow type of individual needs are submerged.
5. Affection is submerged in one's formal interpersonal relationships and roles.
6. There is virtual absence of legal consciousness and economic consciousness.

In this model, face is earned through showing concern toward others. Face hardly exists without others and relationships that constitute a community, or an audience. Therefore, face always relies on others in its efforts to construct and maintain itself in interaction with the community. A sufficient level of individual agency is lost through giving face to others in all directions. This is well illustrated by Ms. Huang in

Chapter 6 and Mi Lan in Chapter 7. Almost all of this happens within a web or a tight circle which invites closure and which draws a sharp line between the inside and the outside. Face dynamics occur only inside, thus creating the closed-ended, static and homogeneous nature of the Chinese *lian/mian* culture. This is true in both cases. Ms. Huang, the director and all the other characters in the first case, and Mi Lan and many other characters in the second case, all seem to be encircled within the web of the *lian/mian* culture and act according to its age-old rules and logics, even after they and their society have been exposed to both communism and capitalism for the past several decades.

However, the concept of web does not tell us everything about face dynamics. It is a half-truth to say that the *lian/mian* culture is concerned with social and interpersonal harmony. If we say that Ms. Huang and Mi Lan value harmony because neither of them nor their friends seek to confront the wrongdoers, we omit to say that they all give in reluctantly to those who are powerful or those who are above them in the social hierarchy. Therefore, while the model described above illustrates harmony in a web, it unavoidably masks the hierarchy which is a major source and goal of harmony or face-giving, leaving the false impression that the *lian/mian* culture is characterized by equality. The alternative model uncovers the hierarchy masked by the superficial harmony within a social or communal web and thus functions as a critique of the ethnocultural model of face shown above.

The hierarchical dimension masked by the ethnocultural model of face can be described as follows:

1. The bigger the circle, the more expansive face becomes.
2. Social hierarchy underlies the web on the surface.
3. The smaller the circle, the less face s/he has but the more face s/he has to give to the bigger circle. This shows the unequal and oppressive nature of the *lian/mian* dynamics within Chinese culture.
4. Face concerns about others can be said to be directed only toward people of a higher social status—which is built upon, maintained, and enhanced by face-giving acts from smaller circles.
5. The circles within the web only flow according to the rigid rules of hierarchy preestablished and prescribed by Confucius and Confucians.

The alternative model functions as a critique of the ethnocultural model of face. What shall we do with them once we have uncovered the hierarchical substance of the rhetoric of harmony as a cultural ideal of the *lian/mian* culture and undesirable social consequences? Consequences such as inequality, injustice, and loss individual rights warrant an ethical transformation of the *lian/mian* culture. Hence, we need a model of change.

The social constructionist model of *lian/mian* transformation can be described as a web without a circle:

1. It proactively makes Chinese culture open to influences from other cultures.
2. It also promotes the influence from Chinese culture on other cultures.
3. It views reality as a tentative and infinitely open process.
4. It favors mutual and equal face concerns.
5. It maintains a relatively independent agency.
6. Openness of Chinese culture can be enabled by a social constructionist communication perspective.
7. Face, economy, law, and others such as religion are equally important and function in relationship to one another as separate but interrelated domains.

The social constructionist model as sketched above attempts to transform the ethnocultural model of face. Seven cultural values embedded in social constructionist theory and its instrument circular questioning can be used to transform the Chinese *lian/mian* culture. These are:

1. Equality in lieu of hierarchy;
2. Moderation in lieu of excessive communalism (close-ended web) dominant in China and the Western type of excessive individualism emergent in China due to the blind quest for the free market economy;
3. Open-endedness and flexibility in lieu of closure, certainty and rigidity;
4. A view of reality as conflicts underlying the surface of harmony and processes, in lieu of a perennial quest for the end result of surface harmony and unity;
5. Pluralism in lieu of homogeneity;
6. Bottom-up and autonomous change in lieu of top-down elitist change.
7. Personhood with individual agency in a nexus of relationships, in lieu of personhood constituted only by a nexus of relationships.
8. In addition, I would treat social justice instead of harmony as a primary end goal. Harmony can be retained as a secondary end goal in the new Chinese culture.

These eight values constitute the essence of the social constructionist model of *lian/mian* transformation. As is illustrated in the two case studies, this social constructionist model functions well with the use of circular questioning, which tries to incorporate these values into the interview process. This model works toward helping create a new type of Chinese personhood which is reflective and critical in thinking, open-minded and pluralistic, moderate and pragmatic, confrontational and consensual; a personhood which has a strong sense of equality and individual agency in the nexus of relationships.

# 9

# A Theoretical Discussion

## IMPLICATIONS AND FUTURE DIRECTIONS FOR *LIAN/MIAN* TRANSFORMATION

### Different Research Agendas

In this book, I explore the possibility of *lian/mian* transformation in light of a systemic theory of communication that I call "the social constructionist theory of communication." By "transformation" here, I mean a meaningful engagement with and facilitation of a gradual and process-oriented systemic evolution of cultural communication patterns such as the Chinese *lianmian* patterns through creatively integrating an outside cultural communication system such as the modern Western one and the basic communication system of Chinese culture into a unified, complex, and open communication system. I do not mean to abandon the native Chinese culture or communication patterns and mechanically replace them with a non-native culture or communication patterns. I mean to form a creative blend of the two.

Transformation of the *lian/mian* practices in the Chinese context entails the following steps: (1) deconstruction, which means to prune the thickets of rules, rituals, feelings, and emotions constituting *lian/mian* that often overwhelm individual agency and constrain Chinese cultural members from constructive discourse and action; (2) reconstruction, which means to inject the fresh blood of modern Western culture into Chinese culture; and (3) protection, which means to protect the face, as the foundation of the ethics of cohumanity, against the dehumanization caused by impersonalization, effacement, complete objectivization, and by overreliance on law, capital, technology, and science in human affairs. This transformation aims for the middle ground (a Confucian concept of *zhongyong*) between the excess of face concerns and the excess of effacement. The steps can occur simultaneously.

In China as in modern Western societies, technology and capital are disintegrating human relations and providing increasingly impersonal forms of communication, thus challenging positive humanistic values embodied in *lian/main*. We need to rescue such values, which are fundamental to human survival. Emmanuel Levinas's philosophical-ethical ideas on face represent one attempt to do so (1985; Robbins, 1991). He argues that face is the very fountain of discourse, social interaction, and human ethics, for "it orders me and ordains me" (1985, p. 97) to be responsible for the other. Levinas suggests that the fact that everyone has a face and exposes his or her face to the other or the public is the reason that humanity is still alive. To give up face completely means to give up humanity, for the face-face constitutes the substance of humanity or cohumanity. This is consistent with the assumptions underlying the interchangeability of the Chinese terms "*diou lian*" (loss of face) and "*diou ren*" (loss of personhood).

On the other hand, the traditional reliance on *lian/mian* to regulate human behavior, motivate social interaction, and distribute resources is becoming increasingly ineffective in the increasingly economically and technologically modernized Chinese world, as the two cases illustrate. We need to juxtapose the mechanism of law and the interpersonal system of *lian/mian* as an informal but pervasive system of rules and norms. The *lian/mian* practices may have to be reconstructed to make room for the implementation of law, which should significantly participate in the regulation of human affairs, motivation of human behavior, and distribution of resources.

This discussion suggests that there are different research agendas for social constructionism. In the West, social constructionism aims to recover the social and systemic view of the human world in order to modify radical and rugged individualism, to reclaim a sense of community, and to repair the broken fabric of society. However, in the current Chinese situation, there seem to be two different research agendas beckoning us social constructionists. On one hand, as the two case studies illustrate, we should alleviate the face consciousness (*danhua mianzi yishi*) or weed out the excessive communalism enacted by face dynamics defined by hierarchy and coated by harmony and stability. On the other hand, we should also stop some sectors of the society from their slippage into a wanton emulation of excessive individualism, impersonalization, and technologization in the West.

Future studies of *lian/mian* transformation in the Chinese context should not only continue the research agenda I have initiated but also extend the research agenda originally developed in the West to the Chinese context, to address social concerns similar to those emerging at a fast pace in the West, due to an excess of individualism. For example, although Chinese people formerly tended to treat good human relationships or *guanxi* as ends in themselves, nowadays more and more Chinese are using such relationships as mere instruments for economic and personal gain. The article "A Circle of Friends, a Web of Troubles: Rotating Credit Associations in China" (Tsai, 1998) tells such a story. A Chinese woman formed a credit association and recruited all her time-tested friends in the community, who put two hundred Chinese dollars each month to the association. After four months, this woman fled from the community with her friends' money. Similar stories happen very often these days in China. They show that the social fabric in some areas of China are torn and masks or faces are shed for sheerly individual wants. These two extremes constitute a dual research agenda for social constructionists grounded in the Chinese context— one more complex and challenging than in the Western context.

Western transnational business practice in China poses an even more complex research question. In order to maximize profit, Western companies in China are adopting Chinese face-centered communication strategies, such as giving face to corrupt officials by bribing them. Such a practice affirms the Chinese communication status quo, reassures the Chinese of the superiority of their *lian/mian* culture, and opposes the social constructionist effort to transform *lian/mian* practices. Helping Western transnationals in China reflect upon such practices and transform themselves into social constructionist agents for change in China, as well as in the West upon their return, could be a unique research agenda, to be shared by both social constructionists originally grounded in the West and social constructionists originally grounded in the Chinese context. This is where both groups of social constructionists can meet and collaborate. Since overreliance on law, technology, and capital as a triad in solving human problems has already subverted face-to-face ethics in the West, social constructionists are also responsible for constraining the forces of impersonalization, objectivization, and dehumanization of human life and creating sufficient space for humans to see a face. To see the face of the other with the naked eye or to meet the eyes of the other prevents one from acting violently against the other, as suggested by Levinas (1985).

However, the Chinese situation is somewhat different. *Lian/mian* or face, what Derrida refers to as "the ethics of the ethics" (Robbins, 1991, p. 135), so dominates Chinese life in all its spheres that codified law, nominally existent, is almost nullified by the ethics of face—the informal but pervasive and traditional substitute for law. The face ethics must be deconstructed to allow law to play a central role where necessary to insure justice, equality, and efficiency. However, capital and technology are destroying the minimal ethics of face in more and more urbanized areas of China, as they have destroyed them in the West. Social constructionists should also be keen and courageous enough to counteract such destructive forces through engagement with other people who are promoting positive processes at the micro, mezzo, and macro levels.

## SOCIAL CONSTRUCTIONISM RECONSIDERED

### Chinese Social Constructionism versus Western Social Constructionism

In the previous chapters, I have discussed at length how social constructionism in the postmodern West can contribute to the study and transformation of the Chinese *lian/mian* practices. The latter lack a sense of the Western type of equality, individuality, or agency. Multiple views of the Chinese as a group are needed to help Chinese incorporate healthy modernity and useful elements of postmodernism such as a non-Sinocentric multicultural consciousness.

Social constructionism in the contemporary West has been generally a thoughtful revision of the modern Western view of personhood, which has fallen into a conceptual dead end, and a critical affirmation of some useful elements from other cultural traditions. It seems to have incorporated some healthy elements of the Eastern tradition, such as morality and responsibility/obligation, that may have been ignored or devalued by modern Western culture. It has reinterpreted/maintained some useful elements in modern Western culture, such as equality, individuality, and justice and has incorporated the notion of contingency. In this sense, social constructionism, in its ideal form (after it has best incorporated the Eastern and Western traditions), offers the best hope for Chinese who have been suffering an intellectual personality split between the Chinese tradition and Western modernity. In this sense, social constructionism portends a possible creative synthesis of the Chinese and Western cultures, or *zhong xi jie he* in Chinese.

Intellectuals concerned about the quality of life of Chinese people should avoid either a wholesale imitation of the modern West or a wholesale dumping of Chinese tradition in reconstructing the modern Chinese personhood when the modern West is trying to transform itself into a post-modern persona. By sharing the social constructionist orientation, the classic myth of the cultural split between the East and West can be discounted. Coordination and cooperation, instead of conflict and confrontation, would become a major theme in exploratory and creative intercultural communication between Cultural China and the West.

Here, I discuss what the Chinese pragmatic and social constructionist tradition can offer to help reflect upon and possibly enrich and expand the growing intellectual enterprise of social constructionism in the contemporary West. Social constructionism in the contemporary West has its intellectual roots in the Ancient Greek philosophy embodied by the Aristotelian concept of praxis. However, the ancient tradition was marginalized by the analytical philosophies of the modern West. John Dewey and George Herbert Mead and so on in the early twentieth century reinvented and expanded the ancient Greek tradition of praxis, only to be eclipsed by the onslaught of scientism in social sciences. This tradition was picked up and further expanded by scholars like Peter Berger and Thomas Luckman (1966), Rom Harré, Kenneth Gergen and later by John Shotter, James Averill, Vernon Cronen, and Barnett Pearce in various fields such as psychology, sociology, rhetoric, philosophy, and communication. Therefore, the social constructionist tradition in the West can be characterized by marginality, breaks, and repeated expansions. While it is becoming more and more intellectually and socially influential, it is still far from a received view.

However, in the Chinese context, a different social construction-ist/pragmatic tradition since the era of Confucius and his roots has been a mainstream tradition, characterized by consistent dominance, continuity, and nonreflection, until China began to be affected by the challenge from the modern West. Modern Chinese intellectuals, en-grossed by the ignorance and iconoclastic negation of the Chinese tradition, have failed to explore the pragmatic nuances of the Chinese tradition. It is Western Sinologists such as Herbert Fingarette (1972) and David Hall and Roger Ames (1998) who have made more remarkable discoveries about the Chinese pragmatic tradition than the Chinese scholars.

Chinese social constructionism is bent more on the elitist design of a moral hierarchy of personhood, with *sheng ren* or the sacred person-hood/sagehood on the top, *ren zhe* or the kind and philosophical on the next lower level, *junzi* or the exemplary person further down the line, then *chen ren* or a mature person, *da ren* or big person, with *xiaoren* or little person at the bottom. One has the potential to climb from the bottom to the top through self-moral cultivation or to degenerate into a little person who would be faceless or invisible (Hall and Ames, 1998, p. 158). This design is explicitly elitist. Believing that such and such constitute the *Dao* or the way to sagehood, scholar-officials are to disseminate the Dao on how to make or construct personhood (*zuo ren*) in their interaction with members of the society. This process has to follow the rules and rituals that are "the rhyme and rhythm of society"

(Hall and Ames, 1998, p. 270) and constitute the grammar of daily communication.

Chinese social constructionism is also unique in its moment-to-moment use of the minutest secular details of proper ritual as displayed/reproduced by the whole human body. The living human body is originally like a thing-like vessel. By partaking of the community through observing or enacting the ritual, the beastlike person transforms himself or herself into a sacred vessel that contributes to communal harmony, of which the person constitutes a share and enjoys a share (Ingarette, 1972). This is why I would call the Chinese social construction of communication a "bodily ritual–centric" model, in contrast to the Western model of logocentrism or talk centrism.

Finally, the social historical context in which the Chinese social constructionist theory of communication represented by Confucius came into being differs from the social historical context in which social constructionism is emerging in the West. The latter is rising against the fixation and constraint of human imagination, open-endedness in construction of humanity, and the assimilation of other cultures on the part of the triad of scientism, individualism, and capitalism. The former rose as a solution to the social chaos in the Period of Warring States (475-221 B.C.). Confucius and his disciples relied on a ritual-centric model of communication to help transform primitive cultures, to homogenize local cultures and acculturate the "barbarians" *(yi ren)*, and to produce social harmony and social order. Social constructionists in the West, however, such as Cronen and Pearce and their associates, affirm cultural diversity and promote multiracial and multicultural harmony through coordination in communication.

The Chinese social constructionism of communication is characterized by elitism, ritual, a sense of shame, and *lian/mian* practices, and has harmony as its ideal. It constrains Chinese imagination, freedom of action, and social innovation during the Chinese quest for modernity by its practices of social hierarchy, Sino-centrism, and personal contingency in moral cultivation. However, Chinese social constructionism can function as a heuristic for the development of social constructionism in the West. First, informed by the Chinese elitist method of constructing personhood, social constructionism in the West could formulate and disseminate operationalized ethical and moral rules and rituals that embody the spirit of social constructionism. Furthermore, since Chinese personhood has been produced and reproduced very effectively through Confucianist ritual, the bodily ritual has demonstrated its power and operationalizability in constructing a given type of person. The practice of ritual constitutes the perfect wedding of theory and practice in its incremental and accumulative process of becoming an ideal person through a bit-by-bit build-up of bodily control and enactment. Social constructionism in the West should give more scholarly attention to how to usefully wed its theory with practice through the creation and use of bodily rituals. Still further, since Chinese social constructionist theory regards the human body as of central cultural significance in building a culture of order and harmony, the embodiment of a social constructionist is of more cultural significance.

Embodying the spirit of social constructionism, a Western social constructionist may cultivate himself or herself according to the ideal through daily rituals and daily interaction as well as through scholarly publications and presentations. Theoretically, the incorporation of ritual that also includes speech may overcome the talk centrism inherent in social constructionism in the West. Finally, socialization is not enough in achieving the social (re)constructionist goal. Cultivation of a more purposeful and more strategic socialization could be the most direct route to social reconstruction.

### Social Constructionism as a Joint Venture

Social constructionism is an enlightened intellectual response to excessive individualism and other social ills of Western modernity. A less known response to the same ills in the West, particularly in the United States, is New Confucianism, championed by Tu Wei-Ming, Roger T. Ames, David L. Hall, and their associates. Appealing to Confucianist philosophical ideals in the classical philosophical texts, which have rarely been achieved even in the Chinese context, their attempt to transform the individualism-crippled American society has had little practical effect. Here, social constructionism, as elucidated in earlier chapters, can act to critique and modify such idealization of the Eastern world and attempts at wholesale easternization of Western society. It can help New Confucianism redefine and operationalize its agenda for social change in North America.

While the modern Chinese intellectuals' perennial advocacy of a complete Westernization of Chinese society has existed much longer than has New Confucianism in North America, it also has been a constant failure. Here again, social constructionism can modify the idea of complete Westernization, which ignores the social and communal dynamics and values of Chinese society. Both New Confucianism in the West and support for complete Westernization in China constitute a love affair on the basis of self-negation and self-obliteration, which will never produce healthy self-renewal. Social constructionism, identifying with the healthy aspects of both Chinese culture and Western culture, can also critique their mutual ignorance, suspicion, hatred, and attempts to obliterate each other and itself. Indeed, the Eastern and

Western cultures, if used well, can shed light on each other and offer transformative resources to each other.

In this sense, social constructionism can help create the synergy necessary for peaceful and productive interaction between the two cultures, creating more commonality and establishing more links. It can work toward building a culture that is neither Eastern nor Western and that is both Eastern and Western. This alternative to the dead end both New Confucianism and the movement for the complete Westernization of China can open up creative space for pragmatic cultural change in the East and the West, as needed in the twenty-first century—the century, or so it now appears, of the globalization of information.

## CONCLUSION

Social constructionism incorporating both Eastern and Western traditions should use policymaking, media, technology, capital, and law as forces of construction. The responsibility of social constructionism is not only to transform modernity into postmodernity (a goal of Western social constructionism), but also to transform tradition into healthy modernity, in the Chinese context. The humanistic values embodied by *lian/mian* should be retained to counter the increasingly dehumanizing forces of capital, technology, and law—a triad that enslaves human beings in the name of empowering humanity. Indeed, scholars and practitioners committed to social constructionist research projects can be joint-venture entrepreneurs, carrying two loads and going in two seemingly opposite directions at the same time—a very challenging task.

# 10

# Remaking the Chinese Character

## THE RELATIONSHIP BETWEEN *LIAN/MIAN* AND THE CHINESE CHARACTER

According to Zai (1995), Chinese self-awareness of their own national or cultural character began to emerge around the late nineteenth century, when China was forced to be frequently at war with the modern powers, as in the Opium War with Britain and a war with Japan. The intermittent introduction of Western social sciences such as anthropology, coupled with China's military confrontations with the modern powers at its own door, helped generate a modern view of China as a living racial, national, and cultural entity in contrast to the West. In this period, for the first time, the Chinese sense of cultural/racial superiority in the form of "the Middle Kingdom Syndrome" was shattered. Chinese intellectuals were forced to examine their everyday life, to become suspicious of their own group superiority and even critical of their own cultural practices, cultural institutions, and classical canons. This was the beginning of modern academic studies of the Chinese character.

The ultimate goal of such studies was to modernize Chinese behavior, Chinese culture, and the Chinese character to save and strengthen the Chinese nation/race. Authors covered in Chapter 4, such as Li Zongwu, Lin Yutang, Lu Xun, Bo Yang, Mao Tse-tung, and Su Xiaokang and his associates, and authors covered in Chapter 3, such as Yi Zongtian and Lu Zeng, belong to this scholarly tradition. They share with a majority of modern Chinese intellectuals the view that the traditional Chinese character, molded after traditional Chinese culture, is responsible for

China's political and economic backwardness. However, what is unique about these authors is that they tend to agree that the Chinese *lian/mian* practices constitute the core of the Chinese character and identity and that therefore a substantial transformation can occur only when the Chinese *lian/mian* practices are changed.

## How to Remake the Chinese Character

The two case studies illustrate how we can begin to remake the Chinese character. They show how we can gradually transform our character, enrich and expand our identity, by systematically observing, reflecting upon, discussing and altering our minutest mundane social/cultural behaviors, feelings, and emotions in a group context. Specifically, such a transformation may occur through the creation of a unique civic discourse. This discourse can be constituted by the following dimensions.

First, ordinary people can enable each other to communicate in a rational-relational way by means of a new type of communication, a hybrid formed by the *lian/mian* patterns of communication and a neo-rationalist form of metacommunication—the social constructionist form of group consultation. This rational-relational form of communication blends the instrumental and procedural values embodied by capital, technology, and law and the constructive dimensions of *lian/mian*, such as the values of good human relations and social harmony. I call this new form of communication by a new term: *reralational*. The reralational form lies between the excess of rationality, which marginalizes relationship, and the excess of relationality, which marginalizes rationality. This form of communication should be able to harmoniously incorporate the monetary, technological, and legal codes and the humanized ethics of *lian/mian*, *guanxi* (good human relations), and *renqing* (human feelings), the three pillars of Chinese culture of communication. It certainly should start by resisting the colonization of Chinese cultural discourse by these all-too-humanized practices, which tend to corrupt the seeds of democracy. The goal of this balanced blend is to maximize the happiness of as many individuals as possible.

Second, equality and freedom in discursive practices should also be a constituent of the civic discourse. The social hierarchy and social control associated with the *lian/mian* discourse should be minimized. This will occur only if the coproduction of discourse, knowledge, and truths is ensured. Since equal and free communication is a vital process of knowledge making, to speak to be heard not only is one's right but also becomes one's social responsibility. The listener-centered communication pattern deeply engrained in Chinese culture should be complemented by a speaker-centered communication pattern.

Third, discourse for and of diversity should also be a significant dimension of Chinese civic discourse. This is closely related to Confucius' ideal of "social harmony in difference" (*he er bu tong*). The Chinese *lian/mian* practices, preoccupied with the Chinese valuation of interpersonal relationships, is more inclined to generate the groupthink that carries Sinocentric and monolithic biases. Cultural discourse for / of diversity in terms of gender, race, class, and region would legitimize many subaltern cultures and invite multiple views of the Chinese *lian/mian* practices. It not only could unearth the Sinocentric and monolithic biases but also could uncover the possible gender (Chinese women may have a different type of *lian/mian* practices), ethnic / racial (the Han nationality versus many other ethnic groups, primarily on the Chinese border), class (city people versus country people), and regional (north versus south) biases. Such open-minded discourse would encourage mindful, critical, and creative thinking and interaction in forging an increasingly expansive social harmony within discord.

In conclusion, the Chinese character and identity lodge themselves in discourse. If the *lian/mian* discourse has shaped and maintains the living Chinese character, the needed civic discourse of relationality and rationality, of equality and freedom in speech, and of diversity and harmony can certainly reshape the Chinese character and identity into a newer, richer, and more expansive one.

# References

Altheide, D. L., & Johnson, J. M. (1994). Criteria for assessing interpretive validity in qualitative research. In N. K. Denzin & Y. S. Lincoln (Eds.), *Handbook of qualitative research* (pp. 485–499). Thousand Oaks, CA: Sage.

Averill, J. R. (1990). Inner feelings, works of the flesh, the beast within, diseases of the mind, driving force, and putting on a show: Six metaphors of emotion and their theoretical extensions. In D. E. Leary (Ed.), *Metaphors in the history of psychology* (pp. 104–132). Cambridge: Cambridge University Press.

Averill, J. R. (1991). Intellectual emotions. In C. D. Spielberger, I. G. Sarason, Z. Kulcsár, & G. L. Van Heck (Eds.), *Stress and anxiety* (Vol. 14, pp. 3–16). Washington, DC: Hemisphere.

Averill, J. R. (1992). The structural bases of emotional behavior: A metatheoretical analysis. In M. S. Clark (Ed.), *Emotion-Review of personality and social psychology* (pp. 1–25). Newbury Park, CA: Sage.

Bai, J. M. (1988). *dan shi xi le pian He Shang ji qi qi shi* [*He Shang* and its inspirations]. In W. H. Tsui (Ed.), *Hai wai He Shang da tao lun* [Great debates on *He Shang* Overseas] (pp. 19–5). Harbin, China: Hei Long Jiang Educational Press.

Bantam Books, Inc. (Ed.). (1967). *Quotations from Chairman Mao Tse-tung*. New York: Bantam Books.

Bateson, G. (1972). *Steps to an ecology of mind*. New York: Ballantine.

Benedict, R. (1946). *The Chrysanthemum and the sword*. Boston, MA: Houghton Mifflin.

Berger, P., & Luckman, T. (1966) *The social construction of reality*. Garden City, N.Y.: Doubleday.

Bernstein, R. J. (1983). *Beyond objectivism and relativism: Science, hermeneutics, and praxis*. Philadelphia: University of Pennsylvania Press.

Bo, Y. (1991). *The Ugly Chinaman and the Crisis of Chinese Culture*. D. J. Cohn and J. Qing (Trans., Eds.). North Sydney, Australia: Allen & Unwin.

Bond, M. H., & Lee, P. W. H. (1981). Face saving in Chinese culture: A discussion and experimental study of Hong Kong students. In A. Y. King & R. P. L. Lee (Eds.), *Social life and development in Hong* Kong (pp. 289–304). Hong Kong: The Chinese University of Hong Kong.

Brown, P., & Levinson, S. (1987). *Politeness.* Cambridge: Cambridge University Press.

Carbaugh, D. (1988). *Talking American: cultural discourses on Donahue.* Norwood, NJ: Ablex.

Carbaugh, D. (1996). *Situating selves: the communication of social identifies in American scenes.* Albany, NY: SUNY Press.

Chang, H., & Holt, L. (1994). A Chinese perspective on face as inter-relational concern. In S. Ting-Toomey (Ed.), *The challenge of facework* (pp. 95–132). Albany: State University of New York Press.

Chen, A. S. (1964). The ideal local party secretary and the "model" man. *China Quarterly, 17*, 229–240.

Chen, L. (1996). *Gu dai zong jiao yu lun li-ru jia si xang de geng yuan* [Religions and ethics in Ancient China: On the roots of Confucianism]. Beijing: The Tri-Union *(San Lian).*

Chen, V. (1990–1991). *Mien tze* at the Chinese dinner table: A study of the interactional accomplishment of face. *Research on Language and Social Interaction, 24*, 109–140.

Chen, V., & Pearce, W. B. (1995). Even if a thing of beauty, can a case study be a joy forever? A social constructionist approach to theory and research. In W. Leeds- Hurwitz (Ed.), *Social approaches to communication* (pp. 135–154). New York: Guilford Press.

Chen, Z. (1988). The theoretical analysis and practical studies of the *mianzi* psychology [*Mianzi xinli de lilun fenxi yu shiji yanjou*]. In G. Yang (Ed.), *The psychology of the Chinese* [*Zhongguoren de xinli*] (pp. 155–237). Taibei, Taiwan: Guiguan Press.

Cheng, C. (1986). The concept of face and its Confucian roots. *Journal of Chinese Philosophy, 13*, 329–348.

Cheng, C. (1996). *Zhouyi* and philosophy of *wei* (positions). *Extreme-Orient, Extreme-Occident, 18*, 150–175.

Choi, S., & Choi, S. C. (1996). Che-myon: *Korea's social face.* Unpublished paper. Chung-Ang University, Seoul, Korea.

Chong, H. (1997). *Coordination and conflict in a multicultural organization.* Unpublished dissertation. Amherst: University of Massachusetts.

Collingwood, R. G. (1946). *The idea of history.* Oxford: Oxford at the Clarendon Press.

Craig, R. T. (1989). Communication as a practical discipline. In B. Dervin, L. Grossberg, B. J. O'Keefe, & E. Wartella (Eds.), *Rethinking communication: Vol. 1. Paradigm issues* (pp. 97–122). Newbury Park, CA: Sage.

Craig, R. T., & Tracy, K. (1995). Grounded practical theory: The case of intellectual discussion. *Communication Theory, 5*, 248–272.

Cronen, V. E. (1994). Coordinated management of meaning: Practical theory for the complexities and contradictions of everyday life. In J. Sigfried (Ed.), *The status of common sense in psychology* (pp. 183–207). Stamford, CT: Ablex.

Cronen, V. E. (1995a). Coordinated management of meaning: The consequentiality of communication and recapturing of experience. In S. J. Sigman

(Ed.), *The consequentiality of communication* (pp. 17–65). Hillsdale, NJ: Lawrence Erlbaum.

Cronen, V. E. (1995b). Practical theory and the tasks ahead for social approaches to communication. In W. Leeds-Hurwitz (Ed.), *Social approaches to communication* (pp. 217–242). New York: Guilford Press.

Cronen, V. E. (1996). *Practical theory and the logic of inquiry.* Paper presented at the Speech Communication Association Convention, San Diego, CA, November 25, 1996.

Cronen, V. E., & Lang, P. (1994). Language and action: Wittgenstein and Dewey in the practice of therapy and consultation. *Human Systems, 5,* 5–43.

Cupach, W. R., & Metts, S. (1994). *Facework.* Thousand Oaks, CA: Sage.

Derrida, J. (1978). *Writing and difference.* A. Bass (trans.). Chicago: University of Chicago Press.

Dewey, J. (1916/1966). *Democracy and education.* New York: Free Press.

Dewey, J. (1929/1960). *The quest for certainty.* New York: Capricorn.

Dewey, J. (1934). *Art as experience.* New York: Minton, Balch.

Dewey, J. (1958). *Experience and nature.* New York: Dover. (Original work published in 1925).

Doi, T. (1971). *The anatomy of dependence.* J. Bester (Trans.). Tokyo: Kodansha International.

Editorial Board of *China Times* (1988). *Cong He Shang tan Zhong guo wen hua qian tu* [On the future of the Chinese culture from the perspective of *He Shang*]. In W. H. Tsui (Ed.), *hai wai He Shang da tao lun (Great debates on He Shang overseas)* (pp. 67–69). Harbin, China: Hei Long Jiang Educational Press.

Editorial Board of *Teacher Zhang Monthly* (1990). *Zhong guo de renqing he mianzi* [Chinese feelings and face]. Beijing: Friendship Publishing, Inc.

Education Bureau of Changzhou City (1981). *Chenyu Tsidian* [Dictionary of Idiomatic Phrases]. Jiangsu, China: Jiangsu People's Press.

Fingarette, H. (1972). *Confucius: Secular as sacred.* New York: Harper & Row, Publishers.

Fitzgerald, J. (1993). The invention of the modern Chinese self. In M. Lee & A. D. Syrokomla-Stefanowska (Eds.), *Modernizing the Chinese Past* (pp. 25–41). Sydney, Australia: Wild Peony.

Fleuridas, C., Nelson, T. S., & Rosenthal, D. M. (1986). The evolution of circular questionings: Training family therapists. *Journal of Marital and Family Therapy, 12,* 113–127.

Fraser, B. (1990). Perspectives on politeness. *Journal of Pragmatics, 14,* 219–236.

Fu, P. R. (1988). *pi pan yu chang xin* [Criticism and innovation]. In W. H. Tsui (Ed.), *Hai wai He Shang da tao lun* [Great Debates on *He Shang* Overseas] (p. 41). Harbin, China: Hei Long Jiang Educational Press.

Gao, G. (1996). Self and other: A Chinese perspective on interpersonal relationships. In W. B. Gudykunst, S. Ting-Toomey, & T. Nishida (Eds.), *Communication in personal relationships across cultures* (pp. 81–101). Thousand Oaks, CA: Sage.

Gao, G., Ting-Toomey, S., & Gudykunst, W. (1996). Chinese communication process. In M. H. Bond (Ed.), *The handbook of Chinese psychology* (pp. 280–293). Hong Kong: Oxford University Press.

Gergen, K. J. (1973). Social psychology as history. *Journal of Personality and Social Psychology*, 2, 309–320.

Gergen, K.J. (1991). *The saturated self: Dilemmas of identity in contemporary life.* New York: Basic.

Gergen, K. J. (1994). *Toward transformation in social knowledge* (2nd ed.). Thousand Oaks, CA: Sage.

Goffman, E. (1967). On face work: An analysis of ritual elements in social interaction. In E. Goffman, *Interaction ritual* ( pp. 5–45). New York: Pantheon Books.

Hall, D.L. (1987). *Thinking through Confucius.* Albany: State University of New York Press.

Hall, D. L. (1994). To be or not to be: The postmodern self and the wu-forms of Taoism. In R. T. Ames, W. Dissanayake, and T. P. Kasulis (Eds.), *Self as person in Asian theory and practice* (pp. 213–233). Albany: State University of New York Press.

Hall, D. L. (1995). *Anticipating China: Thinking through the narratives of Chinese and Western culture.* Albany: State University of New York Press.

Hall, D. L., & Ames, R. T. (1998). *Thinking from the Han-self: Truth and transcendence in Chinese and Western Culture.* Albany: State University of New York Press.

Hansen, C. (1995). *Qing* [Emotions] in pre-Buddhist Chinese thought. In J. Marks & R. T. Ames (Eds.), *Emotions in Asian thought* (pp. 181–211). Albany: State University of New York Press.

Harré, R. (1983). *Personal being: A rationale for the natural sciences.* Oxford: Blackwell.

Harré, R. (Ed.) (1987). *The social construction of emotions.* Oxford: Blackwell.

Harré, R. (1991). The discursive production of selves. *Theory and Psychology, 1,* 51–63.

Harré, R. (1994). *The discursive mind.* Thousand Oaks, CA: Sage.

He, P. (1995). Perception of identity in Modern China. *Journal for the Study of Race, Nation and Culture, 1,* 127–154.

Ho, D. Y. (1976). On the concept of face. *American Journal of Sociologist, 81,* 867–884.

Hu, H. C. (1944). The Chinese concepts of "face." *American Anthropologist, 46,* 45–64.

Hu, W., & Grove, C. L. (1991). *Encountering the Chinese.* Yarmouth, ME: Intercultural Press.

Huang, L. (1996). *Facework strategies and interpersonal negotiations: A Chinese perspective.* Paper presented at National Communication Association Annual Convention, San Diego, CA.

Huang, R. (1990). *Bu yao chuan pan fou din chuan tong wen hua* [Do not completely negate the traditional culture]. In F. X. Li (Ed.), *He Shang bai niou* [Many mistakes of *He Shang*] (pp. 68–69). Beijing: China Writers Association Press.

Hsu, C. (1996). *"Face": An ethnographic study of Chinese social behavior.* Ann Arbor, MI: UMI Dissertation Services.

Hsu, F. L. K. (1985). The self in cross-cultural perspective. In A. Marsella, G. DeVos, & F. L. K. Hsu (Eds.), *Culture and self: Asian and Western perspectives* (pp. 24–55). New York: Tavistock Publications.

Hwang, K. (1987). Face and favor: The Chinese power game. *American Journal of Sociology, 92*, 944–974.

Hwang, K. (1997-1998). *Guanxi* and *Mientze*: Conflict resolution in Chinese society. In G. Chen (Ed.), *Conflict resolution in Chinese* (special issue). *Intercultural Communication Studies* 7: 1, 43–61.

Jacobs, B. (1979). A preliminary model of particularistic ties in Chinese political alliances: *Kan-ch'ing* and *Kuan-hsi* in a rural Taiwanese township. *China Quarterly, 78*, 237–273.

Jia, W. (1997-1998). Facework as a Chinese conflict-preventive mechanism: A cultural/discourse analysis. In G. Chen (Ed.), *Conflict resolution in Chinese* (special issue). *Intercultural Communication Studies* 7: 1, 43–61.

King, A. Y. (1988). *"Mian," "chi" yu zhongguoren xinwei zhi fenxi* [Face, shame, and the analysis of behavior patterns of the Chinese]. In G. Yang (Ed.), *Zhongguoren de xinli* [The psychology of the Chinese] (pp. 319–345). Taibei, Taiwan: Guiguan Press.

Kipnis, A. (1995). "face": An adaptable discourse of social surfaces. *positions, 1(3)*, 119–147.

Kiyoto, S.C. (1984). *World Communication*, 24, 1, 23–31.

Kuhn, T. (1962). *The structure of scientific revolutions*. Chicago: University of Chicago Press.

Lang, P. (1996). Presentation at the Workshop on CQ. Amherst: University of Massachusetts at Amherst.

Legge, J. (1967). *Li Chi*, Book of rites: An encyclopedia of ancient ceremonial usages, religious creeds, and social institutions (Trans.). New Hyde Park, NY: University Books.

Levinas, E. (1985). *Ethics and Infinity: Conversation with Philippe Nemo*. R. A. Cohen (Trans.). Pittsburgh: Duquesne University Press.

Li, F. (1996). *The cultural meanings and social functions of "face" in Sino-US business negotiations*. Ann Arbor, MI: UMI Dissertation Services.

Li, Z. (1917/1989). *Houhei daquan* [The anthology of studies of thickness of face and blackness of heart]. Beijing: China Economics Press.

Lin, Y. (1935). *My country and my people*. New York: Reynal & Hitchcock.

Liu, J. T. C. (1957). An early Sung reformer: Fan Chung-yen. In J. K. Fairbank (Ed.), *Chinese thought and institutions*. Chicago: University of Chicago Press.

Lu, X. (1934/1960). On "face." In H. Yang & G. Yang (Trans.), *Selected works of Lu Xun, Vol. 4*. Beijing: Foreign Language Press.

Lu, Z. (1996). Insights into the worldly affairs constitute knowledge and experience in dealing with issues concerning human feelings is as good as ability to write good articles: *shishi dongming jie xuewen, renqing lianda ji wenzhang* [On the psychology of *renqing* and *mianzi*]. In Z. Lu, *Zhonggueren de chuantong xintai* [The social psychology of the Chinese tradition] (pp. 141–152). Hangzhou, Zhejiang, China: Zhejiang People's Press.

Luo, X. (1997). The new trend in the cultural transformation in Mainland China: A reconstruction of *guanxi* and the imaginary identity. *Dong Yia Ji Kan, [Quarterly Journal of East Asian Studies] 28*, 1–28.

Ma, R. (1992). The role of unofficial intermediaries in interpersonal conflicts in Chinese culture. *Communication Quarterly 40, 3*, 269–278.

Mao, L. R. (1994). Beyond politeness theory: "Face" revisited and renewed. *Journal of Pragmatics, 21,* 451–486.

Matsumoto, Y. (1988). Reexamination of the universality of face: Politeness phenomena in Japanese. *Journal of Pragmatics, 12,* 403–420.

Maturana, H. R., & Varela, F. (1987). *The tree of knowledge: The biological roots of human understanding.* Boston: New Science Library.

Mead, G. H. (1934). *Mind, self and society.* Chicago: University of Chicago Press.

Morgan, C., & Averill, J. R. (1992). True feelings, the self, and authenticity. In D. Franks & V. Gecas (Eds.), *Social perspectives on emotion* (pp. 95–123). Greenwich, CT: JAI Press.

Pearce, W. B. (1994). *Interpersonal communication: Making social worlds.* New York: Harper Collins.

O'Driscoll, J. (1996). About face: A defense and elaboration of universal dualism. *Journal of Pragmatics, 25,* 1–32.

Penman, R. (1994). Facework in communication: Conceptual and moral challenges. In S. Ting-Toomey (Ed.), *The challenge of facework* (pp. 15–45). Albany: State University of New York Press.

Potter, S. H. (1988). The cultural construction of emotion in rural Chinese social life. *Ethos, 16: 2,* 181-208. Society for Psychological Anthropology.

Pye, L. W. (1968). *The spirit of Chinese politics.* Cambridge, MA: MIT Press.

Redding, S. G., & Ng, M. (1982). The role of "face" in the organizational perceptions of Chinese managers. *Organizational Studies, 3,* 201–219.

Reding, S. (1997). *The repatriation of Hong Kong and the concept of face.* Unpublished master's thesis, University of Indiana at Bloomington, Indiana.

Reischauer, E. O. (1962). *The United States and Japan.* New York: Viking Press.

Robbins, J. (1991). Visage, figure: Reading Levinas's *Totality and infinity.* In C. Nouvet (Ed.), *YFS 79: Literature and the ethical question.* Yale Station, CT: Yale University Press.

Rosenwein, B. H. (1998). *Anger's past: The social uses of emotion in the Middle Ages.* Ithaca, NY: Cornell University.

Scheff, T. J. (1990). *Microsociology.* Chicago: University of Chicago Press.

Scheff, T. J. (1994). *Bloody revenge.* Boulder, CO: Westview Press.

Schwarcz, V. (1997). The pane of sorrow: Public uses of personal grief in Modern China. In A. Kleinman, V. Das, & M. Lock (Eds.), *Social suffering* (pp. 119–148). Berkeley: University of California Press.

Scollon, R., & Scollon, S. B. K. (1981). *Narrative, literacy and face in interethnic communication.* Norwood, NJ: ABLEX.

Scott, W. (1994). *About face: Social networks and prestige politics in contemporary Shanghai villages.* Ann Arbor, MI: UMI Dissertation Services.

Selvini-Palazzoli M., Boscolo, L., Cecchin, G. and Prata, G. (1980). Hypothesizing–Circularity–Neutrality: Three guidelines for the conductor of the session. *Family Process, 19,* 3–12).

Shao, Y. M. (1988). Literature is not history and there are more emotions than reason; but where are our achievements? In W. H. Tsui (Ed.), *Hai wai He Shang da tao lun* [Great debates on *He Shang* overseas] (pp. 50–52). Harbin, China: Hei Long Jiang Educational Press.

Shotter, J. (1984). *Social accountability and selfhood.* Oxford: Blackwell.

Shotter, J. (1993). *Conversational realities.* London: Sage.

Smith, A. (1894). *The Chinese characteristics*. New York: Fleming H. Revell Company.

Smith, M. B. (1985). The metaphorical basis of selfhood. In A. L. Marsella, G. DeVos, & F. L. K. Hsu (Eds.), *Culture and self: Asian and Western perspectives* (pp. 56–88). New York: Tavistock Publications.

Solomon, R. C. (1995). Some notes on emotion, "East and West." *Philosophy East and West, 45*, 171–202.

Stelzer, L. (1998). Trust and law in China's socialist market economy. *Asian American Review, 16: 4*, 137–147.

Stewart, J. (1995). *Language as articulate contact: Toward a post-semiotic philosophy of communication*. Albany: State University of New York Press.

Stover, L. E. (1962). *"Face" and verbal analogues of interaction in Chinese culture*. Ann Arbor, MI: UMI Dissertation Services.

Stover, L. E. (1974). *China: An anthropological perspective*. Pacific Palisades, CA: Goodyear Publishing Company.

Su, X. K., & Wang, L. X. (1988). *He Shang [The Deathsong of the river ] Xian dai chu ban she* Beijing, China: The Modern Press] .

Sun, L. (1991). Contemporary Chinese culture: Structure and emotionality. *Australian Journal of Chinese Affairs, 26*, 1–41.

Tao, S. (Ed.). (1995). *Zhongguoren de mianzi* [The Chinese *mianzi*]. Taibei, Taiwan: Wangwenshe.

Ting-Toomey, S. (Ed.) (1994). *The challenge of facework*. Albany: State University of New York Press.

Tomm, K. (1987a). Interventive interviewing: Part I. Strategizing as a fourth guideline for the therapist. *Family Process, 26*, 3–13.

Tomm, K. (1987b). Interventive interviewing: Part II. Reflexive questioning as a means to enable self healing. *Family Process, 26*, 167–183.

Tomm, K. (1988). Interventive interviewing: Part III. Intending to ask circular, strategic, or reflexive questions? *Family Process, 26*, 1–16.

Tracy, K., & Baratz, S. (1994). The case for case studies of facework. In S. Ting-Toomey (Ed.), *The challenge of facework*. Albany: State University of New York Press.

Tracy, K., & Tracy, S. (1997). *Rudeness at 911: Re-conceptualizing face and face attack*. Paper presented at the Top Four Panel on Language and Social Interaction, National Communication Association Annual Convention, Chicago.

Tsai, K. S. (1998). A circle of friends, a web of troubles: Rotating credit associations in China. *Harvard China Review, 1*. Http://www.harvardchina.org/magazine/article/rotating%20credit.html.

Tsui, L. D. (1990). *hua er bu shi de xue feng* [Unauthentic academic style]. In The Division of Films and TV, Bureau of Culture and Arts, Ministry of Propaganda, Chinese Communist Party Committee (Ed.), *He Shang wu chu-cong He Shang dao wu si* [Erroneous areas of *He Shang:* From *He Shang* to the May 4th Movement] (pp. 183-185). Nanchang, China: Jiangxi People's Press.

Tu, W., & Leung, I. (1995). Rebuilding rational communication and an open mind. *Cultural China, 4*. Burnaby, Canada: Culture Regeneration Research Society.

Watzlawick, P., Beavin, J., & Jackson, D. D. (1967). *Pragmatics of human communication*. New York: W. W. Norton.

Wilson, R. W. (1970). *Learning to be Chinese: The political socialization of children in Taiwan*. Cambridge: MIT Press.

Wittgenstein, L. (1958). *Philosophical investigations*. G. E. M. Anscombe (trans.). New York: Macmillan Company.

Xinhua (1997). Peking University plans to renovate its *menmian* to celebrate its centennial anniversary. *The World Daily*, A9.

Xu, Z. S. (1988). *jia gu wen tsi dian* [The Dictionary of Tortoise Shell Characters]. Chengdu, China: Sichuan Dictionaries Press.

Yan, H. (1995). The concept of "face" in Chinese proverbs and phrases. *Proverbium: Yearbook of International Proverb Scholarship, 12*, 357–373.

Yang, L. (1957). The concept of Dao as a basis for social relations in China. In J. Fairbank (Ed.), *Chinese Thought and Institutions*. Chicago: University of Chicago Press.

Yang, M. (1994). *Gifts, favors and banquets: The art of social relationships in China*. Ithaca, NY: Cornell University.

Yang, Z. (1991). *Huigu gangtai zi'ou yanjiou: Fanxing yu zhanwang* [In retrospect upon the studies on self in Hong Kong and Taiwan: Reflection and prospect]. In Z. Yang & S. Gao (Eds.), *Zhongguoren, Zhongguoxin* [Chinese people, Chinese heart] (pp. 16–91). Taibei, Taiwan: *Yuanliou quban shiye gufen xouxian gongsi* [Far Flow Publishing Inc.].

Yi, Z. (1996). *Chatting about Chinese*. Beijing: Hualin Press.

Yu, D. (1991). An analysis of interpersonal sufferings in the Chinese society. In Z. Yang & S. Gao (Eds.), *Zhongguoren, Zhongguoxin* [Chinese people, Chinese heart] (pp. 292–362). Taibei, Taiwan: *Yuanliuo quban shiyie gufen youxian gunsi* [Far Flow Publishing Inc.].

Yu, W. H. (1990). *He Shang hu huan shen mo yi zhong fan xing yi shi* [What kind of "reflective consciousness" is He Shang fanning?]. In The Editorial Board (Ed.), *He Shang xuan yang le sheng mo?* [What is *He Shang* propagandizing?] (pp. 73–88). Beijing: China Broadcasting and TV Press.

Zai, X. (1995). *Zhongguoren de lianmian guan* [The Chinese perspective or *lianmian*]. Taibei, Taiwan: Guiguan Press.

Zeng, J. F. (director). (1997). *Elder sisters and younger sisters' adventures in Beijing* (Thirty-episode TV film series). Beijing: Beijing Tianpin Economic and Culture Development Inc., Runnan Province Red River Tobacco Company, & Beijing Power Film and TV Consulting Inc.

Zhang, Y. J. (1989). He Shang san wen [Questioning *He Shang*]. In N. Hua (Ed.), Criticisms of He Shang [*He Shang pi pan*] (pp. 8–13). Beijing: Culture and Arts Press [*Wen hua yi shu chu ban she*].

Zhao, L. M. (1988). *He Shang* negates the Chinese cultural values. In W. H. Tsui (Ed.), *Hai wai He Shang da tao lun* [*Great debates over He Shang overseas*] (pp. 55-59). Harbin, China: Hei Long Jiang Educational Press.

Zhong, H. M., et al. (1989). *On He Shang again*. Hangzhou, China: Hongzhou University Press.

Zhou, M., & Ho, D. Y. (1992). *Cong kuawenhua de quandian fenxi mianzi de neihan yu chi zai shehui jiaowang zhong de yunzuo* [An analysis of the meanings and functions of *mianzi* in social interaction from a cross-cultural perspective]. In G. S. Yang & G. Huang (Eds.), *Chinese psychology and Chinese behavior: Concepts and methods* (pp. 205–252). Taibei, Taiwan: Guiguan Press.

Zhu, C. (1989). *Cong shehuigeren ru wenhua de guanxi lun zhongguoren xinge de chigan chuxiang* [On the shame orientation of the Chinese personality in light of the relationship between the social individual and culture). In L. Li & G. Yang (Eds.), *Zhongguoren de xinge* [The Chinese personality] (pp. 91-131). Taibei, Taiwan: Guiguan Press.

Zhu, R. (1987). *Zhongguoren de shehui hudong: Lun mianzi wenti* [Social interactions among the Chinese: On the issue of face]. In G. Yang (Ed.), *Zhongguoren de xinli* [The Psychology of the Chinese] (pp. 239–288). Taibei, Taiwan: Guiguan Press.

Zi, Q. (1998, February 9). Why Ms. Huang knelt down so sadly. *Jiefang Ribao* [Liberation daily], Vol. 1206 (3–15), p. 4. Shanghai, China: Jiefang Ribao Press.

Zito, A. (1994). Silk and skin: Significant boundaries. In A. Zito & T. E. Barlow (Eds.), *Body, subject and power in China* (pp. 103–130). Chicago: University of Chicago Press.

Zito, A., & T. E. Barlow (1994). *Body, subject and power in China.* Chicago: University of Chicago Press.

Zuo, B. (1997). *Zhongguoren de lian yu mianzi* [Chinese *lian* and *mianzi*]. Hubei, China: Central China Normal University Press.

# Subject Index

Advantages of using *lian/mian* as a central framework, 25–26
Apology (East and West), 130
Appreciative inquiry, 96

*Bao en*, 157

Case study method, 106
Chinese: identity, x; culture, xi; character, 179–181; personhood, 12–13; expatriates, 154
CCP's face-giving strategies, 81–82
Communication defined, xiii, 97
Civic discourse, xiii–xiv, 180–181
Cultural: identity, ix; change, ix–x; transformation, xi–xii, strategies, 101–102
Culture: *wenhua*, 67; defined in diverse ways, 78–79
Circular questioning, 91–96; its critique, 97–99; as used in China, 99–103, 138–142, 163–164
Criticism, 79–80

*Duqi*, 116–117, 129–130

Eight values, 169–170
Emotive actions, 26

Historical method, 90

Intellectual approaches (to face-related cultural change), 68–77; a social constructionist critique of them, 77–80

*Lian/mian:* The social constructionist view, 5, 10–13; a historically grounded social constructionist view, 15–22; Confucianism and, 18–19; face discourse genres, 22; its central position in Chinese culture, 22–26; its emotional dimension, 26–38; its communicative dimension, 37–50; its social consequences, 50–55; social constructionist critique, 58–61, 61–62, 62–64, 64–66, 77–80, 83; its universal theories, 58–61; its cultural theories, 61–62; in light of grounded practical theory, 62–64; its ethnocultural views, 64–66; its roots, 117–118; its transformation, 100–105, 165–170, 171–174; and law, 121, 150; and power, 115; anger and loss of, 131; emotions and, 26–33, 133; idiomatic phrases related to, 38–50

# Author Index

## ABOUT THE AUTHOR

WENSHAN JIA is Assistant Professor of Communication, State University of New York at New Paltz, New York, and was Research Chair of The Association of Chinese Communication Studies. His research concentrations are intercultural communication, Chinese communication and social change, and communication theory.